HISTORIC VIRGINIA GARDENS

HISTORIC VIRGINIA GARDENS

Preservation Work of
The Garden Club of Virginia

1975–2007

Margaret Page Bemiss

PHOTOGRAPHS BY ROGER FOLEY

UNIVERSITY OF VIRGINIA PRESS

CHARLOTTESVILLE AND LONDON

University of Virginia Press
© 2009 by the Rector and Visitors of the University of Virginia
All rights reserved
Printed in China on acid-free paper

First published 2009

9 8 7 6 5 4 3 2 1

LIBRARY OF CONGRESS CATALOGING-IN-PUBLICATION DATA
Bemiss, Margaret Page.
    Historic Virginia gardens : preservation work of the Garden Club of Virginia,
1975–2007 / Margaret Page Bemiss ; photographs by Roger Foley.
        p. cm.
    Includes bibliographical references and index.
    ISBN 978-0-8139-2659-9 (alk. paper)
    1. Historic gardens—Virginia—History. 2. Historic gardens—Conservation
and restoration—Virginia—History. 3. Garden Club of Virginia—History.
I. Foley, Roger. II. Title. III. Title: Preservation work of the Garden Club of
Virginia, 1975–2007.
    SB466.U65V83 2009
    712.09755—dc22

                                                                                    2008029771

All photos © Roger Foley unless otherwise indicated below.

Photo, p. 56, by William D. Rieley; photos, pp. 114 and 119, by Peter J. Hatch; photo, p. 124, courtesy
of Thomas Jefferson Foundation/Leonard Phillips; illustration, p. 120, courtesy of Thomas Jefferson Foundation/Monticello; illustration, p. 128, courtesy of Réunion de Musées Nationaux/
Art Resource, NY

To the members of The Garden Club of Virginia,
who spend countless hours every year
carrying on the tradition of Historic Garden Week in Virginia,
enabling the undertaking of new restoration projects,
and continuing the oversight of the old,

and to the ladies and gentlemen who saved these places and
designed the gardens described herein

Our human landscape is our unwitting autobiography, reflecting our tastes, our values, our aspirations, and even our fears, in tangible, visible form. . . . The cultural record we have written in the landscape is liable to be more truthful than most autobiographies because we are less self-conscious about how we describe ourselves.

Pierce E. Lewis, *The Interpretation of Ordinary Landscapes*

By preserving its historic gardens and the grounds of its churches and universities, Virginia has become an outdoor museum of an art that has, since the beginning, challenged man's ingenuity.

Ralph E. Griswold

CONTENTS

FOREWORD

In 1923, just three years after the founding of the Garden Club of Virginia, *Historic Gardens of Virginia* was published by the James River Garden Club of Richmond. In the introduction to that pioneering, 355-page, richly illustrated tour, which served as a foundational cornerstone for other garden surveys that followed (both in Virginia and throughout the United States), Mary Johnson noted, "For—at least in Virginia—women and gardens go together."

This happy marriage, between the "ladies" and the land, which began with Ann Pamela Cunningham and the Mount Vernon Ladies Association of the Union in 1856 and their battle to save Virginia's Mount Vernon estate, has not only been realized, but it has continued to evolve, blossom, and bear fruit, over the past eighty years under the careful watch of the Garden Club of Virginia. The present volume is evidence that the Club tradition of thoughtful stewardship and patronage continues today at such historically significant gardens as Bacon's Castle, Oatlands, and Lee Hall. The book also serves as an unparalleled chronicle of the maturation of the historic garden and landscape preservation movement in America.

Historic Virginia Gardens: Preservation Work of The Garden Club of Virginia, 1975–2007 builds on the 1923 foundational survey of the James River Garden Club, and on the groundbreaking work and unrivaled publishing legacy of the Garden Club of Virginia, which includes *Homes and Gardens in Old Virginia* (Susanne Williams Massie and Frances Archer Christian, 1931), and, more recently, *Historic Virginia Gardens: Preservations by The Garden Club of Virginia* (Dorothy Hunt Williams, 1975). As with the 1975 publication, this latest work places the restoration projects of the past three decades into their rightful historical contexts.

Besides its ongoing relationship with the land, the Garden Club of Virginia has also had a long-term connection with the landscape architecture profession that has provided fertile ground for landscape architects to advance and test current practice. In the 1920s and 1930s, for example, two of the earliest landscape architects to provide consulting services to the Club's Restoration Committee, Ralph E. Griswold (whose work included Saint John's Mews and the Mary Washington House) and Alden Hopkins (Stratford Hall and the University of Virginia), had been Fellows in Landscape Architecture at the American Academy in Rome. During their two-year fellowships abroad, these early practitioners immersed themselves in the rich, and at times complex, layered Italian villa landscape. They measured and carefully documented these landscapes and created restoration plans, and in the process not only learned how to "see" but developed a nature-culture stewardship ethic that they then brought back to the United States. Thus, Griswold and Hopkins, along with other early Virginia practitioners, such as Charles Gillette, brought a unique sensitivity to any particular garden's narrative and evolution. Under the careful stewardship of the Garden Club of Virginia, this perspective has been adopted and promoted, and standards for professional practice have been established. The present work not only provides a context for these earlier collaborations, but it also places the later work of Rudy J. Favretti and the current work of William D. Rieley in their rightful contexts as well.

When Griswold died in 1981, Dorothy Hunt Williams wrote in the *Garden Club of Virginia Journal* that his work had possessed an "instinctive sense of suitable design in landscape that was sharpened by previous experience." As the present volume shows, this same philosophy—one of sympathetic change and continuity—holds true for the restorations undertaken by the Garden Club of Virginia. As garden lovers, historians, horticulturists, landscape architects, and historic preservationists, all of us are grateful for this diverse and accessible legacy of gardens, guidebooks, and guidelines.

Charles A. Birnbaum, FASLA, FAAR
Founder and President, The Cultural Landscape Foundation Washington, D.C.

PREFACE

THE GARDEN CLUB OF VIRGINIA WAS ORGANIZED IN 1920 AS A FEDERATION of eight separate clubs within the Commonwealth of Virginia. Within a few years, the members decided that their commonality of interests was such that the federation should be reorganized into a single entity. Presently, there are forty-seven member clubs, ranging geographically from the Eastern Shore to western Virginia. The Garden Club's mission statement, printed in its annual Register, is clear and direct: to restore historic gardens and landscapes, conserve Virginia's natural resources, inspire a love of gardening, and provide education for its members and the general public.

The present volume documents—in words, photographs, and drawings—the efforts of the Garden Club of Virginia for the period 1975–2007 in the field of historic landscape preservation. Each of the landscapes herein is presented in its historical context. The photographs show the gardens as they appear today, and the accompanying text explains why each landscape was considered worthy of restoration or recreation. The sites documented here were chosen for rehabilitation either because of their architecture or because of who originally designed them, or for what they tell us about the political and social history of Virginia, founded four hundred years ago when three square-rigged English ships improbably sailed up the James River.

An earlier volume documenting the work of the Garden Club, entitled *Historic Virginia Gardens: Preservations by The Garden Club of Virginia,* was published more than thirty years ago, in 1975. As Dorothy Hunt Williams wrote in the preface to that work, Virginia's gardens have national relevance: the history of Virginia and its landscapes, beginning in 1607 when the first permanent English-speaking settlement was established at Jamestown, is the history of the beginnings of the United States of America. With this new volume, we have attempted to bring that history up to date.

Since 1975, the Garden Club of Virginia has restored, preserved, or documented more than forty historic landscapes. This labor of love has been financed by the proceeds from Historic Garden Week, a statewide house-and-garden tour that holds the distinction of having been the first such organized fundraiser of its kind in America. Garden Week began in 1929, skipped 1930, and since then has continued without interruption, except for the years of the Second World War.

As gardens mature, shade patterns change, shrubs die, trees fall, and walls must be repaired and walks replaced. Many of Virginia's historic gardens are continuously and heavily used by the public, and their functions also are modified. All these changes require certain adaptations and alterations in the design of the garden. Accordingly, a few of the gardens that appeared in the Club's 1975 catalogue of historic Virginia gardens have been revisited here. In the main, however, the gardens in the present volume have not been documented before.

The stories of the gardens begin with Bacon's Castle, built in the seventeenth century, where an archaeological study commissioned to uncover a vanished nineteenth-century garden found a previously unknown, formally laid-out seventeenth-century garden instead. And they end with an entirely new garden at Yeardley House, one created in the twenty-first century as the Garden Club's contribution to the 400th anniversary celebration at Jamestown. Sandwiched between the stories of these two gardens, the reader will find many others. Among them, the stories of two historically significant colonial churchyards—the seventeenth-century St. Luke's, in Isle of Wight County, and Williamsburg's eighteenth-century Bruton Parish. Also, we relate the history and restoration of the gardens of three successful nineteenth- and early twentieth-century businessmen. The nineteenth-century birthplace of one president, and the much-loved eighteenth- and nineteenth-century gardens of two others are chronicled, as is the story of the twentieth-century duPont garden at the home of yet a fourth. The gardens and landscapes of four institutions of higher learning are also included: Hollins University, Sweet Briar College, the University of Virginia, and Washington and Lee University. Plus, the eighteenth-century landscape and demonstration gardens at a remarkably sophisticated frontier house, owned by APVA Preservation Virginia (formerly the Association for the Preservation of Virginia Antiquities) but sitting more or less in the middle of the Virginia Tech university campus. Two other well-documented twentieth-century gardens that are found within these pages are that of Mrs. Gari Melchers' Belmont, in Falmouth, and the garden at the Executive Mansion in Richmond, designed for Mrs. Thomas B. Stanley when her husband was governor of Virginia in the 1950s.

The existence of contemporary documentation for an old garden is a great, and rare, luxury for the Garden Club's Restoration Committee. Among the gardens for which such documentation could be found are those of George Washington and Thomas Jefferson, who were among America's first landscape gardeners and who left copious and detailed records. Similarly, the elegant eighteenth-century wooden picket fence around the Moses Myers House in Norfolk was carefully researched and meticulously re-created, as was the Victorian picket fence around the Sutherlin House in Danville. Neither were there problems with documentation in the restoration of Jefferson's serpentine walls at the University of Virginia. (The problem there was persuading the Virginia Department of Transportation to move a road so that the walls could be properly restored!) And in the rebuilding of the dry stone wall at the State Arboretum at Blandy we were even able to preserve a vanishing technique along with the wall. But for others of these gardens, there is, unfortunately, little or no contemporary documentation, and their "restorations" have in fact been the informed and sensitive original creations of a succession of talented landscape architects who have worked with the Restoration Committee over the years: Charles F. Gillette, Arthur A. Shurcliff, Morley J. Williams, Alden Hopkins, Donald H. Parker, Ralph E. Griswold, Meade Palmer, Rudy J. Favretti, and William D. Rieley.

As archaeological techniques become more and more sophisticated and precise, future restorations may be truly that, but these new techniques are also giving rise to some interesting new tensions for the GCV. The Colonial Revival style is now a recognized and respected style of garden design; it is a formal, ordered style that arose in the mid-nineteenth century, harking back, in the words of F. Scott Fitzgerald, to a "simpler, nobler time," and it continues in use today. Several of the best-known restorations in Virginia—most notably those at Kenmore and Montpelier—are in fact restorations of Colonial Revival gardens that were themselves superimposed on the original garden sites. As these gardens age and begin to require refurbishing, the question has become, Where is their real intrinsic value? Should they be respected and restored to their Colonial Revival designs, or should they be ripped out and the gardens redone as nearly as possible in accordance with new archaeological evidence? One problem with the latter approach is that such evidence is often incomplete. Archaeology can show you where a path was, or a building or a fence or a road. Sometimes it can identify particular plants that grew in a given garden. But it cannot tell you, without contemporary documentary evidence, exactly which plants grew where. In addition, in most cases, the eighteenth- or nineteenth-century landscape is completely gone, so that the relationship of the house to its surroundings is totally altered. Thus, a return to eighteenth- or nineteenth-century purity in the landscape setting of any of these houses amounts to nothing more than a twentieth-century artifact in itself. But, these days, there is pressure to return a garden as far as possible to its original state, insofar as this can be determined. Thus, we believe that with the passage of time the present volume may come to provide the most complete, and perhaps the only, record of the history of many of these gardens.

The restoration process itself can be fraught with complications. Churchyards are a particular hazard. The Bruton Parish restoration went fairly smoothly; no bones were disturbed. But the historic St. Luke's Church sits down in a bowl, and drainage problems developed in conjunction with construction of the new walkways. When excavation for a new drainage pipe uncovered a group of ancient gravesites, right at the church door, the work had to be stopped dead in its tracks until permission could be obtained for the bones to be removed and re-interred, with the proper ceremony, out of the path of the new pipe.

Another constant difficulty is landscape maintenance. Virginia's horticultural zones range from zone 6 in the mountains to zone 8 at the beach. Summer, except in the mountains, is searingly hot and humid. At the same time, the summer season is generally very dry all across the state. Mountain winters are frigid, and coastal winters gentle, though frost does occur. The plant palette, then, must vary for each location, as well as taking into account the original date of the garden, and all the plants must be drought- and disease-tolerant, and tough. Photographs of a perennial border from the 1920s might show an abundance of towering delphiniums, for example, but for some reason these plants do not survive now. Similarly, the signature mainstays of dogwood and box have fallen victim to anthracnose and decline, so substitutions must be found. Moreover, the original Colonial gardens and their Colonial Revival descendants were labor-intensive in the extreme; very few of the restored gardens have the luxury of being able to provide that kind of upkeep. In designing each restoration, then, the landscape architect must take into consideration the degree of maintenance available.

The changes in garden design from the seventeenth to the twenty-first century reflect related changes in the ways people have thought about gardens and about themselves, the ways they have used their gardens, the ways they were able to maintain them, and the ways they furnished them. The introduction of new plants was often the result of new explorations of the American continent, new commercial connections with the rest of the world, and, in the nineteenth century, of the American passion for the European Grand Tour. It is our hope that this book will give the reader not only specific knowledge of the gardens of a particular era, including specific illustrations of garden layout along with adjacent buildings, fences, and ornaments, but that it will also foster a greater understanding of the men and women who made these beautiful landscapes, and the society in which they lived.

ACKNOWLEDGMENTS

W. Walker Cowen, a former director of the University of Virginia Press (1969–87), once told me that no committee ever wrote a book. In the case of this volume, that is certainly true: it took the better part of a Commonwealth. The process lasted through the terms of three presidents of the Garden Club of Virginia and three chairs of the Restoration Committee. Because these positions quite often overlap, the numbers don't add up, but Bessie Carter, Mina Wood, Mary Hart Darden, Deedy Bumgardner, Sally Guy Brown, Lucy Ellett, and Mary Lou Seilheimer all share responsibility for bringing this book to fruition. They had the vision and the faith, not to mention the patience, to start it and to see it through to completion. If not for them, it would never have seen the light of day.

Walker Cowen's dictum notwithstanding, this book did have an ad hoc committee of writers: Madeline Hutcheson, Mary Ann Johnson, Nancy St. Clair Talley, and myself. Mary Ann and Nancy have also been generous and able copy editors, improving the pieces they didn't write.

In my view, the real authors of the book are Will Rieley and Roxanne Brouse. Will has designed all the restorations undertaken since the year 2000, and in several cases he has had to act as contractor as well as designer of the installation. He is also, directly or indirectly, responsible for whatever part of this book that is without error; he has most tactfully steered that part of the text he didn't write in the right direction, and has clarified endless confusions. In addition, he took on the very demanding job of overseeing the illustrations. Roxanne Brouse has been project manager, nanny, counselor, psychologist, fire-putter-outer, and friend, organizing and reorganizing reams of e-mailed text into a coherent whole, and then formatting it according to the very precise demands of the University of Virginia Press. In addition to Will and Roxanne, I must acknowledge the contributions of Rachel Lloyd, Jennifer Esser, Jill Trischman-Marks, and Shay Aulie, who are the genii behind the appearance and legibility of all the plans and working drawings throughout the book; they also produced the perspective drawings, without which the layout of some of the larger gardens would be incomprehensible. Jill also coped with the master plant list.

The archival resources at the Virginia Historical Society and at the Library of Virginia have provided the backbone of the text. At the Historical Society, E. Lee Shepard, Director of Manuscripts and Archives, and Frances Pollard, Director of Library Services, interrupted whatever they were doing whenever there was a call for help; John McClure, Reference Department Manager, searched the stacks when I couldn't come up with the proper call number, always finding the book; Library Clerks Margaret T. Kidd and Greg Hansard and Library Assistant Katherine Wilkins cheerfully hauled boxes and boxes of GCV records, copied endless pages of text, and understood that the Virginia Historical Society's computer search function was beyond me. In the Gillette Archive at the Library of Virginia, Chris Colby, Senior Research Archivist, and a bevy of lovely ladies behind the desk explained the mysteries of their system, printed out the necessary records, produced the unwieldy canisters we needed, and helped to lay out and reroll the fragile plans (no easy job) for our inspection; Mark Sagerburg, Photographic and Digital Imaging Manager, worked our cumbersome requests into his busy schedule to produce the required CDs in record time.

The directors of all the properties profiled here, as well as the directors of grounds and horticulture, the horticulturists, the gardeners, the curators, and the historians, have been unfailing sources of information and encouragement. They welcomed and worked with the photographers, and read and re-read the text, correcting mistakes and offering valuable suggestions for its improvement. Beate Jensen and Joanna Catron at Belmont, Peter Hatch at Monticello, Ann Miller at Montpelier, and Dean Norton at Mount Vernon have located or led me to diaries and other valuable and hard-to-find sources.

The owners of all the private houses documented by the Favretti Fellows and the Garden Club of Virginia Fellows have generously given permission to lead the reader to the Fellows' reports, which have been deposited at the Virginia Historical Society, the University of Virginia Library, the Kent-Valentine House, and the Colonial Williamsburg Foundation Library. I particularly wish to thank H. Furlong Baldwin, Joseph F. Johnston Jr., and the Rosewell Foundation for permission to include pictures of Eyre Hall, Bremo, and Rosewell.

Virginia's First Lady, Anne Holton Kaine, took the time to read and correct the essay on the Executive Mansion. Architect John Paul C. Hanbury, FAIA, was equally gracious, as was James E. Wootton, Executive Director of the Capitol Square Preservation Council. Paula Felder, Fredericksburg historian and author, was enormously helpful in straightening out the convoluted histories of Kenmore and Mary Washington's house and garden. Mary Lynn Bayliss, author of a forthcoming book on Major Dooley, provided anecdotes and sources of information about Maymont.

We have offered new conclusions about the historical importance of the Bacon's Castle garden. Archaeologists Nicholas M. Luccketti and William M. Kelso gave generously of time and counsel. Kevin Kelly led me by the hand to the letter in the files of Governor Nicholson that verified the background of the Allen family.

The responsibility for any mistakes is all mine.

Penelope Kaiserlian, director of the University of Virginia Press, was our acquisitions editor; her faith in the project was the greatest gift of all. Her assistants, Mary MacNeil and Angie Hogan have fielded our questions and calmed our fears. The project editor, Ruth Steinberg, has organized reams of confusing text into an organized whole and bridged the chasm between Press style and Virginia vernacular. With the aid of Roger Foley's glorious pictures, production manager Martha Farlow has made it a beautiful book.

INTRODUCTION

Margaret Bemiss's invitation to write this introduction has provided me the privilege to extend my thanks to the Garden Club of Virginia for all the time, treasure, talent—and, indeed, love—that it has expended over the past eighty years to create places of lasting beauty in our Commonwealth. The Garden Club's many projects form a record of remarkable achievement and dedication. It is also an effort that, fortunately, has no end in sight.

Mrs. Bemiss's volume, in many respects, is a progress report: a catalogue of the Garden Club's more recent restoration projects. A particular strength of this work is that it not only describes the garden restorations themselves, but lays out their historic contexts. Her entries provide substantive background information on the personalities and events associated with these places over the course of their histories, all of which enhances our understanding of the genesis and evolution of the various gardens and landscapes.

Perhaps my earliest firsthand encounter with the Garden Club's efforts was as an undergraduate at the University of Virginia in the early 1960s. Since I was enrolled in the architectural history program, I naturally paid due respect to the university's Jeffersonian buildings. But a magical discovery for me during my first year was the West Lawn gardens. It was the first time I had ever encountered such a complex of interesting and varied garden rooms. It was truly a nourishing experience to walk through these spaces and observe how diverse they were, how carefully tended, and how they changed character through the seasons. A couple of years later I summoned up enough self-confidence to ask the Department of Buildings and Grounds if I could work as a gardener for a summer. So, in my third year, I was duly employed for three months, with a salary of $1.05 per hour, spending most of my time pulling weeds in the Garden Club's newly created East Lawn gardens. That summer taught me something of what it takes to maintain a garden.

During my career as an architectural historian for the state of Virginia, I have devoted my energies primarily to the study of old buildings. I study why they look the way they do; I try to figure out what's happened to them over the years; and I offer advice on their preservation and restoration. My gardening venture at the University of Virginia, however, kindled my awareness of the importance of the relationship between landscape and historic buildings. This relationship is something every architectural historian needs to appreciate. As with buildings, we need to understand why these landscape settings look the way they do. We also need to understand what's happened to them over the years, and to take an interest in their preservation and restoration. Working in the university's pavilion gardens helped me realize that buildings are inseparable from their landscape contexts. A building and its setting form a cohesive unit, whether what surrounds the building is an expansive garden or park, or an urban work yard. The landscape context greatly affects the visual character of a building, and it also helps us understand the lifestyle and interests of its generations of occupants. Each generation leaves its stamp on both its buildings and their settings.

Landscapes, particularly gardens, change constantly, whether we tend them or not. Plant materials, being living organisms, are changing every day. I think my more focused interest in the landscape settings of historic buildings grew out of my concern at seeing many improperly managed landscapes, and the effect uninformed or absent management has on historic architecture. Moreover, a collegial association in the early 1990s with the distinguished garden historian John Dixon Hunt taught me the necessity of constant critical evaluation of works of landscape architecture. He prodded me to question whether a garden was performing as it was intended. As for understanding the proper visual relation between a historic house and its setting, John taught me always to ask what is supposed to be doing the speaking. Most historic grounds were laid out to complement a work of architecture, not obscure or dominate it. Thus, perhaps one of the greatest benefits of the Garden Club's many projects is their demonstration of a keen awareness of the balance between architecture and landscape, and the importance of having architecture and landscape work in tandem to maintain the intended effect. Indeed, in a number of the club's projects, the object was not to restore or create a garden but to enhance the landscape setting of a historic landmark or complex.

Interestingly, if I were to be asked to define a garden with one word, that word would be "control." Being composed of living plant materials, whether ornamentals or edibles or both, a garden is a controlled space. It takes constant labor to maintain both its intended character and function; otherwise, a garden degenerates into wilderness, an uncontrolled landscape. Be that as it may, whether it's the terraces of a grand estate or just a simple cottage garden, a garden is a controlled space, an unnatural landscape. This concept of control applies not just to gardens but to broader landscapes as well, particularly the grounds of country houses, suburban villas, churches, and even educational institutions, many of which were designed to have a naturalistic or picturesque look. These too require constant control to keep the scenes looking natural, and to have them properly complement the architecture they surround.

Not only have the Garden Club's many projects been informed essays in the proper balance between architecture and landscape, they also are demonstrations of the importance of proper, ongoing control. Any entity fortunate enough to be a beneficiary of a Garden Club restoration project, whether a house museum or a university, must commit to a strict maintenance agreement to ensure that the Club's investment in the property will be sustained. The Garden Club's Restoration Committee takes its projects very seriously. The committee formally revisits its gardens from time to time to satisfy itself that its maintenance agreements are being respected and that any necessary amendments are adequately justified. A number of gardens covered in this book reflect recent re-workings of early Garden Club projects. Such adjustments can result from new research or from practical considerations—an admission that some plant varieties just don't perform well in a particular space, for example. This is another great strength of the Garden Club's program: the realization that gardens are not static, and require regular evaluation and, oftentimes, corrections. Such long-term oversight has set a standard for the treatment of many other historic gardens and landscapes in Virginia, including private gardens.

Virginia has a long and esteemed tradition of gardening, owing in large part to the fact that Virginia's early settlers came from a mother country where gardening was, and remains, a revered institution. The creation of fine gardens, however, was not a high priority when the settlers first set foot on the shores of the James River. They had to contend with a wilderness. Their foremost need was basic habitable space. Thus, for the first half-century of settlement, eastern Virginia's cultural landscape was largely characterized by rude wooden cottages set in small clearings surrounded by palisades or barriers of tree stumps. It was not a pretty scene, but frontier occupation rarely is. Our earliest known instance of serious gardening on a grand scale came through extensive archaeological investigation sponsored by the Garden Club beginning in 1983, which revealed evidence of the huge rectilinear garden at Bacon's Castle, laid out in the last third of the seventeenth century. Even though the Bacon's Castle garden was exceptional for its time and place, it marks the genesis of a solid gardening tradition in the Old Dominion that has lasted for over three hundred years and is continuing on a healthy basis today.

By the beginning of the eighteenth century, extensive gardens had become a hallmark of Virginia's large plantations. Planters, including George Washington and Thomas Jefferson, took a keen interest in their gardens and created some of the country's most outstanding horticultural endeavors. Regrettably, by the beginning of the twentieth century, many of Virginia's earliest gardens had disappeared, or survived in only skeletal form. The loss of labor, particularly after the Civil War, made the maintenance of large gardens a low priority. Many old gardens were simply plowed under. Others were allowed to return to wilderness.

During the 1920s, Virginia witnessed an intensification of interest in the preservation of its historic landmarks, particularly those relating to its eighteenth-century heritage. Efforts were made to acquire and restore as museums some of our most noted works of colonial architecture. The restoration of Colonial Williamsburg, beginning in 1928, set a standard for comprehensive, professional treatment of historic sites. Williamsburg was an all-encompassing effort, involving not just the restoration and reconstruction of the town's buildings, but also of its landscape and gardens. The expertise in garden history and landscape architecture assembled in Williamsburg greatly stimulated Virginians' interest in historic gardens and made a new level of professionalism available to the Commonwealth. The Garden Club was quick to recognize the value of Williamsburg's expertise as a resource and drew a number of its early consultants from the Colonial Williamsburg Foundation staff.

With the guidance of Williamsburg scholars, as well as that of Virginia's noted landscape architect Charles F. Gillette, many of the Garden Club's early efforts involved the gardens of eighteenth-century plantation houses, including Monticello, Stratford, and Kenmore. Over the years, however, the Club's interests have expanded to embrace a remarkable variety of garden and landscaping projects, including Victorian estates, university grounds, old churchyards, and twentieth-century gardens. The projected restoration of General George C. Marshall's mid-twentieth-century garden at his Leesburg home, for which a plan has been presented, would take the Club's projects into a period very close to the present. Together, these projects comprise a living textbook of historic gardening and landscaping of many periods and styles unmatched anywhere else in the country.

Supplementing the restoration projects is one of the Garden Club's most important programs, one launched barely ten years ago. This involves the documentation of surviving privately owned historic gardens. Grants are given to graduate students in landscape architecture to spend the summer months recording garden features, plant materials, and historic documents relating to specific gardens. Several of the recording projects have focused on important colonial plantation gardens, including Sabine Hall,

Eyre Hall, Old Mansion (Bowling Green), Tuckahoe, and Rosewell. A few of these early gardens, such as Sabine Hall and Eyre Hall, survive relatively intact. Others, such as Rosewell, maintain only hints of their original appearance. Nonetheless, the surviving features of Virginia's colonial plantation gardens form a corpus of tangible relics of an exceptionally significant phase of America's gardening tradition. More recently, however, the Garden Club's documentation program has involved two outstanding twentieth-century gardens: Mirador, created by the famed Nancy Lancaster, and the Ellen Shipman garden at Chatham Manor. The site plans, photographs, and narrative descriptions produced through all these projects will be an invaluable archive for garden historians for years to come.

In summary, this catalogue of the Garden Club's recent projects and documentation efforts is a loving presentation of the remarkable accomplishments of this venerable and industrious organization. Margaret Bemiss offers us a window onto one of America's oldest, richest, and most sustained traditions of gardening and landscaping. While her text and the accompanying illustrations increase our understanding of and appreciation for the Garden Club's many gifts to the Commonwealth, it does not excuse us from directly experiencing the fruits of the Club's labors. The only way to truly know a garden is to visit it, and the Garden Club of Virginia has given us much to visit.

Calder Loth
Senior Architectural Historian
Virginia Department of Historic Resources

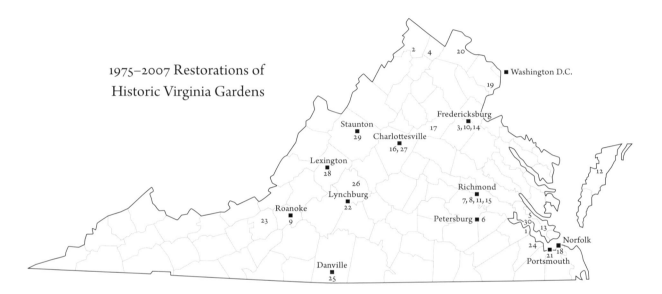

1975–2007 Restorations of Historic Virginia Gardens

1	Bacon's Castle	11	Kent-Valentine House	21	Old Portsmouth Courthouse
2	Belle Grove	12	Ker Place	22	Point of Honor
3	Belmont	13	Lee Hall Mansion	23	Smithfield
4	Blandy	14	Mary Washington House	24	St. Luke's Churchyard
5	Bruton Parish Churchyard	15	Maymont	25	Sutherlin House
6	Centre Hill	16	Monticello	26	Sweet Briar College
7	The Executive Mansion	17	Montpelier	27	University of Virginia Pavilions III and VI
8	Grace Arents Garden	18	Moses Myers House	28	Washington and Lee University
9	Hollins University	19	Mount Vernon	29	Woodrow Wilson Presidential Library at His Birthplace
10	Kenmore	20	Oatlands	30	Yeardley House

HISTORIC VIRGINIA GARDENS

The north end of the garden
at Bacon's Castle

Bacon's Castle

SURRY COUNTY

*A rare example of Jacobean architecture with its garden restored
to 1680s form based on archaeological evidence*

THE ASTONISHING DISCOVERY, IN 1983, OF THE LARGEST DOCUMENTED SEV-
enteenth-century garden in America, at Bacon's Castle, in Surry County, Virginia,
changed the history of landscape gardening in America. Before that, the scholarship
of Virginia's garden history began with the eighteenth century. Moreover, until then,
it was thought that all seventeenth-century gardens were, as Ann Leighton put it, "for
Meate or Medicine,"[1] and that the American pleasure garden was years away. Yet at
Bacon's Castle, in the middle of more or less nowhere, there was irrefutable archaeological evidence of a very large garden of a formal English Renaissance design, with
alcoves in the hedge on the west side that almost certainly were exedras—places to sit
and enjoy the garden! Glass fragments—wine-bottle seals marked "AA"—and bits of
bell jars that were used to protect seedlings from frost pointed to a construction date
of between 1680 and 1690.[2]

Bacon's Castle, according to the *Virginia Landmarks Register,* is "the oldest documented house in Virginia" and "the nation's outstanding example" of high-style, seventeenth-century domestic architecture.[3] However, until the archaeological exploration of the 1980s, there had been only two known references to a garden there: a 1911
map that was said to be a reproduction of an 1843 survey signed by a surveyor named
Morrison, and that showed "a large fenced garden in the west yard";[4] and a 1935 sketch
by Richard P. Hankins of the garden around 1871 as his grandfather, John Hankins,
remembered it from his childhood. For years, the house had been seen as an anomaly,
unique among Virginia's surviving Colonial houses: it sat in the middle of an open
field, surrounded by only a few trees, and with its outbuildings scattered in no particular pattern. Its existence conjured up many questions: Why was such a house built
there? And who was the man who had built it? Where did the design of the house come
from, much less the garden? Why, until 1983, had there been no thought of a contemporary garden? And how did it happen that such an extensive garden could have been

made in the seventeenth century at a time when life in Virginia was still so precarious? And not just any garden, but a "regular" garden—one with features suggesting that it could have been a place designed for strolling and sitting as well as weeding and harvesting, for pleasure as well as sustenance.[5] And, even more puzzling, at a time when there was no American garden literature to use as a resource, and therefore virtually no contemporary mention of garden design. Indeed, the few references to gardening that appear during this period are to be found only in estate inventories, where garden tools and "flower potts" were sometimes included in lists of household goods.

From the time of its construction, in 1665, until it was put up for auction and bought by the Association for the Preservation of Virginia Antiquities, in 1972, Bacon's Castle was a private home. In the spring of 1972, the APVA commissioned Kevin P. Kelly, a historian at Colonial Williamsburg, to research the site's history. His report, dated April 1, 1972, covered everything then known about the residence.[6] Missing from Kelly's report, however, was any information about the background of the original owner, Arthur Allen, or any discussion of how or why Allen could afford to build a brick house when most contemporary dwellings from the period were constructed as simple frame buildings. Nor is there any mention of an early garden on the grounds, much less such a remarkable one.

Interestingly, in 1976, archaeologists working at Richneck Plantation in Denbigh discovered a cruciform foundation almost identical to that of Bacon's Castle, but the plantation house, probably built during the 1660s by Miles Cary II, was completely gone. It is known, however, that Cary was both wealthy and prominent. Two years later, in 1978, the APVA initiated its own archaeological survey of the Bacon's Castle site, necessary to the formation of a plan to preserve Virginia's oldest remaining seventeenth-century house. Exploration to the south of the house revealed evidence of forecourt buildings, the dates of which could not be determined. Further excavations, nearer to the house, showed evidence of various alterations that had been made over the three-hundred-year history of the house's occupation. One of the more telling discoveries was that originally the house had probably had a stone roof.[7] The importation to the colonies of such a quantity of stone shingles would have been quite expensive. This was yet another indication that Arthur Allen had been a man of considerable wealth, and also that he was aware of comparable English houses of the period and the materials used to build them.

In 1983, the APVA turned its attention to the west side of the house, after infrared photography exposed a large dark rectangle at just the spot where the 1843 Morrison map had shown there was a garden. At this stage, the APVA applied to the Garden Club of Virginia for a grant to fund its archaeological research on this site. It was unusual for the GCV to fund archaeological research, but the Club decided to support the project because the research would make possible a more accurate restoration of the nineteenth-century Hankins garden. The result—the uncovering of a geometrically designed seventeenth-century garden longer than a football field—was unanticipated and astounding.

DENDROCHRONOLOGICAL STUDY DATED THE BUILDING OF BACON'S CASTLE to 1665. Arthur Allen, the owner and builder, was known to have come to Virginia in 1649, and for two hundred years the house was known as "Arthur Allen's brick house." The nineteenth-century appellation, "Bacon's Castle," came from the fact that for a few months in 1676, by which time the house belonged to Arthur Allen II, the followers of Nathaniel Bacon had taken it over for their headquarters, plundering and stealing much of Allen's household goods. Bacon and his followers were finally driven out by a detachment of British marines, and Allen was able to return home. He later sued the rebels—successfully—for 25,000 pounds of tobacco. The house passed down through seven generations of the Allen family, and sometime before 1800 a frame addition was added. In 1774, the property was left to Allen Cocke, a grandson of Arthur Allen III, and it continued to belong to Allen descendants until 1843, when it was sold at auction. In 1852, owner John Hankins moved the frame addition, now the caretaker's cottage, and replaced it with a large Neoclassical brick wing that connected to the 1665 house with a two-story hyphen. The Hankins family lived there until 1872, but after the Civil War, farming with wage labor was no way to make a living. Hankins had to mortgage the place in 1870, and the family was forced to sell it two years later to the mortgage holder, Edwin White. White moved in but died soon after, and when his estate was finally settled, Bacon's Castle was bought by William Allen Warren, whose descendants kept it for the next hundred years. It was designated a National Historic Landmark in 1960. In 1972, the last Warren owners died childless, and the APVA bought the house and the surrounding forty acres from the Warren estate in September of that year.[8]

Until 1984, Arthur Allen was essentially unknown to history, being one of a number of shadowy figures who surface in the archives but whose origins are a mystery. But as the archaeological work on the garden site progressed, Kevin Kelly discovered, among the papers of Royal Governor Francis Nicholson, part of an unsigned letter written in 1704/5 that gave a clue as to Allen's past. The letter appears to have been an answer to a request by Governor Nicholson for information about the Allen family of Surry County, and with its discovery the pieces of the puzzle began to fall into place.[9]

It seems that Arthur Allen was a younger son of one John Allen of Droitwich, in

Worcestershire. John Allen was "a Gentleman of an Antient family and of three hundred pound per annum Paternal Estate." Arthur Allen emigrated to Jamestown in 1649, the year that Virginia "announced its allegiance to the Stuart House after the execution of Charles I and gave refuge to prominent Cavaliers." Though not a prominent Cavalier, Allen was clearly a Royalist, and he became a loyal follower of Governor William Berkeley.[10]

On March 14, 1650, Allen patented two hundred acres of land on the south side of the James River, in what would two years later become Surry County. With this patent, he was allowed to transport three servants and one Alice Tucker, who either "was, or would shortly become, his wife." Their first son, named for his father, was born in 1651. When Surry County was split off from James City County in 1652, Arthur Allen was appointed one of Surry's first county commissioners and a justice of the peace. In 1661, he was elected to the vestry of Lawne's (or Lyon's, or Lane's, depending on the source) Creek Parish. In measuring Allen's political influence, this is an important fact. Each county was divided into parishes, depending on the number of tithable households; thus, the Lawne's Creek Parish would have been the first political subdivision of the original county, a measure of the size of the population. There were two parishes in Surry County at its founding, and the county therefore elected two members to the House of Burgesses. Tithes were due to the parish; taxes were assessed by poll count. Though Arthur Allen himself never served in the House of Burgesses, he was nonetheless a leading citizen of Surry County.[11]

In 1656, Allen added to his holdings by buying 350 acres from one John Richards. The deed refers to "Arthur Allen, Merchant." Kelly says that "as a merchant, he may well have acted as a factor for an English firm. He may also have operated as a middleman for neighboring planters, collecting their small amounts of tobacco, and in return, selling them English goods. In all likelihood, Allen probably combined whatever his role as a merchant entailed with that of being a tobacco planter himself." Whatever he did, it was obviously successful; in 1661, he bought another 500 acres, in Lawne's Creek Parish, from John and Peleg Dunstan. There, in 1665, he built his grand brick house with its English stone roof. And then, in 1669, not too long before he died, he bought another 1,000 acres, "somewhere inland from his home plantation." Kelly writes: "As time went on, and his properties increased, tobacco planting may have become his primary concern. His eleven adult laborers in 1668 were certainly numerous enough to engage in extensive tobacco cultivation." He was close to the top of the county lists in tithable household size and recorded land ownership.[12] Arthur Allen's brick house, then, was a statement of his position in society and in the power structure of Surry County.

There is very little seventeenth-century architecture left in Virginia, and most of the domestic foundations that have been uncovered are of much simpler, frame dwellings. However, in 1995, archaeologists working at Colonial Williamsburg uncovered the foundation of yet another cross-shaped, all-brick house, very similar to the foundations for Bacon's Castle and the Miles Cary house. This one was built by John Page in 1662, three years before Arthur Allen's. In a newspaper article on the discovery, Edward Chappell, Colonial Williamsburg's director of architectural research, is quoted as saying that the Page house, like Bacon's Castle, represented "the real high end of Colonial Society."[13]

Arthur Allen died in June 1669, leaving the house entailed to his son, Arthur Allen II. Allen's son had been born in Virginia in 1651, and in 1660 he had been sent to England for six or seven years to be educated. He would have been eighteen when his father died, and not long back from England.[14] The younger Allen built on his father's legacies of position and wealth. He served in the Surry militia, rising to the rank of major, then moved into the larger sphere of colonial government. In 1682 Major Allen was elected to the House of Burgesses, and in 1686 he was elected Speaker by his fellow Burgesses.[15]

Though successful, Major Allen's political career was a stormy one. He was twice

suspended from the Surry County Commission for opposing gubernatorial power, and as Speaker of the House was twice responsible for the dissolution of the House, for the same reason. From 1691 until 1702, Allen was retired from public life, having refused to swear allegiance to King William and Queen Mary. On the death of James II, he took the new oath and was back in the swim, receiving new, distinguished, and lucrative appointments.[16] It is interesting to note the development of a young and ambitious Virginian, native-born but English-schooled, from loyal follower of Lord Berkeley, to strong proponent of the power of the colonists, to respected elder statesman enjoying important appointments from another royal governor.

Given what we now know about the position of wealth and prestige that he held, as well as the great interest in seventeenth-century England in horticulture and garden design, it is not surprising that the younger Allen laid out such an impressive garden, sometime around 1680. When this garden was uncovered three hundred years later, it was a stunning surprise. Aspects of its plan are common to many eighteenth-century Virginia gardens, but that there was a garden of English Renaissance design, of that size, in Surry County in 1680 was totally unexpected. One is forced to wonder: Were there others like it in the colony at that time? And why did Allen put the garden where he did, on the west side of the house and visible from the inside? There is no documentation to prove it, but it seems fair to speculate that young Arthur Allen, during his seven or eight years in England, would have been exposed to the intense interest

BACON'S CASTLE

there in horticulture and garden design. He could well have seen John Parkinson's *Paradisi in Sole Paradisus Terrestris; or, A Garden of All Sorts of Pleasant Flowers . . .* (1629), or William Lawson's *A New Orchard and Garden . . .* (1614). Both of these books, then widely known in England, show gardens in the configuration of the one Allen was to develop in Virginia.

There is another entertaining basis for speculation about the genesis of the Bacon's Castle garden. In 1664, the year before Arthur Allen built his brick house, the English diarist and writer John Evelyn published his *Sylva: or, a Discourse of Forest Trees,* with the "Kalendarium Hortense" as an appendix. As it happens, the Evelyn family was well known in Virginia. John Evelyn's uncle, Robert Evelyn, was an investor in the Virginia Company in 1609 and was on the list of Company "Adventurers" in 1618 and 1620. His two sons, George and Robert, first cousins of John, moved to Virginia around 1634. Robert was surveyor general of Virginia, and a member of the council in 1637. George moved to Maryland. In 1649, the year that Arthur Allen arrived in Virginia, George Evelyn made a trip to England and visited his cousin, John. In that same year, George Evelyn also bought 650 acres in James City County, Virginia, which he gave to his son, Montjoy, in 1650. He also had a daughter, Rebecca, whose first husband, Bartholomew Knipe, owned more than 500 acres in James City County.[17] One plausible possibility is that George might have brought back to his daughter Rebecca some gardening books. Having just returned from a visit with his cousin, the author John Evelyn, he would certainly have been aware of that man's interest in gardening and horticulture. To add to the mix is the fact that Arthur Allen and Daniel Parke, who would become Rebecca Evelyn's second husband, both sailed to Virginia in 1649. It may not be too far-fetched to think that they and George Evelyn could have crossed the Atlantic together on Evelyn's voyage home. And there is every reason to think that Arthur Allen would have come to know Rebecca Evelyn Knipe and her husband. They were prosperous landowners in James City County when Allen took out his first patent there, although his land was in that part of the county which later became Surry. Be that as it may, given all the comings and goings between England and the colonies, the wealthier Virginians would certainly have been aware of the fascination with garden design and horticulture that was all the rage in England in the mid-seventeenth century.

So when Major Allen laid out his grand garden in 1680, applying well-known principles of garden design, he might conceivably have been finishing his father's work. But it is more likely that he was making a statement about his own financial and political successes. His brick house and elegant formal garden were "appropriate symbols of his prestige." The archaeological discoveries give evidence that this was a

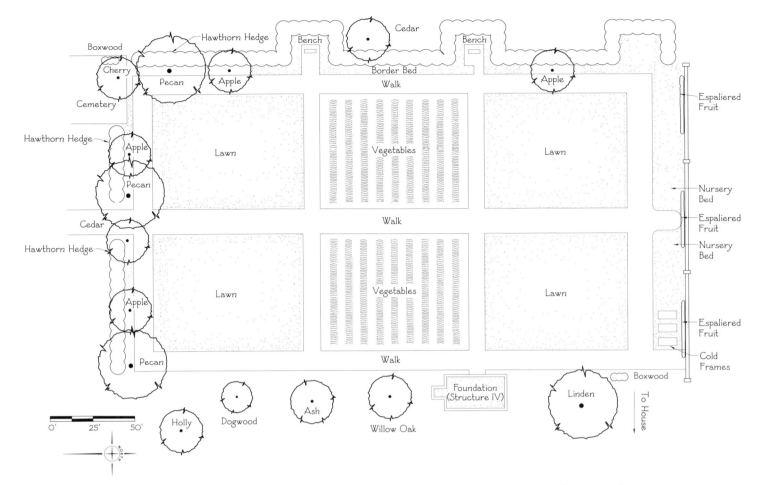

garden to be admired and enjoyed, laid out by a gentleman of taste and imagination, with a knowledge of garden design. It was a Virginia garden of vegetables and medicinal herbs, embellished with some unusual English amenities.[18]

Major Allen's garden was, by the standards of his time in Virginia, unusual in size and detail. It was probably not unique; other gentlemen of substance doubtless enjoyed similar ones. Governor Berkeley's garden at Green Springs was legendary, although no archaeological evidence for it has been found. But the fact that Surry became something of a backwater early in its history protected this particular garden from the plow or later development, which would have obliterated all traces of its existence. In its basic outline, the garden was similar to many more-elaborate English pleasure gardens. The space was outlined by a ten-foot walkway. Within this walkway, six large, rectangular, raised planting beds were defined by a twelve-foot-wide central north-south walkway and two eight-foot crosswalks, the whole surrounded by a six-foot-wide border bed and a hedge. At the north end were signs of a brick forcing wall with two long, narrow planting beds in front of it.[19] There was no evidence, however, of an orchard or a vineyard within any of the six large planting beds; it was clear that there had been no trees in the beds, and that everything had been planted in rows. But at the crosswalks on the west side of the garden were the remains of structures bearing a "strong similarity to the footprint of buildings seen frequently in depictions of medieval English gardens. These buildings, called exedras, had only three sides, often, but not always, with a bench along all three sides. With a bench against only the back wall, the Bacon's Castle example seems to be a close parallel to these English predecessors."[20] In addition, the central walk did not stop at the edge of the northern perimeter walkway, as it did at the opposite end. Instead, it crossed the northern walkway and terminated in a graceful, bell-shaped space which almost bisected the planting bed between the walkway and the forcing wall. In this space, slightly off-center, was a circular hole that possibly had held the base of a sundial or some other decorative garden ornament.[21]

Rudy J. Favretti, the Garden Club of Virginia's landscape architect at the time of the garden restoration, analyzed the research for the Bacon's Castle garden, categorizing its conclusions as either "positive" or "conjectural." The conclusion that the fragmentary foundations at the west termini of the crosswalks were exedras, he places in the conjectural column, saying that they could also have been compost bins or cold frames. True, but equally conjectural. The archaeological team that uncovered the garden was led by Nicholas Luccketti, who feels quite strongly that the alcove spaces were exedras, although he readily admits that they would have been unusual in seventeenth-century Surry County. Luccketti has no doubt but that Major Allen's garden was a garden to be enjoyed, as well as one to sustain the family.

WHEN THE APVA'S ARCHAEOLOGICAL SURVEY WAS COMPLETE, IT WAS DEcided to cover the original garden with a layer of sand, to ensure that the historical evidence that had miraculously survived unplowed for three hundred years would remain undisturbed. The sand would act as a "bookmark," in case there should ever be further excavation. Any future restoration will be done on top of this protective layer. Both the scraping away of the wind-deposited top layer, which it had been determined contained no information of archaeological interest, and its subsequent replacement, were accomplished using an excavation machine, called a Gradall, in "a process proven to be both safe for subsurface deposits and the most realistic and economical way to excavate sites as large as gardens."[22] While it is true that historical evidence was saved, the resulting compaction of the soil has produced some intractable drainage problems in the restored garden. The excavation of this garden was thus a learning experience, both for the archaeologists and for the Garden Club of Virginia.

The garden itself was not replaced until 1988, after the archaeological work was

Bell-shaped terminus of central walkway and brick forcing wall

BACON'S CASTLE

brought to a close. To maintain a garden of the size of the original in the late twentieth century would not have been practical, so the two north and south pairs of planting beds were seeded as lawn. Only the two central beds are planted in vegetables, with flowers and herbs in the north planting beds and the west border bed. On the east side, the hedge and border were not replaced. Instead, a historical marker is there and the view of the garden is open from the house. As the archaeologists had found no sign of an enclosure fence, Favretti specified a hawthorn hedge on the west side. But because it was not possible to obtain enough hawthorn in time for the scheduled presentation of the garden, this was changed to mockorange, which proved unsuccessful, and the hawthorn has now been installed. Apricots, first specified for the espaliered fruit trees along the north forcing wall, succumbed to fire blight and were replaced with Hewes crabapples. In the summer of 2006, they too perished, and they have been replaced by peaches, which are thought to be less susceptible to fire blight. Favretti specified the hedge material, the trees, and the planting scheme for the west border beds. He also provided a list of authentic vegetables to be planted in the vegetable plots, leaving the choice of vegetables each year to the Bacon's Castle gardener.

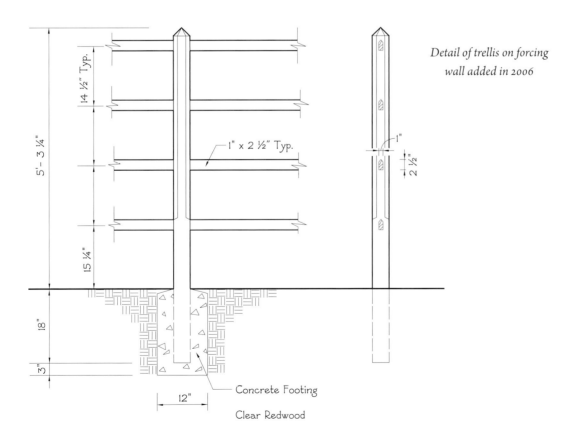

Detail of trellis on forcing wall added in 2006

There are still unanswered questions about the garden, some of which might be cleared up by further archaeological investigation, but some of which can probably never be answered. Among them: In 1680, what was the entire landscape—which would have included the house and garden and other buildings—like? Was Arthur Allen familiar with some of the great houses in England whose similar formal gardens were situated to the side of the main house?[23] What was the basis for the garden's axial relationship, or lack of one, to the main house? Was there another building balancing Structure IV to the east of the house as one approached from the south? Could the garden have had a paling fence that left no archaeological traces? If there were exedras, were they roofed? And were the seats only in the back, or did they extend around three sides? Were there ever any decorative objects, like topiaries, at the intersections of the paths? And is it possible that the planting rows were not the only pattern that ever existed, but just the last pattern in that layer? Is it conceivable that the creation of rows might have superceded an earlier, and perhaps more elaborate, pattern in some of the beds? There is also some very interesting geometry at work in the design of the garden, but Major Allen was a surveyor, so it is perhaps not surprising that the garden is laid out in even increments of the standard measurement units of his time.[24]

Although questions remain, Arthur Allen's garden tells us a great deal about the growing tensions in the colony and the political relationship of the native-born Virginians to the English colonial government. To succeed in politics in Virginia in the late seventeenth and early eighteenth centuries, it was necessary to have one foot in each camp. In a way, the design of this garden can be read as a metaphor for Arthur Allen's political career. His was a "regular" garden, common in early Virginia, though larger than most, to be sure. At the same time, its unusual decorative elements showed him to be an educated English gentleman, a position his father had worked hard to solidify and one that Major Allen valued greatly, judging from his loyalty to Governor Berkeley. But finally, and above all, he was a Virginian, having suffered through several periods of ostracism, from both the Surry County Courthouse and the House of Burgesses at Jamestown, for defending the interests of the colonists against the power of the king.

*Demonstration garden behind
the Belle Grove house*

Belle Grove

The landscape for Isaac Hite's elegant dwelling

BELLE GROVE COMMANDS THE LANDSCAPE SOUTH OF MIDDLETOWN, RIS-
ing massive in the western view from the Valley Pike, originally the Great Wagon
Road from Pennsylvania through southern Appalachia. It was completed by 1797 and
is now a historic site of the National Trust for Historic Preservation. Minus its 1815
wing, the house recalls a Palladian villa, with the same balance and symmetry, and
somewhat the same agricultural function, as those sixteenth-century monuments of
the Veneto. The dressed-stone southern façade, the corner quoining, and the pedimented second-story portico suggest the influence of the Commonwealth's architectural arbiter of the period. Just imagine stone replaced with brick to see a typical Jeffersonian pavilion.

Belle Grove is a third-generation statement of pioneer success. Hans Jost Hite,
grandfather of the builder and the first of the family to cross the Atlantic, sailed from
Rotterdam to London in 1709, and thence to New York in 1710, where he settled in
Kingston with his wife and small daughter.[1] His trek began in his native Bonfeld, Kreich-
gau, Germany, where he had worked as a linen weaver. Records show that by 1717 he
was living in Pennsylvania, and that by 1720 he had established a successful mill, which
came to be known as Pennypacker's Mills, on the Schuylkill River there. After receiving less than the desired assistance when he petitioned the governor of Pennsylvania for protection from increasing Indian hostilities, Jost Hite sold his Pennsylvania
holdings in 1730 and moved early the next year to the virgin Shenandoah Valley of
42Virginia. From John Van Meter he bought 40,000 acres, which came to be known as
Hite's Grant, and in partnership with his friend, Robert McKay, another 100,000 acres
from Governor Gooch, on August 15, 1731. He then set about finding settlers to improve them, making at least one recruiting voyage to Ireland. By June 1734 the Council
of Virginia judged Hite to have settled the required number of families and granted
him his patents.

Belle Grove endured. After the war, it had a succession of owners before the Brumback family bought it in 1907, using it first as a family farm and later as an inn. One of their summer regulars was Francis Welles Hunnewell, secretary to the Harvard Corporation and phaenogamic curator of the New England Botanical Club. He came to the Valley in the 1920s to collect botanical species, later giving his celebrated plant collection to Virginia Polytechnic Institute and State University. Among his specimens were an adder's tongue fern (*Ophioglossum engelmanii*), chiefly southern and western in distribution; *Woodsia ilvensis,* a fern northern in range; and *Paxistima canbyi,* a small rare evergreen shrub of limited range and found in the Valley in only a handful of obscure locations.

In 1929 Hunnewell purchased Belle Grove from the Brumback family, and in 1964 he bequeathed it to the National Trust for Historic Preservation with the stipulation that the Brumbacks be given rights to remain.

In 1983, at the request of Belle Grove Incorporated, the Garden Club of Virginia chose Belle Grove for its thirty-eighth landscape restoration. The two-year project, designed and implemented by Rudy J. Favretti, provided a detailed interpretation for the nineteenth-century plantation landscape. Despite meticulous recordkeeping at Belle Grove even before 1794, no document has surfaced regarding garden design or specific plantings by the original owners or subsequent stewards. Archaeological investigations have so far revealed nothing about a garden. The earliest nineteenth-century engraving of the house shows light foundation planting but little else about the landscape. With this single visual link, Favretti developed plans for a re-creation to suit the period 1800–1830. This was a time of unequalled agricultural prosperity in the Valley, when the Hites operated one of Virginia's most successful plantations. Relying upon the lay of the land, the siting of the house, and the tastes of the day, Favretti concluded that Belle Grove's few clues indicated a residence set in trees and overlooking tilled fields, the only garden, a sustenance garden for the culinary and medical needs of a large family and its many servants, having probably been behind the house.

Favretti's plan began with a survey of existing trees and the addition of new ones. He redesigned the demonstration garden behind the house, enclosing it on three sides with a lattice fence reproduced from one shown in an old photograph. He chose plants for their historical authenticity, with varieties conforming as closely as possible to those available to a Shenandoah Valley working farm before 1830. Plants included those used in cooking, medicine, and commerce.

Following Favretti's suggestions, the Garden Club sanctioned the removal of

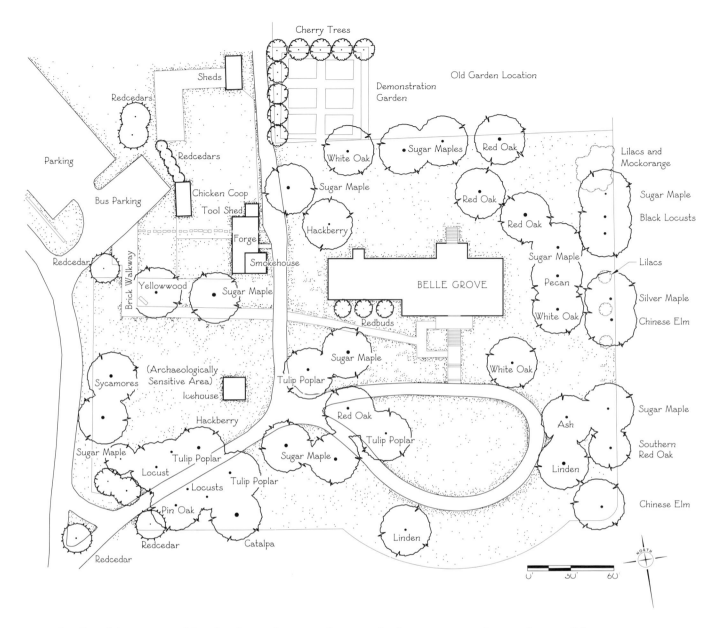

Cherry Trees

Old Garden Location

Sheds

Demonstration
Garden

Redcedars

Lilacs and
Mockorange

Parking

Redcedars

White Oak

Sugar Maples

Red Oak

Sugar Maple

Black Locusts

Bus Parking

Sugar Maple

Red Oak

Chicken Coop

Tool Shed

Red Oak

Lilacs

Redcedar

Hackberry

Forge

Sugar Maple

Silver Maple

Yellowwood

Smokehouse

BELLE GROVE

Pecan

Brick Walkway

Sugar Maple

White Oak

Chinese Elm

Redbuds

Sugar Maple

(Archaeologically
Sensitive Area)

White Oak

Sugar Maple

Sycamores

Icehouse

Red Oak

Ash

Hackberry

Tulip Poplar

Southern
Red Oak

Tulip Poplar

Linden

Sugar Maple

Tulip Poplar

Sugar Maple

Locust

Tulip Poplar

Locusts

Chinese Elm

Pin Oak

Redcedar

Catalpa

Linden

Redcedar

NORTH

0'   30'   60'

dead and/or unsuitable shrubs and trees, along with the pruning of some huge old
trees that obscured both the view of the house and the one from the house looking
out across the fields. At the request of the Belle Grove board of directors, the plan
called for low-growing and low-maintenance plants to soften the foundation, although
foundation planting was not customary in the period 1800–1830.

An important element in the project was the construction of an entrance ramp
from a new parking lot outside the restored area, with directional fencing and signs,
and of a long brick walk to the front entrance of the house.[2] An existing fence around
the landscaped area was repaired and extended to the entrance.

In 1993, the Restoration Committee revisited the garden at Belle Grove. At this time, Favretti drew up a master plan for the replacement and addition of trees; his plan was never completed in its entirety, and has subsequently been modified.

In 1998, William D. Rieley was retained as landscape architect by the Garden Club of Virginia to succeed Favretti, reporting to the Restoration Committee. When he took over the care of Belle Grove, he noted that the demonstration garden covers one corner of a large flat rectangle of ground just outside the lawn and the west fence. The dimensions of that rectangle led him to conclude that the entire area had been the site of the original garden. It would most probably have been laid out in planting squares defined by a central path and crosswalks, in the manner of earlier "regular" gardens, a form that appeared in the colonies in the early seventeenth century and continues in modified forms to this day. The Montpelier garden of Nelly Hite's childhood must have been of that old pattern; that now vanished garden put in by the older James Madison (Dolley Madison later called this the "old lady's garden") is almost certain to have been laid out in squares. Though this has not been archaeologically verified at Montpelier, similar Madison family gardens in Orange County support the notion. And the size of the Hite household would have required a very large garden, to feed all those children and the people who took care of them.

When the Restoration Committee revisited Belle Grove in 2003, the Belle Grove board agreed to the removal of the foundation planting, and today Belle Grove rises spare and uncluttered from the ground, as it would have done originally. At the request of Belle Grove, new trees have been planted according to the modified master plan.

Outlasting weather, war, family triumphs, and tragedies, Belle Grove testifies to the persistence and courage of the settlers who built their homes so as to make a lasting mark on future generations. It is a prized survivor, of regional and national significance. In 2002, the National Trust for Historic Preservation and Belle Grove Incorporated joined a private/public partnership with the National Park Service and helped establish the Cedar Creek and Belle Grove National Historic Park. Together, they share jointly in the protection of the hallowed ground of the Civil War battlefield and of the original prosperous plantation with its open farmland and glorious views of Belle Grove.

Belmont

*The garden of two artists restored
to their original vision*

BELMONT SITS ON A HILL IN THE TOWN OF FALMOUTH, ACROSS THE RAP-
pahannock River from Fredericksburg. The north half of the frame house, with an
entrance passage on its south side, was built about 1790.[1] Deeds of ownership have
disappeared, probably during the Civil War, but surviving documents indicate that
there were two owners of the property between 1785 and 1804—a Mr. Voss and a Mr.
Horner. In 1807, Thomas Knox bought the house for his mother, Susannah Fitzhugh
Knox. When she died, in 1823, it was sold to Joseph Burwell Ficklen, an ambitious and
successful young businessman who ended up owning the Bridgewater and Bellemont
Flour Mills as well as the Falmouth toll bridge. He did not live in the house until his
first marriage, in 1843, to Ella McGee. Both she and their infant daughter died within
a year or two.

Ficklen later married Anne Eliza Fitzhugh, with whom he had six children. To
house this burgeoning brood, the Ficklens enlarged the house to its present size in
several stages during the 1850s, and they laid out the structure of the present garden.
They also added the east porch and its horseshoe stone steps with the magnificent
wrought iron railing. The steps go down to the "long walk" leading south along the
brow of the hill, defining the east edge of the lawn with its triangular planting beds at
either end, or north to what was a circular carriage drive and a long flight of brick steps
down to the village of Falmouth at the bottom of the hill. This was the route taken
every day by Mr. Ficklen to work at his mill. The Ficklen family lived at Belmont until
1916, when they sold it to the American Impressionist painter Gari Melchers and his
much younger wife, Corinne.

It was the Melchers garden that the Garden Club of Virginia was asked to restore
in 1991, and it was an unusual experience for the Restoration Committee and their
landscape architect: an eighteenth-century house surrounded by a twentieth-century
garden that had been designed by two artists. Their paintings were full of flamboyant

Belmont in the late 1920s

color, and so was their garden. Fortunately, they had left a trove of diaries and letters upon which to base the restoration.

Julius Garibaldi Melchers was born in Detroit in 1860. His father, also named Julius, a Prussian-born sculptor, was his son's first art teacher. When it turned out that the son's bent was for painting, the young Melchers was packed off to Dusseldorf at the age of seventeen to study at the Royal Prussian Academy of Art. There, the emphasis was on rigorous classical training; religious and historical themes and anecdotal figure painting were the requirements. By the late 1870s, painting styles in the rest of Europe had changed and the artistic action had moved to Paris. But Melchers's mother considered Paris a "den of iniquity." Gari finally did get to Paris, four years later, but by then his style was firmly grounded in the "hard-edged realism" he had learned at Dusseldorf. Nonetheless, his work was widely acclaimed in Paris. In 1889 he was one of two Americans to win a Grand Prize at the Paris Universal Exposition; the other was John Singer Sargent. Toward the turn of the century, however, his realistic paintings of rural subjects fell out of fashion, and he adopted a more impressionistic style, turning his attention to religious rites of passage and other popular subjects of the day. Romantic love, family life, the world of women, and particularly young motherhood, became his forte. His work became more colorful and decorative, and he was very successful.

About this time, in 1902, he met Corinne Mackall, a gifted young art student from Baltimore and Savannah. Twenty years younger than Melchers, her own plans to become a painter had brought her to study in Europe. It seems that Gari kept turning up wherever she was, and that she occasionally returned the compliment. By the end of 1902, they were engaged. They were married in 1903, and for all intents and purposes Corinne gave up her own painting and devoted her life to his. The couple lived in Europe until the First World War drove them back to New York. Life in New York was frenetic: Melchers was much in demand as a painter of portraits and large-scale murals. He was also elected an academician of the American Academy of Arts and Letters, and he served as president of the New Society of Artists, dealing tactfully with his temperamental peers.

As a retreat from this too-busy life, he bought Belmont, an easy half-day's train ride from New York. But he couldn't resist accepting new involvements in Washington and Richmond: he served on the board of the Corcoran Gallery of Art and was a member of the Virginia Art Commission, and he was president of the Smithsonian Commission to Establish a National Gallery of Art, now the Smithsonian American Art Museum. His new home also provided a base for a successful new direction in his work. He transferred his earlier European interests to American counterparts, painting impressionistic scenes of urban and small-town southern life that were very popular with the buying public.

Corinne, for her part, launched seriously into developing Belmont into a proper country estate. Black-and-white photographs taken in the late twenties by Frances Benjamin Johnston show that the house itself was rose-bowered and vine-clad.[2] According to Belmont's grounds preservation supervisor Beate Jensen, this was "an esthetic shared by many of her contemporaries and other artists as well. Think of Monet. Like the Melchers, many people covered their houses in vines and roses, added foundation plantings edged by boxwood, and had plants and pots sitting on steps and stoops. It looks busy to our eye today, but was [then] considered 'old fashioned' and 'charming.'"[3]

Corinne began by improving the immediate surroundings of the house. On the east front and south side of the house, she retained the long walk, the lawn, and the triangular beds, but rebuilt the arches, embellished the walkway, filled the beds with spring bulbs and summer annuals, and added roses wherever she could. Her planting lists are prodigious. Another early project was the planting of fruit trees, both around the house and in the area of the garage and stables. Her diary contains long lists of apples, cherries, peaches, pears, plums, and quinces, with shipping tags from various nurseries. One entry for June 6, 1923, notes: "Have peaches for first time off new trees." Other entries record the first strawberries, the first raspberries, the first asparagus. One mentions "putting grapevine posts in the garden."[4]

Also in 1923, Corinne designed a new entrance to the drive and planted six American elms on the west side of the house, to provide shade and "a stately ambience" to the approach from the road. The new entrance was flanked by stone walls, with lions capping the posts for a new wooden gate. That June, work was begun on the stone house that was to serve as a studio and gallery; the last stone was laid on October 28. This was also the month in which she had hot beds built, to get an early start on the spring planting.

In 1931, Corinne tackled the "grove," as she called the wooded hillside at the south end of the long walk, making a garden filled with laurel and shade-loving flowers, with

a path winding down to the river and along the streambed. Her diary of that year tells the story:

JANUARY 26: Nannie and I walk over the grove and choose location for winding paths down the hill.

JANUARY 27: Direct the work on the place and stake paths in grove.

JANUARY 30: Men lay steps in grove.

MARCH 11: Plant laurel in the grove.

APRIL 17: Mason and Fox put up bird house in grove. I try to plant flower seed.

APRIL 21: Visit Mt. Vernon, I admire little summer house and plan to have one.

The next year, before her husband died, she added the octagonal summerhouse at the crest of the hill overlooking the grove.

The diaries, calendars, letters, receipts, notes, and photographs from the period 1921–31 paint an amazingly detailed picture of the life that Corinne Melchers set up for herself at Belmont. Though she and her situation were unusually—she was remarkably gifted and her husband was a well-known artist who spent a lot of time in New York and elsewhere—the life she led was not unique, but rather had much in common with the life of any well-born, well-educated, well-traveled, and well-to-do woman of her time. There are references to friends who share her love of gardening, guests to take for a walk by the river, friends to go driving with, ice to be cut for the ice house, trees to be trimmed or sprayed, bulbs to be dried, roses to be pruned, seeds to be planted, wheat to be cut, cuttings to be potted up, sunflowers to be picked, roses to be arranged, cherries to be stoned. It is the rhythm of life on a farm in Fredericksburg, Virginia, in the 1920s that she evokes so clearly in her letters and diaries.

Three of the diary entries describe the close and affectionate relationship she had with her husband, and her pleasure at having him home:

NOVEMBER 24, 1921: Plant white lilac bush and visit Gari painting George Young as hunter at foot of grove.

December 1, 1921: Work with vines, etc. in garden with Gari.

October 17, 1924: Take G. to town to find flowers to paint—to Chatham—Gari paints delphiniums in yellow vase.

As he grew older, Gari Melchers painted more and more at Belmont, prevailing upon his portrait subjects to come to Virginia for their sittings and devoting the rest of his time to his impressionistic renderings of life in the South. He died at Belmont in 1932. Corinne then devoted the rest of her life to maintaining his reputation through a series of retrospective exhibitions.

In 1942, Corinne gave Belmont to the Commonwealth of Virginia to serve as a Gari Melchers Memorial and Art Center. It took the state government a while to find the proper administrative home for Corinne's gift; it was moved from the aegis of the Virginia Museum of Fine Arts to that of the University of Virginia, and then to Mary Washington College (then part of the University of Virginia, more recently the University of Mary Washington) in Fredericksburg. It is now exhibited as the Gari Melchers Home and Studio.

By the time the Garden Club of Virginia was asked to help, there was not much garden left at Belmont. It had been fifty years since Mrs. Melchers gave the property to the Commonwealth, and the administration of Belmont had been passed around from pillar to post. The garden had suffered greatly, although the bones were still there to guide the restoration process. Though the Ficklens' mid-nineteenth-century Federal design was the basis for the garden immediately to the south of the house, and is part of the restoration, the rest of the Melcherses' landscape was decidedly theirs—that of a twentieth-century country estate. It is this joint project of the two artists who were Belmont's last private owners that is being re-created as accurately as possible.

The Garden Club of Virginia began its restoration in 1993 under the direction of its landscape architect, Rudy J. Favretti. Favretti based his work on the records from the Melchers archive that had been studied up to that point. The first move was to restore the long walk on the east side of the house. To make it passable for brides, as the Belmont management had requested, the much overgrown boxwood was cut way back and the derelict rose arbors, originally built by the Ficklens in the mid-nineteenth century and restored in 1916 by the Melchers, were again rebuilt and replanted with climbing roses. Oakleaf and Annabelle hydrangeas carpeted with periwinkle were planted close to the house. Documentary evidence for these had not been found in Corinne's letters or lists, and the Johnston images, which might have provided spe-

West front with replanted Valley Forge elms

cific information on the Melcherses' plants, had not yet been microscopically studied, but the plants Favretti specified were suitable to the period, as well as being sturdy, low-maintenance plants, which at the time was a necessary requirement. Part of this 1993 renovation included the replacement of trees, to re-create Corinne's "stately ambience" on the west front of the house, as five of the original elms planted in 1923 had been lost to disease and lightning. Since the species American elm was out of the question, scarlet oaks and disease-resistant Liberty elms were substituted.[5] The 1993 restoration also called for plantings in a bed that was situated between the stairs to the long walk; this bed was later removed, since it was not original to the Melchers period. A panicled goldenraintree anchored the planting around the newly opened Marguerite Stroh Visitors' Center; several Adam's-needle yuccas and two mockoranges were put in to screen the air-conditioning units. This first phase of the restoration was presented in 1994.

The Restoration Committee next addressed the Belmont garden, in the spring of 1999, when it approved the plans for lawn restoration and a sprinkler system. These plans were drawn by William D. Rieley, who had succeeded Favretti after his retirement the year before. A landscape lighting plan was approved in 2000 and subsequently installed at the property's expense. Meanwhile, Belmont's grounds supervisor,

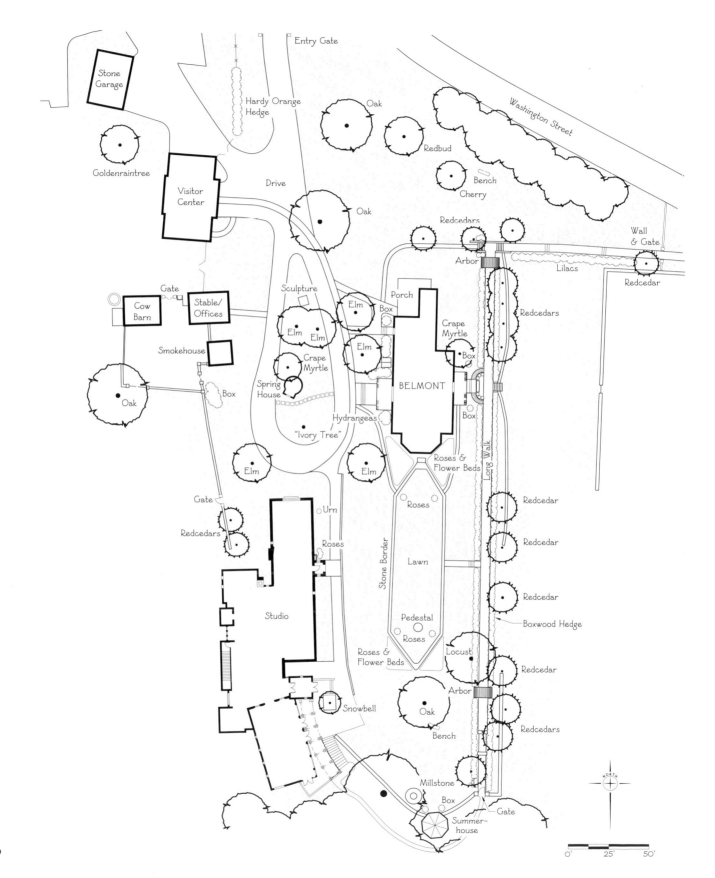

Entry Gate

Stone Garage

Hardy Orange Hedge

Washington Street

Oak

Redbud

Bench

Cherry

Goldenraintree

Visitor Center

Drive

Oak

Redcedars

Arbor

Wall & Gate

Lilacs

Redcedar

Gate

Sculpture

Porch

Redcedars

Cow Barn

Stable/ Offices

Elm

Elm

Box

Crape Myrtle

Smokehouse

Elm

Elm

Elm

Box

Crape Myrtle

Box

Oak

Box

Spring House

"Ivory Tree"

BELMONT

Hydrangeas

Roses & Flower Beds

Elm

Elm

Long Walk

Urn

Roses

Redcedar

Gate

Roses

Redcedar

Redcedars

Stone Border

Lawn

Redcedar

Studio

Pedestal Roses

Boxwood Hedge

Roses & Flower Beds

Locust

Redcedar

Arbor

Snowbell

Oak

Bench

Redcedars

Millstone

Box

Gate

Summer- house

NORTH

30

0'   25'   50'

Beate Jensen, approached the Garden Club to see if the original 1923 planting could be restored with a new, disease-resistant Valley Forge elm. She felt strongly that the branching structure of the Valley Forge elm was closer to that of the species American elm, and that the mixture of oaks and elms did not create the "stately ambience" so prized by Corinne Melchers. The Restoration Committee was at first reluctant to cut down perfectly good trees, but in 2004 the tree planting was reexamined. Hurricane Isabel had damaged the last original elm, so it was removed, along with the 1993 planting of oaks and elms, and the driveway restored according to the 1921 plan.

During the Melcherses' time, the ivy-covered trunk of a dead tree stood within the circular drive. It had been a favorite of theirs ever since one of the workmen had christened it the "ivory tree." Since that time, a large magnolia had grown very near the spot where the "ivory tree" stood. In the post-Isabel replanting, Beate Jensen made an imaginative request: instead of getting rid of the misplaced magnolia, why not leave in place a fifteen-foot piece of the trunk and then plant ivy to grow on it, in effect, reproducing the "ivory tree."

Further improvements were approved in 2005: a rotten garden gate was meticulously replicated and a Melchers-era antique stone eagle restored. Since then, the Restoration Committee has approved the replanting of the hardy-orange hedge, which used to separate the driveway from the service yard of the garage; it is now in place. Next on the list are the conservation of the stone entrance gateposts and wooden entrance gate, restoration of additional garden gates, and a durable reproduction of the little putto (cherub) that once sat in the garden but is now too fragile to be left outside.

Because of Corinne Melchers's journals, her copious and meticulous lists, and the many contemporary photographs that exist, the ongoing work at Belmont comes close to being a true restoration. The Restoration Committee is most grateful for the documentation, and for the dedication of the Belmont staff, which keeps turning up treasures. All of the sources continue to be subjected to the diligent sleuthing of Beate Jensen and Curator Joanna Catron, with the full support of Director David Berreth.

Blandy

BOYCE

*Restoration of the ½-mile-long stone wall along
the historic Dogwood Lane*

THE REBUILDING OF A DRY STONE WALL AT THE STATE ARBORETUM OF VIR-
ginia may look to be a bit off the path of the preservation work of the Garden Club of
Virginia, but the lane defined by that stone wall leads straight into the rich history
of the Valley of Virginia. The Arboretum is part of the Blandy Experimental Farm,
carved in 1926 from the Tuleyries, an early nineteenth-century estate built on part of
what was originally the Northern Neck Proprietary, the huge royal grant inherited by
Thomas, Lord Fairfax.[1] Since Robert "King" Carter was his factor, or land agent, several of Carter's great-grandsons, among them Nathaniel Burwell Jr., the last entailed
owner of Carter's Grove, inherited large acreages in the northern Shenandoah Valley.

These descendants, who grew up in the splendid Georgian houses of the Tidewater, built many of the impressive Federal mansions gracing the western hillsides of
the Blue Ridge in the Lower Shenandoah Valley. The Tuleyries, however, sprang from
another source a generation later; its builder was the son of a tanner from New Jersey,
one among the many immigrants who streamed into the Valley of Virginia by way of
the northern colonies. This young man's path crossed early with that of the Tidewater
gentry, after he established a tannery in Millwood, the village that became a landowners' merchant center from the later eighteenth century on.

In 1785, Carter's grandson, Nathaniel Burwell Jr., entered into a partnership with
that colorful hero of the Revolutionary War, General Daniel Morgan. Together, they
"contracted with William Clark, a millwright, to build a commercial mill on what Burwell called his 'Shenandoah lands.'" By June of 1786, according to historian Margaret
Peters, "surveyor John Cordell recorded two acres with a merchant mill held in partnership with Burwell and Morgan and a parcel leased to Joseph Tuley to construct a
tanyard below the mill." And seven years later, in 1793, Tuley recorded "a proper lease
for two acres of land lying on Spout Run as laid off by Mr. John Cordell, with a plenti-
ful supply of water for a tanyard from the millrace."[2]

Dogwood Lane

The tanyard next to the Burwell-Morgan mill was extremely successful. Tuley extended his tanyards and other business interests as far as Pennsylvania, but when the tanner's son, Colonel Joseph Tuley Jr., could afford a splendid new mansion, he decided to return to happy childhood haunts. His house, a combination of grace and space, was completed in 1834 on a large tract of land amassed by his father somewhat southwest of Millwood. Apparently, Tuley the younger gave some thought to naming the property Hide Park, but passed that up in favor of a grander pun on his own name, the Tuleyries.

When Colonel Tuley died, in 1860, the place passed to Mrs. Tuley's niece, Belinda, and her husband, Colonel Upton Boyce. Colonel Boyce's efforts to extend the Shenandoah Valley Railroad resulted in his name being given to the town that grew up around the local depot. But after the Boyces died, the Tuleyries was sold, in 1904, to Graham F. Blandy of New York.

The Blandys lived at the Tuleyries for eleven years, maintaining it as a proper Gilded Age estate. Georgette Blandy's notable garden included a boxwood maze. When Graham Blandy died, in 1926, the Tuleyries, along with 200 acres, descended to her niece, Mrs. Orme Wilson, and later to Mrs. Wilson's son, Orme Wilson Jr. He had completed a careful restoration of the house, the grounds, and the stone walls on the property just before his untimely death in 1966. His widow lives now in another house on the grounds.

Blandy left the other 700 acres of Joseph Tuley's original tract to the University of Virginia, to be used "to teach young men farming." That directive has evolved into a program of basic environmental research and public outreach. In 1986, the Virginia General Assembly designated 165 acres as the State Arboretum of Virginia. In addition to a remarkable collection of eight thousand trees and woody shrubs, the Arboretum also contains a number of other interesting features. There is a Virginia Native Plant Trail which showcases plants that grew in Virginia before the European immigrations of the 1600s. A boxwood garden designed by the American Boxwood Society contains the largest collection of boxwood cultivars in the United States, including *B. sempervirens* 'Graham Blandy'. An ornamental herb garden devoted to culinary and medicinal herbs, horticultural plantings for sun and shade, and a traditional perennial border in the old courtyard all gain increased beauty from the vistas of pasture, water, and of the venerable Blue Ridge.

The Arboretum's main building is known as the Quarters; it is a large, two-story brick edifice with a double wooden portico forming covered walkways upstairs and down. It was built around 1830, just before the main residence, and enlarged in the 1940s to make more office and dormitory space. Its name implies slave quarters; if so, the Quarters was a radical departure from what constituted the usual plantation street. Early local historians thought the building was constructed initially as a residence for craftsmen living on the place while the Tuleyries was being completed. There is a hint that the building may have been a stable with living quarters above. In any case, the structure was a vital part of the plantation complex, connected to the main house by a lane bordered with dogwoods and dry stone walls on either side.

As its major millennium project, the Winchester-Clarke Garden Club replanted the trees along Dogwood Lane, many of which had succumbed to old age and disease. The Garden Club of Virginia was asked to rebuild the historic stone walls. This was one of the more unusual projects the Restoration Committee had undertaken. The first step was to find a stonemason versed in that time-honored technique, almost a lost art. The chosen craftsman, John Fletcher, worked at a very deliberate pace, finally hiring—and teaching—his own son to help. This was a true restoration, a revitalization of a disappearing trade as well as the preservation of a Shenandoah Valley landmark. The Garden Club of Virginia did not diverge from its path; it just made that path a little wider.

Bruton Parish Church from
Duke of Gloucester Street

Bruton Parish Churchyard

A seventeenth-century churchyard

BRUTON PARISH, THE THIRD PARISH OF ITS COMMUNITY, WAS ESTABLISHED in 1674, twenty-five years before the Virginia capital was moved to Williamsburg from Jamestown.[1] It could be said that the settlement, known for sixty-odd years as Middle Plantation, was America's first planned community: it was established by an Act of Assembly in 1633. The Act for the seating of Middle Plantation ordered "that every for-tyeth man be chosen and maynteyned out of the tithable persons of all the inhabitants within the compass of the forest contained between Queenc's Creek in Charles River [later the York] and Archer's Hope Creek in James River, with all the lands included, to the bay of Chesepiake." The men so chosen were to be employed in building houses and securing the tract of land lying between the two creeks. Further, the Act provided that "if any free man shall this yeare before the first of May voluntarily go and seate upon the sayd place of the middle plantation, they shall have fifty acres of land inheritance and be free from all taxes and public chardges."[2]

At first, Middle Plantation was a single parish. There is no record of the whereabouts or design of its first church. In 1645, it was divided. Harrup Parish was split off, and remained independent until 1658, when the two parishes were recombined into Middletowne Parish, which implies that a town had grown up in the former forest. In 1674, Middletowne Parish was joined to Marston Parish (founded 1654) to form Bruton Parish, named for the English village that was the ancestral home of a prominent local family, the Ludwells, and of the Royal Governor, Sir William Berkeley. From its beginnings, then, Bruton Parish was identified with wealth and power. The earliest vestry records, of April 18, 1674, name the Reverend Roland Jones as the first minister and authorize the purchase of glebe lands. Three years later, the vestry voted to build a new brick church on land that had been donated by Colonel John Page, who also contributed £20 sterling toward the new church. The foundations of this first brick church, about 60 feet by 24 feet, can be seen in the churchyard today, to the north and west of the present church, outlined in stone in the most recent restoration. This first Bruton Parish Church was similar to St. Luke's Church in Newport Parish: a simple, rectangular structure with buttressed side walls. It was completed in 1683, except for the "steeple and a ring of bells," which were soon added.

In 1693, the College of William and Mary was founded by James Blair, commissary of the Bishop of London in Virginia. Then, in 1699, the colonial capital was moved from malarial Jamestown to the higher ground of Middletowne, which was renamed Williamsburg. The small Bruton Parish Church was quickly overwhelmed by the influx of professors and students, the governor, his council and their entourage, and the members of the House of Burgesses. In 1706 the vestry began wrestling with the need for a bigger church, and in 1710 the General Assembly agreed to fund pews for the governor, his council, and the burgesses. Governor Alexander Spotswood himself drafted the plans for the first cruciform church in Virginia; it would be 75 feet long and 28 feet wide, with transepts 19 feet long, and would take five years to build. Finished in 1715, its first rector was James Blair, who was also the president of the College of William and Mary.

Until the American Revolution, Bruton Parish Church was the center of political as well as religious life in the colonial capital. It was a wealthy and richly appointed church, and its cemetery held the graves of royal governors and councillors as well as local leaders. During the years leading up to the Revolution, the church was at the center of all the political drama unfolding in Williamsburg. But in 1776 the House of Burgesses disestablished the Anglican Church and ended its tax support. Then, in 1779, Thomas Jefferson moved the capital of Virginia to Richmond, taking large numbers of the Bruton Parish congregation along. By 1813, the church's glebe lands had been sold and the church was destitute. The congregation diminished further, and the building fell into real disrepair. A "modernization," beginning in 1828, destroyed much of the colonial interior, and by 1840 it was almost all gone, although some of the chancel paneling is thought to be original. During the Civil War, the church was used as a hospital.

After the Civil War, there were efforts at repair and restoration, but the real success story began after the turn of the century, when the Reverend William Archer Rutherford Goodwin arrived for his first stint as rector from 1903 to 1909. Between 1905 and 1907 the church was partially returned to its original form and a new organ was installed. The 300th anniversary of Jamestown brought a large Bible from King Edward VII and a bronze lectern to hold it from President Theodore Roosevelt. Dr. Goodwin left in 1909, but in 1926 he came back for a second term as rector, this time for twelve years. It was during this term that he persuaded John D. Rockefeller Jr. to

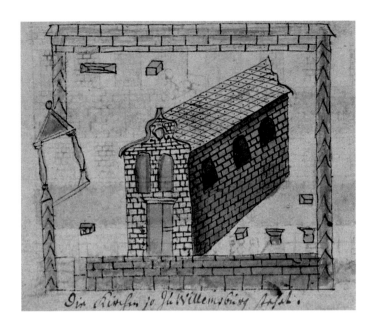

Left: *Contemporary sketch of the first Bruton Parish Church, completed 1683*

Below: *Foundation of 1683 church outlined in stone*

BRUTON PARISH CHURCHYARD

Gate leading from Bruton Parish churchyard onto the Palace Green

restore the town of Williamsburg, and Colonial Williamsburg was born.

In 1936, the Williamsburg Garden Club asked the Garden Club of Virginia for help in restoring the Bruton Parish churchyard. This was before Mr. Rockefeller's involvement, but Dr. Goodwin had already begun to work on the tombstones and the 1745 brick wall. Repairs to the wall were paid for by the church, but the Garden Club replaced ten trees and planted shrubs. Three years later, Colonial Williamsburg authorized Arthur Shurcliff to draw up a plan for landscaping the churchyard. Shurcliff's plan put in brick walks and pedestrian areas in a right-angled pattern, replacing earlier diagonal walks. Approved by the vestry and the Garden Club of Virginia, which funded the work, the plan was executed by Colonial Williamsburg. In the 1950s, Alden Hopkins, who succeeded Shurcliff as landscape architect at Colonial Williamsburg, expanded on these areas, attempting to protect the areas adjacent to the church from erosion and compaction. As the number of visitors increased over the years, more paving was added, but the resulting patchwork did not cope with the problems.

By the end of the twentieth century, the Bruton Parish churchyard was in a sorry state. In the early summer of 1997, the Restoration Committee of the Garden Club of Virginia received a letter from the Bruton Parish vestry requesting that it "look at conditions relating to drainage, the bare area of lawn . . . competing tree roots . . . and the grounds in general." The report of a site committee consisting of committee member Mrs. W. Tayloe Murphy Jr. and Rudy J. Favretti, at that time the landscape architect to the Restoration Committee, concluded that the vestry itself would have to address the structural and policy problems that had caused the trouble. This report was presented to the Restoration Committee at its July 1997 meeting.[3]

But the vestry came back to the Restoration Committee and repeated its request for help. William D. Rieley, who succeeded Favretti after his retirement in 1998, proposed that the Restoration Committee present Bruton Parish with a plan that the church would implement. This suggestion was adopted, and the vestry employed Rieley to oversee the work. The following report, published in the *Church Bulletin,* describes the situation:

> Bruton Parish Church announced today that, beginning on July 1, 2000 it will undergo a major renovation of its churchyard. During the period of the

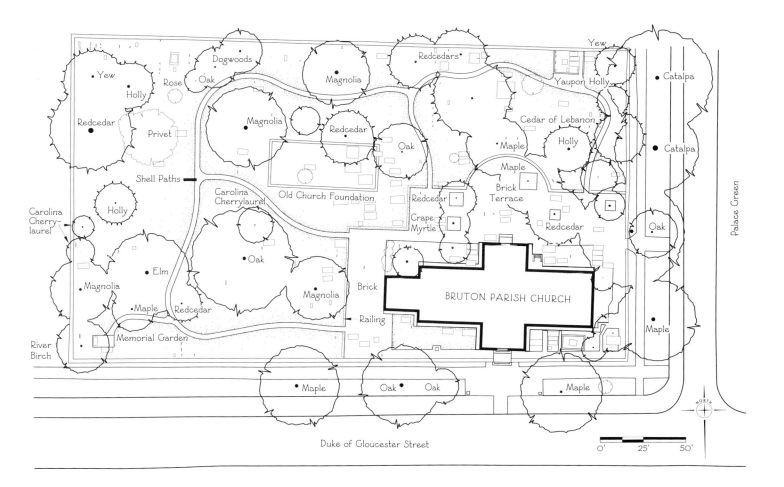

Yew · · Catalpa

Redcedars·

Yew

Magnolia

Dogwoods

· Yew

Rose · Oak

Holly

Yaupon Holly

Redcedar ·

Privet

Magnolia

Redcedar

Cedar of Lebanon

· Catalpa

· Maple

Holly

Oak ·

Maple

Shell Paths

Brick Terrace

Holly

Carolina Cherrylaurel

Old Church Foundation

Redcedar

Oak ·

Redcedar

Carolina Cherry- laurel

Crape · Myrtle

· Oak

· Oak

· Elm

Oak ·

· Magnolia

Magnolia

· Maple · Redcedar

Magnolia

Brick

Maple

Memorial Garden

Railing

BRUTON PARISH CHURCH

River Birch

· Maple

Oak · · Oak

· Maple

Palace Green

NORTH

Duke of Gloucester Street

0'   25'   50'

renovation, only the Duke of Gloucester Street entrance to the church will remain open.

The churchyard of Bruton Parish Church in Colonial Williamsburg is on the verge of becoming unraveled. It supports the activities of a congregation of almost two thousand, and is visited by upwards to three million visitors a year. This visitation, poor drainage, and erosion have caused significant damage to a churchyard, which was last restored seventy years ago. This extensive renovation is being made possible by the generosity of the Garden Club of Virginia, the Lettie Pate Evans Foundation of Atlanta, Georgia, and the Bruton Parish Church Endowment Fund.

In early 2000 the church accepted an offer from the Garden Club of Virginia to help. They provided the services of their landscape architect, Mr. William D. Rieley, for both planning and contract administration. . . . The task assigned to Mr. Rieley was to design a renovation that would maintain

BRUTON PARISH CHURCHYARD   41

the eighteenth century character of the churchyard, respect the requirements of an active congregation, and accommodate three million visitors (six million feet) a year. Colonial Williamsburg was invited into planning at the outset, and has fully participated in the plan's development. . . .

The concept for the renovation entails:

—Removing the present brick paving in the north and west of the church, grading, laying a concrete slab base and repaving with brick.

—Expanding the paved brick area to the north of the church, and enclosing the bricked area to the north and west of the church with a low single rail fence as is found in many old English churchyards.

—Servicing the newly graded and paved area by an underground drainage system that will connect into the City of Williamsburg storm sewers.

—Establishing a system of closable pathways throughout the remainder of the churchyard.

—Placing plantings and an area for meditation in a corner of the churchyard now used as a Columbarium.[4]

Rieley's notes describe the project more fully:

Our approach, with the advice of both Colonial Williamsburg and the Church, was to expand once again the paved areas around the church, in essentially the same orthogonal pattern established by Shurcliff and Hopkins, and to add a simple rail as a means of confining the routine pedestrian traffic to the paved areas. This was combined with a new subsurface drainage system to handle the runoff and reduce erosion. Gates were established to allow access for parishioners and those wishing to view specific burial sites and markers. Paths were established which connected these gates to the outer churchyard. In an effort to allow continued interments in the churchyard, the Vestry established an area for interment of ashes and memorial markers on replicas of the raised-tablet memorials common in the churchyard. In this area we established a simple sitting area for visitation and reflection. In addition, the location of the old church near the middle of the site, which predated Williamsburg, was outlined with stone.

Removal of sick or problematic plants was combined with a long-term strategy for replanting that will eventually phase in all native species or plants that could have been seen in Williamsburg in the eighteenth century. This combination of expanding the pavement, handling the drainage and

BRUTON PARISH CHURCHYARD

restoring the park-like setting of the churchyard beyond the paved areas has allowed the grass areas to prosper and has restored the dignity and simple beauty of the site.[5]

What neither the church report nor Rieley's notes describe are the practical complications of such an extensive operation in a cemetery that has been active for more than three hundred years, involving excavations throughout the burial grounds and right up to the foundations of an eighteenth-century church of enormous historical and cultural importance. But under Rieley's direction and oversight the renovation was successfully accomplished, and the Bruton Parish churchyard maintains its unique character.

Centre Hill

Replanted grounds for a Greek Revival house

THE TOWN OF PETERSBURG WAS FOUNDED IN 1702 AS A TOBACCO PORT ON the Appomattox River.[1] It grew slowly through the eighteenth century, serving as an arms depot and a battle site during the Revolutionary War. By the beginning of the nineteenth century, it was a proud small city that managed to muster a company to fight in the War of 1812. There was no fighting in that war on the community's home territory, but its members acquitted themselves so bravely at the Battle of Winchester that they were described as a cockade in the Union's hat, and Petersburg began calling itself the "Cockade City."

At the time of the War of 1812, Petersburg was a flourishing port, shipping flour and tobacco to New York and other cities. Norfolk suffered during the war, and Petersburg took up the slack. The Appomattox River drops 120 feet in the five miles above Petersburg, so there is plenty of water power, and in addition to the grain mills, a prosperous textile industry sprung up there, adding to the success of the shipping industry. The city grew rapidly, with fortunes being made in land development as well as tobacco, industry, and shipping. It was during this period of great prosperity that Centre Hill was built.

It is hard, coming now to Centre Hill, to envision it as it was in its heyday, crowning a nine-acre hilltop that looks down on the Appomattox River. Its expansive grounds, with service buildings and terraced gardens on the east side, were defined by an elegant wrought iron fence that wrapped around the entire place. The imposing, Federal-style house was built in 1823 by Robert Bolling (1759–1839), a member of a distinguished family whose history goes back to Jamestown. Bolling was a man of considerable consequence. He had amassed a fortune in industry and tobacco inspections and land development. A major landholder in Petersburg, he contributed some of his land to the city. In 1794, he gave a piece of land on Walnut Street for a cemetery for the African Americans of Petersburg. He also donated the site for the courthouse,

South front with restored iron fence

on the theory that the presence of public buildings would enhance the value of the adjacent lots that he still owned. Unfortunately, the city erected a jail on the land he had donated for the courthouse, in a spot that he considered far too close to his property.

Bolling died in 1839, and his son inherited Centre Hill. Robert Buckner Bolling was a bird of a different feather; his letters show that he had a gentler and less confrontational temperament than his father. In 1858, for example, a vacancy occurred on the Petersburg Common Council and Bolling was elected, without consultation, to fill it; he was also appointed alderman for Petersburg's East Ward. He declined both offers, in a letter so gracious and so descriptive of nineteenth-century Petersburg that I quote an excerpt here:

> Although about, with the closing year [I plan] to change permanently to another part of our State, my residence, & thereby sever ties, interrupt friendly social relations, valued & dear. I shall ever cherish while I live, the deepest & liveliest interest in the future growth of Petersburg, the place of my birth, the home of my manhood & the home of my father & father's father & never cease to invoke the blessings of Heaven upon our City & its people & continue to rejoice in her prosperity & the welfare & happiness of her Citizens.

I beg, in conclusion, to convey to your body, collectively, and individually, the warmest expression of my kindest wishes for your continued welfare, prosperity & happiness & bid you a *kind, respectful and final farewell.* Robt B. Bolling[2]

In the 1840s, Bolling gave Centre Hill a grand makeover, enlarging and remodeling it in the latest Greek Revival taste. At that time, the east wing was added, and a service tunnel was built on the north side down to Henry Street. There was a circular drive on the south side, and a semicircular carriage drive on the north, or river, side. On the east side of the house, there were outbuildings and a large, elaborate, terraced vegetable and flower garden. This was later removed and replaced by a small formal garden on axis with the east portico. The only bit of the original setting that remains is the circular driveway on the south side of the house, around which, in about 1911, the Centre Hill Court housing development hemmed the house in completely on the east, south, and west. That development, which Calder Loth, the editor of the *Virginia Landmarks Register,* described as "a visually lively collection of primarily Bungalow-Craftsman-style houses," has itself been designated an historic district. As Loth added: "The houses contrast with the great Federal mansion and reflect the early twentieth century interest in creating small planned neighborhoods."[3]

Sometime after 1911, on the north side of the house, a large brick apartment building rose to block the view of the river, obliterating Robert Bolling's carriage drive, which had swept up and down the hill behind the house in a great horseshoe from the northwest to the northeast corners of the block on Henry Street. The apartment building was demolished in 1993, and the steep north hill is open now, as it was in 1910 when

Centre Hill in the nineteenth century

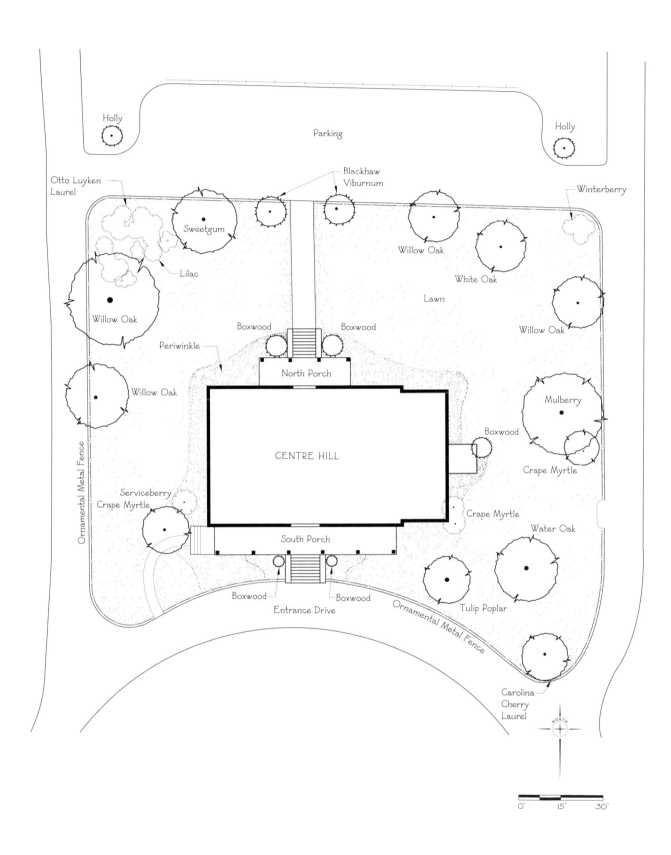

Holly

Parking

Holly

Otto Luyken
Laurel

Blackhaw
Viburnum

Winterberry

Sweetgum

Lilac

Willow Oak

White Oak

Lawn

Willow Oak

Willow Oak

Periwinkle

Boxwood

Boxwood

North Porch

Willow Oak

Mulberry

Boxwood

CENTRE HILL

Crape Myrtle

Ornamental Metal Fence

Serviceberry
Crape Myrtle

Crape Myrtle

Water Oak

South Porch

Boxwood

Boxwood

Tulip Poplar

Entrance Drive

Ornamental Metal Fence

Carolina
Cherry
Laurel

NORTH

0'   15'   30'

President William Howard Taft became the second president to visit Centre Hill. The other president to visit was Abraham Lincoln. Lincoln's visit, on April 7, 1865, was to meet with General George Lucas Hartstuff (or Hartsuff), Centre Hill having been requisitioned for the general's headquarters. One of the soldiers with General Hartstuff was the Civil War photographer Mathew Brady, who made several photographs of Centre Hill, two of which appeared as "images of the Civil War" in Ken Burns's film about that conflict.

IN EARLY 1978, THE PETERSBURG GARDEN CLUB WROTE TO THE GARDEN Club of Virginia asking for help with Centre Hill. The landscape architect to the Garden Club of Virginia was Rudy J. Favretti, who submitted a final plan in March 1979. All of the terraced garden landscape of the 1840s had been built up, so Favretti chose one of Brady's 1865 photographs as his starting point. In the presentation brochure for the completed project, he says that "the restoration philosophy or concept followed

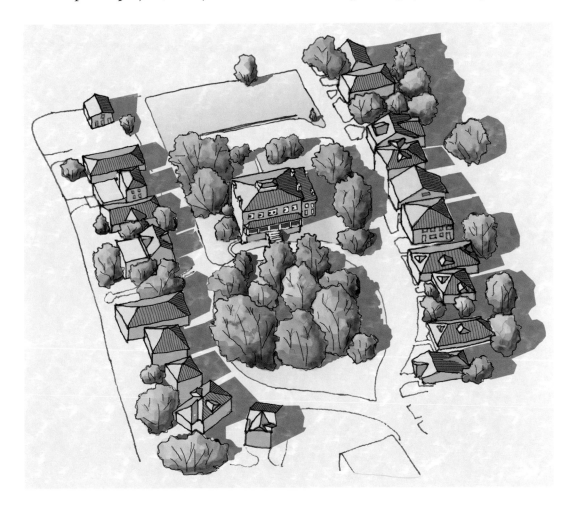

that used for the restoration of the mansion: to show a transition over the years." He described the process further in a 1994 letter to the president of the Petersburg Garden Club:

> First, it was our intent to restore the landscape to its nineteenth century grandeur to the extent that present conditions would permit (i.e. the invasive concrete wall, the revised original contours, the reconfiguration of the roads, and the fact that the site is now public.) . . . The Centre Hill archives provided nineteenth century photographs, a 1909 plan, and some other documents from which we could work.
>
> Second, we carefully preserved the underground tunnel area which is quite fragile especially after all of the soil disturbance regarding both the construction of the apartment building and its destruction. Care was taken not to plant anything over it for fear roots would eventually penetrate.
>
> Third, the plan respects present day conditions and provides for safety on the site.
>
> Fourth, we attempted to screen out unsightly aspects of surrounding properties while enframing desirable views and vistas.[4]

There were two other major pieces of the 1979 Centre Hill project. Access to the mansion is not easy; to drive up to the front door requires knowing the contemporary maze of streets, and there is limited parking space. The city of Petersburg directs visi-

The "Taft Lawn," reproduced on a 1920s era postcard

tors to park on Adams Street, a block west of the mansion, at the bottom of the steep hill. But the steep flight of cement steps climbing up the hill between two of the houses in the surrounding development was hardly recognizable as the entrance to Centre Hill. Favretti transformed this undistinguished stairway into a garden walkway lined with shrubs and trees and with proper signage for visitors. In the same restoration, the Garden Club of Virginia underwrote major repairs to the mansion's stately iron fence, which had been badly bent by trucks and cars. It was beautifully restored by a young Petersburg craftsman.

The Garden Club of Virginia papers at the Virginia Historical Society describe continuing difficulties with this garden, due largely to the difficulties of proper maintenance in the punishing heat and drought of Southside Virginia summers. One letter pleads for plants that will survive these conditions. But throughout the years, the Petersburg Garden Club has supported the city and the GCV in helping to keep Centre Hill presentable, its members in many cases doing the work themselves.

In 1993, after the apartment building north of the mansion was demolished, the Petersburg Garden Club turned once again to the Garden Club of Virginia, this time for help with landscaping the now bare hillside down to Henry Street. William J. Martin, director of tourism for the city of Petersburg, wrote then:

> Centre Hill Mansion will have a sweeping new vista of Old Towne and the Appomattox River. The house with its prominent location will be visible from both the I-95 and Colonial Heights Bridges. With the transfer of the property to the City, the Petersburg Department of Tourism has the rare opportunity to create a new garden on the river side of Centre Hill Mansion. . . . The new landscape plan must compliment the garden created by the Garden Club of Virginia. It is our hope that the Garden Club of Virginia will assist with the development and implementation of these plans.[5]

There is an existing photograph and a detailed plan of this hillside as it looked at the time Centre Hill was preparing for a 1910 visit from President William Howard Taft. Moreover, there is also a preliminary plan for this area prepared by Favretti that was never implemented. In 2003, the question came up again, and William D. Rieley prepared another plan, but so far it has not been implemented either. The Garden Club of Virginia remains interested in the development and interpretation of the area down to Henry Street because of its importance to understanding the Centre Hill landscape over the course of its varied and fascinating history.

*Restored Executive Mansion
garden in summer*

The Executive Mansion

Restoration of the 1953 Charles Gillette design

VIRGINIA'S CAPITAL HAS BEEN MOVED TWICE, FROM JAMESTOWN TO WILliamsburg in 1699, and thence to Richmond in 1780.[1] The first move was to escape the mosquitoes, the second to escape the British. It was Governor Thomas Jefferson who engineered the move to Richmond, where he subsequently took up residence in a house rented from his uncle, Thomas Turpin. Jefferson's gubernatorial successors lived in a two-story frame house facing Governor Street that the General Assembly purchased from James Marsden. Before 1788, there was no state capitol building; the Assembly conducted its business crowded into makeshift quarters in two warehouses near Shockoe Bottom.

Until 1810, the inconvenience of having to live in the almost-dilapidated Marsden house was accepted by most governors. Then, Governor John Tyler decided that it was "intolerable for a private family"[2] to live in the old house, and he persuaded the legislature to appropriate $12,000 for a permanent residence (the appropriation eventually grew to $20,000). The first governor to live in the new mansion was James Barbour; and, except for the period of complete renovation in 1999, it has been continuously occupied since 1813, a national record.

New England architect Alexander Parris (1780–1852) was given the commission to design the new Executive Mansion, which was completed in 1813 at a final cost of $18,871.82. Before coming to Richmond in 1810 to build the businessman John Bell's house, which straddled present-day Main Street at Ryland Street, Parris worked in Portland, Maine, where he had relocated in 1800 to take advantage of a building boom there. After completing his three Virginia commissions (John Wickham also employed him to build his beautiful house on Clay Street, now part of the Valentine Museum), he returned to Boston, where he became one of the best-known architects of the Federal and Greek Revival periods, succeeding his colleague Charles Bulfinch as Boston's leading architect. One of Parris's best-known Boston designs is his 1826 Classical Re-

Restored garden in summer, showing live oak planted by Admiral Byrd

vival Faneuil Market, later named Quincy Market. In the final phase of his distinguished and varied career, Parris also built a string of elegant granite lighthouses along the Maine coast, as well as the Execution Rocks Lighthouse on Long Island Sound.[3]

In 1906, almost a hundred years after the 1813 completion of the governor's mansion, the architect Duncan Lee was commissioned to add an oval dining room and to transform the two rear parlors designed by Parris into one large ballroom. This was done, in part, in preparation for the anticipated festivities of the 1907 Jamestown celebration.

Although Governor Tyler never got to occupy his "private residence," it's fair to say that until recently it wasn't really all that private. True, governors' families since 1813 have been protected from the prying eyes of passers-by, but for most of its history the house was at best only quasi-private. The first floor was always kept open to the citizens of Virginia; anyone ringing the front doorbell was apt to be greeted at the door by the first lady then in residence.

The Barbours had set the standard for hospitality early on. They kept a silver bowl full of iced whiskey punch on the table at all times, in case any of their guests happened to be thirsty. During Prohibition, the punch bowl long gone, Governor Harry F. Byrd played host to Winston Churchill, who was researching his *History of the English-Speaking Peoples*. Churchill stayed about a week in an upstairs bedroom, and it came to be known that he was accustomed to drinking about a quart of brandy every day. The governor knew a certain journalist who had "connections," so he spoke to his friend, and thereafter a "brown bag" appeared every day during the great man's visit.

There are other stories: Governor Littleton Tazewell (1834–36) was a night owl who installed the mansion's first chandeliers; Governor William ("Extra Billy") Smith (1846–49) put in indoor plumbing—an almost unheard-of luxury for the time. In 1926, Billy Trinkle, aged five, set fire to the mansion's Christmas tree with a sparkler, nearly burning the house down. This was the second time the governor's mansion escaped destruction by fire, the first having been during Richmond's Evacuation Fire of 1865.

From this house Governor and Mrs. Linwood Holton (1970–74) accompanied their three children to their new schools. A moving and widely disseminated photograph shows the governor marching with his older daughter, Tayloe, into one of Richmond's integrated public high schools as double ranks of onlookers and the national press look on. The younger Holton daughter, Anne, is now living in the house once again, this time as Virginia's current first lady.

It was Mrs. Thomas B. Stanley, whose husband was governor from 1952 to 1956, who first employed Charles F. Gillette to design and install a suitable garden for entertaining on the south side of the mansion. Mrs. Stanley, herself a gardener, took great pleasure as well as pride in her jewel of a garden, but fifty years later, it had been very much changed. There was very little left of Gillette's formal design, and of the original planting only one holly tree survived.

The Garden Club of Virginia's involvement with the mansion began in 2000, at the suggestion of architect John Paul C. Hanbury, FAIA, who was in charge of a complete overhaul of the building. The renovation project had been initiated by First Lady Roxane Gilmore, who then appealed to the Club for help in restoring the garden. Mr. Hanbury rightly felt that it would be a great pity not to restore the once elegant formal garden to the same standard as the house itself. As he put it, "The Mansion restoration restored historic integrity to the 1813 Alexander Parris original and to the 1906 Duncan Lee addition, equally important in interpreting the structure as it has evolved with equal respect to both architects."

To add to the complications of restoring the garden, a magnificent live oak, planted by Admiral Richard Evelyn Byrd upon his return from the South Pole, was

Garden pool

Restored Gillette garden in spring

causing serious trouble to the brick wall enclosing the garden on the east side. The solution was to reconfigure the wall by devising a structural system that would support it on steel piers, instead of a conventional footing, and thus protect the root system of the splendid tree. As Mr. Hanbury noted, "The restoration of the fountain and its original sculpture, as well as the other bronze figure, are particularly noteworthy for a return of splashing water and a marriage of garden and artwork." The fountain sculpture is the mythological figure "Daphne," by Gertrude Vanderbilt Whitney.

The formal request, when it finally came to the Restoration Committee in January 2000, asked that the garden be completely restored to its original appearance in time for that year's Garden Week at the end of April. Because it had taken several months for the various bodies involved to see eye to eye, the already barely sufficient time for such a complicated installation would need to be considerably shortened. In the end, somehow, it worked. GCV landscape architect Will Rieley reinstalled the entire garden following Gillette's original, very elaborate formal plan, right down to the last tulip. This involved removing everything within the enclosure except for one mature holly tree and starting from scratch.

A great stroke of luck was that Mrs. Stanley's daughter, Mrs. Hugh Chatham (a member of the GCV), had the original urns, which had belonged to her mother. Rieley asked for permission to copy them, which was graciously given. The name of the Alabama foundry where they had been made was decipherable on the urns, and when Rieley called the foundry he found that they still had the original molds and could reproduce the urns exactly. Mrs. Chatham then donated the new urns to the garden in honor of her mother. The mansion's garden was a true restoration in every detail, a rare luxury in the experience of the Restoration Committee.

It is, however, a high-maintenance design. Tulips, one of Gillette's signature plants and a focus of the annual Garden Week display, require yearly replacement and special techniques to ensure proper timing of the blooms. Some of the other plants specified in Gillette's very detailed planting plan are no longer available, or possibly might better be replaced with improved cultivars. Budgetary realities have resulted in cutbacks of the excellent maintenance staff. Younger gubernatorial families are apt to have dogs, who love the garden. Where else can they run? The Executive Mansion is the only one of the GCV's restoration properties that functions as a private home as well as a house-museum open to the public. The balance is hard to keep, but the man-

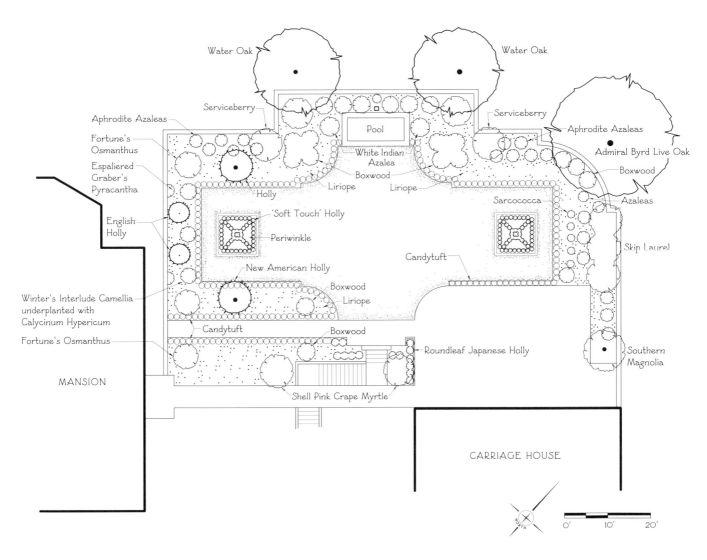

Water Oak

Water Oak

Serviceberry

Aphrodite Azaleas

Fortune's
Osmanthus

Espaliered
Graber's
Pyracantha

English
Holly

Winter's Interlude Camellia
underplanted with
Calycinum Hypericum

Fortune's Osmanthus

MANSION

Pool

Serviceberry

Aphrodite Azaleas

Admiral Byrd Live Oak

Boxwood

Azaleas

White Indian
Azalea

Boxwood

Liriope

Liriope

Holly

'Soft Touch' Holly

Periwinkle

New American Holly

Boxwood

Liriope

Sarcococca

Candytuft

Skip Laurel

Candytuft

Boxwood

Roundleaf Japanese Holly

Southern
Magnolia

Shell Pink Crape Myrtle

CARRIAGE HOUSE

0'   10'   20'

sion staff does a superb job, and the support of each first lady in succession has been
invaluable.

Public tours of the Executive Mansion now end on the terrace overlooking the
garden. From that raised walkway, Gillette's elegant design is seen to its best advantage. The crisp lines of the box-edged borders filled with seasonal bloom, the two urn-
crowned squares facing each other at each end of the rectangular lawn, Daphne's lim-
pid pool flanked by white Indian azaleas with Admiral Byrd's live oak tree shielding
the view at the far corner, all make it a fitting garden for the beautifully restored 1813
house; a private refuge for the governor's family and their guests; and a source of pride
not only to the members of the Garden Club of Virginia, whose statewide hard work
rescued it and brought it back to life, but to all the citizens of Virginia.

*View of Grace Arents Garden
from the summerhouse
looking toward the
Bloemendaal house*

Grace Arents Garden at the
Lewis Ginter Botanical Garden

A garden restoration based on the original early 1900s design

NEW YORK–BORN LEWIS GINTER LOST AND GAINED THREE FORTUNES DUR-
ing his lifetime (1824–1897).[1] He arrived in Richmond at the age of seventeen, or-
phaned and penniless, but he soon catapulted himself into the business of selling toys
and then into the importation of linens and woolens. He developed a reputation as a
creative genius, a master of packaging and presentation.

At the beginning of the Civil War, Ginter sold his business and invested the proceeds in tobacco, sugar, and cotton. He then joined the Confederate Army, ultimately
attaining the rank of major. When the Evacuation Fire of 1865 destroyed Richmond,
Ginter's sugar and tobacco stores were lost, although his cotton escaped the fire. Using the capital from its sale, he returned to New York to tackle Wall Street. Highly
successful, Ginter flourished once again, until the Black Friday stock market crash of
1873 obliterated his second fortune. Broke and middle-aged, he made his way back to
Richmond and partnered with his friend John F. Allen to form Allen & Ginter, which
eventually became the American Tobacco Company.

By 1880, Major Ginter had reestablished himself as a brilliant businessman, en-
trepreneur, and philanthropist. He built the Jefferson Hotel, acquired the *Richmond
Times*, donated land for the Union Theological Seminary and the A. P. Hill Monument, and supported many charities and churches.

Inspired by the attractive residential neighborhoods he had seen in Adelaide,
Sydney, and Melbourne, Australia, on a visit to his company's offices there in 1888–
89, Ginter launched into acquiring land on Richmond's north side for the purpose of
building a residential development close to his own country house, Westbrook. He
was often quoted as saying he had chosen the north side because it was "a foolish waste
of eyesight to drive east into the rising sun each morning and west into the setting
sun each evening." In 1884, Ginter bought an additional ten acres just beyond his up-
scale suburban development; it had once been farmland belonging to Patrick Henry,

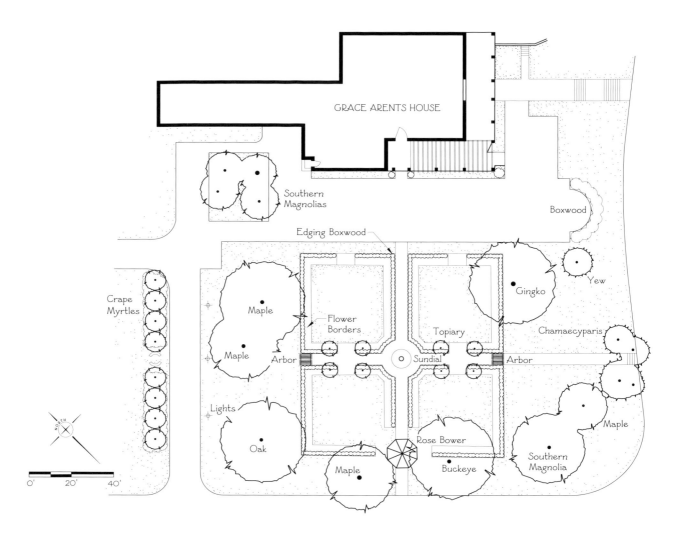

GRACE ARENTS HOUSE

Southern
Magnolias

Boxwood

Edging Boxwood

Yew

Gingko

Crape
Myrtles

Maple

Flower
Borders

Topiary

Chamaecyparis

Maple

Arbor

Sundial

Arbor

Lights

Maple

Oak

Rose Bower

Buckeye

Maple

Southern
Magnolia

NORTH

0'   20'   40'

and more recently an orchard. There, he eventually established the Lakeside Wheel Club, a response to the bicycling craze of the 1890s, but also to provide a place for healthful outdoor recreational activities for the residents of his new neighborhoods. The Lakeside Wheel Club soon grew into a complex of public facilities that included Richmond's first public golf course, its first zoo, a boating lake, and a dance hall. It also included a one-story "wheelhouse," for renting bicycles.

When Lewis Ginter died, in 1897, his favorite niece and heir, Grace Arents, purchased the Lakeside Wheel Club from his landholding company. Arents, a trained nurse, wanted to provide a healthy country environment for children suffering from the crowded living conditions in the polluted areas of the city. She added a second story to the wheelhouse, turning it into a hospital for the sick children of the working-class neighborhood of Oregon Hill. She grew most of the food required for her young patients on the property.

Later, Miss Arents established the Instructional Visiting Nurses Association. Having thereby made her children's hospital obsolete, she decided to convert the building into her own residence. Leaving the Ginter family home on Richmond's Franklin Street, she moved to the country with her companion, Mary Garland Smith. She named her new home Bloemendaal ("Valley of Flowers"), after a village in the Netherlands, the ancestral home of the Ginters.

Miss Arents was inspired to develop the gardens at Bloemendaal by her visits to European botanical gardens. She collected rare trees and shrubs, built a series of three ridge-and-furrow greenhouses, and made a border of herbaceous perennials along one side of the greenhouse range. In front of the house, so it could be viewed from the porch and dining room, was her flower garden. Visitors still marvel at the majesty of a mature, nearly hundred-year-old female ginkgo tree, which is balanced by a massive specimen southern magnolia, at the southwestern perimeter of that garden. Arents's love of roses is evident in vintage photos taken in the 1920s.

Gingko tree planted by Grace Arents

Over the years, "Miss Grace," as she was called, re-purchased some of the original property that had been owned by Patrick Henry, eventually increasing her uncle's initial ten acres to eighty-five. She died in 1926, leaving life rights to her companion, Mary Garland Smith, but she stipulated in her will that at Miss Smith's death Bloemendaal Farm should be developed "as a botanical garden and public park in perpetual memory of my Uncle Lewis Ginter to be known as Lewis Ginter Botanical Garden." Smith lived a quiet life at Bloemendaal for the next forty years and died in 1968. After many trials and tribulations, the Lewis Ginter Botanical Garden officially opened to the public in 1987.

ONE YEAR AFTER THE OPENING OF THE LEWIS GINTER BOTANICAL GARDEN, its Board requested help from the Garden Club of Virginia in re-creating the Arents Garden. Plans were drawn in 1989 by Rudy J. Favretti, and the garden was formally presented in 1990. Miss Grace's garden had been in the classic Renaissance style, with a cruciform walk system forming four garden quadrants. The brick walks were still there.

Summerhouse   The rich documentation for the garden—photographs, plant lists, and other written works—revealed that the only parts that had remained static over the years were the walks, the summerhouse, a rose arbor at each end of the crosswalk, a few rosebushes, and the boxwood edging. Miss Arents changed the other plants in her gardens every year. In its day, this was Bloemendaal's major garden, although today it is only one of the many marvels to be seen at the Lewis Ginter Botanical Garden. The management wanted to use the restored garden as a place to display new plant varieties and new acquisitions, so Favretti provided detailed plans only for the repair of the walks, summerhouse, and arbors, the boxwood edging, and the replacement of some trees. In addition to excellent photographs from which to draw plans for the summerhouse and arbors, remnants of the original structures were discovered underneath the barn. These were only fragments, but enough to give the proper dimensions for the rose arbors and details for the summerhouse.[2]

Grace Arents's original sundial now stands at the intersection of the walkways in the middle of the garden. Roses, vintage perennials, and complementary seasonal herbaceous plants fill the box-edged beds. The summerhouse is festooned with creamy Lady Banks roses and bright pink William Baffin clambers over the arbors to shade the seats.

The Grace Arents Garden continues to develop, under the supervision of the Restoration Committee. The arbors have been repaired as needed, and boxwood replaced. The English box edging declined, and at the request of Holly Shimizu, then managing director of the Lewis Ginter Botanical Garden and now executive director of the National Botanic Garden, it was replaced with the disease-resistant Jensen box. As was the case under Miss Grace's guidance, interesting plants and seasonal color schemes inspire the gardener's creativity. Spiral conifer topiaries, added in recent years, give a dimension of height and internal structure to the garden and provide year-round architectural and horticultural interest. Frank Robinson, the Botanic Garden's current executive director, notes: "The Garden Club of Virginia's contribution is immense in the life of the Garden. This restoration literally helped establish the Lewis Ginter Botanical Garden. We are grateful for the Garden Club's foresight to see the potential of the Botanical Garden and fund the restoration of Grace Arents's garden at her beloved Bloemendaal."[3]

In the past twenty years, the Lewis Ginter Botanical Garden has enjoyed tremendous growth. But Robinson says it is the Grace Arents Garden which remains the Botanical Garden's cornerstone and sentimental favorite: "The Grace Arents Garden is our signature garden. It was the first garden implemented and restored, and while the property continues to evolve, the Grace Arents Garden has almost become our trademark."[4]

None of Lewis Ginter's many philanthropic contributions to the city of Richmond has had a greater impact than this one, made posthumously by his heir in his honor. No one could have dreamed that in barely twenty years' time Richmond would have a botanical garden which can hold its head up in any company. Its gardens, its programs, its education building with its much used auditorium, meeting rooms, and library, its magnificent glass house with its changing exhibits, all are of immeasurable benefit to the city, and to all Virginians within its reach.

Lady Banks roses

View of the restored garden
from the chapel terrace of
Hollins University

Hollins University

*Restoration of the 1930s Beale Garden to honor
alumna Lucy Preston Beale*

IN VIRGINIA EDUCATION WAS AN EARLY PRIORITY, BUT IT DIDN'T HAVE A
very successful start.[1] A first effort to establish a college in the colony met a disastrous end with the massacre of 1622. It would take another seventy-one years before
the College of William and Mary would be chartered, in 1693. In the ensuing century
and a half, the institutions of higher learning in Virginia were mainly for young men;
their sisters, when they were educated, were taught at home. One interesting exception to this rule was the Roanoke Female Seminary, established in 1839 on the site
of the former Botetourt Springs Resort. The idea was way ahead of its time, and the
school unfortunately failed, but not for long. In 1842, the property was sold to the
Reverend Joshua Bradley, who turned it into the Valley Union Education Society of
Virginia, for boys and girls.

Bradley left the school in 1846, turning it over to Charles Lewis Cocke, a twenty-
six-year-old business manager and professor of mathematics at Richmond College.
Cocke accepted the job despite the remarkable stipulation that he would be required
to advance his own money to meet the liabilities of the school. In 1851, apparently
having met those liabilities, the redoubtable Mr. Cocke recommended that the school
dedicate itself to the education of young women rather than men, arguing that, given
the state of society in the country at that time, it was necessary that young women receive the same thorough and rigid mental training as was afforded to young men. The
first session of the Female Seminary at Botetourt Springs was inaugurated in 1852.

Mr. Cocke next faced the challenge of the need for new buildings, as the Botetourt Springs summer cottages had begun to age. A southern institute dedicated to
women's education was not the most popular choice of philanthropists. But, in 1855,
Mrs. John Hollins, whose husband was a miller in neighboring Campbell County, persuaded her husband to give $5,000 to Mr. Cocke's cause. He did so with the stipulation
that the institution would thenceforth operate under a new charter and that it would

be governed by a self-perpetuating board of trustees. The school's name was changed to Hollins Institute, and Mr. Hollins served on its board until he died, in 1859.

Mr. Cocke, the recognized founder of Hollins, served for fifty-five years as president of the growing young institution, and, according to the school's brochure, "was never paid a cent." Indeed, the brochure notes that by 1900, "the Board calculated that the only way to reimburse him was to transfer the school's ownership to the Cocke family." Cocke died the following year, and he was succeeded by his daughter, Matty, who served as president for more than thirty years. During her tenure, the name of the school was changed to Hollins College. In August 1932, Matty Cocke delivered the legal deed of ownership to the president of the board and Hollins once again became a publicly owned institution with a self-perpetuating board of trustees. The school added a select number of graduate programs to its curriculum in 1958, and in 1998 it changed its name once more, to Hollins University. Although its undergraduate college is still a liberal arts women's college, its graduate programs are open to men; the graduate school now accounts for half of the degrees granted each year. Hollins has further broadened its program with community outreach initiatives.

The Hollins campus has been described by the *New York Times* as "achingly beautiful." Situated in the Roanoke Valley between the Appalachian and Allegheny Mountains, the campus is surrounded by spectacular views in all directions. At its center is a classical quadrangle, framed on all sides by the white-columned brick buildings that are the trademark of many institutions of higher learning in Virginia. The original

The Beale Garden in the 1930s

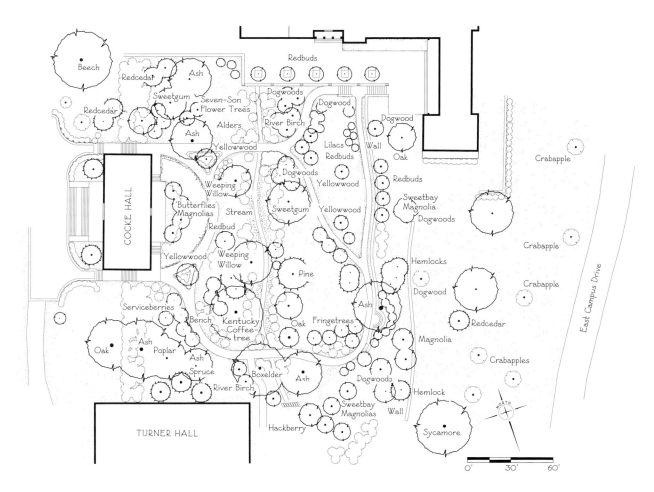

structures of red brick and white columns have been modernized on the inside, but they maintain their classical integrity in their outward appearance. Newer buildings are spread out on the surrounding hillsides. It is a spectacular setting for a university.

IN 1930, LUCY BEALE HUFFMAN, A HOLLINS ALUMNA, DONATED A GARDEN to Hollins in honor of her mother, Lucy Preston Beale, who had graduated from Hollins in 1864.[2] Mrs. Beale was a Virginia representative to both the Chicago World's Fair and the Jamestown Exposition. She remained enormously loyal and generous to Hollins throughout her life. Her two great loves were literature and gardening, so a garden in the heart of the educational institution that she loved is both a fitting tribute and an important link to the university's heritage.

The garden was designed by A. A. Farnham, a Roanoke landscape architect, in 1929. In the 1950s, a dormitory was built near one end of the garden, and a new chapel was constructed on a rise over the streambed. The chapel, built in 1959, took up three-eighths of the existing garden's land. Over time, the paths and stone walls of the

HOLLINS UNIVERSITY

New bridge and paths garden had failed, plants had disappeared or were overgrown, and the streambed had eroded. By the turn of this century, the Beale Garden was obscured and its plantings deteriorated. Hollins turned to the Garden Club of Virginia for help in its revitalization, and the collaboration was announced in 2004. Hollins also wished to repair the terrace that had been built adjacent to the chapel, so this work was undertaken at the same time.

Members of the Hollins staff unearthed some photographs, correspondence between Farnham and the donor, and an illustrative drawing showing the general configuration of the garden but not the specific layout or plant locations. While Farnham's approach guided the revitalization of the garden, the Restoration Committee directed landscape architect William D. Rieley to emphasize the native plants that had been used by Farnham and to limit the number of exotics. Rieley's choices included the Virginia sweetspire, strawberry bush, dogwood, sweet autumn clematis, sweetbay magnolia, witchhazel, swamp white oak, and tulip poplar.

Rieley's approach to revitalizing the garden was to restore or re-create as many elements as possible, keeping to the spirit of the original plan throughout. The circulation pattern was adjusted to meet new conditions: stone-dust paths, edged with brick, once again connect the disparate parts of the garden, just as they did in Farnham's original plan. One path, graced by four 'Butterflies' magnolias donated by Bremo Trees, forms the edge of a formal semicircle behind Cocke Hall. Beautifully crafted wooden bridges, based on the design for the elevated walkway that once formed the southern edge of the garden, cross the little branch of Carvin's Creek that runs through the garden.

The 1957 construction of the chapel and its terrace had truncated the original garden, but Rieley's plan unifies the new landscape. A row of large boxwood, blocking the view into the garden, was replaced with airy redbud trees, and the terrace is now a viewing platform into the restored garden below. Hollins added new railings, brick surfacing on the terrace, and broad steps leading down to the garden to complete the linkage.

New trees and shrubs were added to those which remained in the garden itself. Farnham's stone wall was rebuilt, and a utilitarian culvert-turned-decorative arch, installed when the chapel was built, was turned into a decorative garden feature. Finally, large stones and plants stabilized the stream banks, as they had in Farnham's original plan.

The restored Beale Garden was presented to Hollins University in the fall of 2006. It will be used for entertaining by the administration, for recreation by the students, and as a place for visitors to enjoy. It will thus make Hollins more valuable to the community and broaden the university's exposure. The Garden Club of Virginia takes pride in playing a part in the renovation of this garden at one of Virginia's pioneering, innovative, and most respected educational institutions.

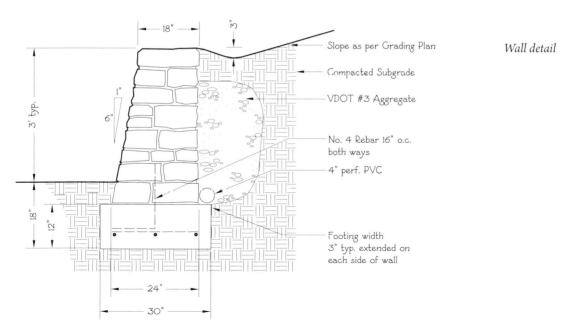

Wall detail

Slope as per Grading Plan

Compacted Subgrade

VDOT #3 Aggregate

No. 4 Rebar 16" o.c. both ways

4" perf. PVC

Footing width 3" typ. extended on each side of wall

Kenmore front entrance

Kenmore

*Dwelling built in the 1770s by Fielding
and Betty Washington Lewis*

KENMORE, NOW COMPLETELY SURROUNDED BY THE CITY OF FREDERICKS-burg, was originally built on the edge of the first expansion of the small frontier town that later engulfed and threatened it. The builder of Kenmore, Fielding Lewis, was the developer of this first expansion of Frederickburg, starting in the 1750s.[1] The western edge of Fielding Lewis's new development abutted a portion of the land that his father, John Lewis, had purchased in 1742—land that Fielding Lewis inherited upon his father's death, in 1754. It was on the eastern edge of this land that he would later build the dwelling now known as Kenmore.

Fielding Lewis was one of eighteenth-century Fredericksburg's most important and influential citizens. As the second son of the wealthy and prominent John Lewis of Warner Hall (located on the Severn River in Gloucester County), he could not inherit the primary estate. In 1742, doubtless with Fielding's future in mind, John Lewis bought 409 acres immediately adjoining the young and sparsely settled town of Fredericksburg, and within two years he had established a store there. In 1744, he brought Fielding, then eighteen, to inspect the store and the property. Two years later, he built a house, as a wedding present for his son, on the northwestern edge of town. It was situated across from the store on the site of the present 1201 Princess Anne Street. The bride was Fielding's first cousin, Catharine Washington, who died in 1750, having given him two sons and a daughter.

Not quite three months later, Fielding Lewis married Betty Washington, his second cousin, who lived with her mother, Mary Ball Washington, at the Ferry Farm across the Rappahannock. Over the next twenty years, he and Betty were to have eleven more children. In 1752, he bought the remaining part of the original Royston patent—681 acres immediately to the west of the town line.[2] It was surveyed by Betty's brother, twenty-year-old George Washington. He and Lewis then laid out a new development which would enlarge the town of Fredericksburg from 64 city lots to 180.

Not until 1759 did an Act of Assembly expand the boundaries of the town to include the new lots.

The French and Indian War began in 1753, and Fredericksburg became a supply depot and staging point for the army. The war went on for ten intense years and was finally settled with the Treaty of Paris in 1763, with sporadic fighting continuing until 1764. Fielding Lewis was right in the middle of the action, as a supplier of the troops and as a respected citizen busy in the defense of the town. For many years, it was thought that Kenmore had been built in either 1752 or 1755, but given the history of Fielding Lewis's land purchases, his other business ventures, and his involvement in the problems of Fredericksburg during the French and Indian War, neither of those dates makes sense. It would not have been until much later that Lewis would have the time or money to devote to building a new house for Betty, which tradition says he had promised Mrs. Washington he would do.

In 1758, having sold his father's store, Lewis went into the shipping business, with mixed success. But the land-development venture flourished, and Lewis realized a profit of more than £1,000 from his lot sales. His bank account thus bolstered, in 1769–70 he imported some sixty craftsmen from Ireland, some of whom were diverted to Mount Vernon. Work began on the Lewises' new house in 1771, but they didn't move into it until 1775. Even then, the interior work was not yet completed; more painting and plastering remained to be done, as Lewis and Washington swapped craftsmen back and forth between them. It was a fine dwelling though, befitting Lewis's position in the community and in the colony.

Directly in front of the Lewis house, two entire blocks of the new suburb had been sold to Mann Page, but they remained open land. Page had by this time already built Mannsfield, for his second family. It is said that Mannsfield was designed by John Ariss, a "shadowy figure" in Virginia's architectural history, according to Calder Loth. It is possible that Ariss also designed the Lewis dwelling: the plans do not survive, but

a bill from Ariss was among Fielding Lewis's papers when he died, and the house is very like one that Ariss designed for Samuel Washington. The Lewises never named their house, which suggests that it was not meant to be a plantation manor, but rather a town villa. It was given the name Kenmore Plantation in 1819 by the Gordon family, who lived there until 1859.

Though Fielding Lewis owned a large quarter in Frederick County and raised wheat on his considerable acreage in Spotsylvania, where he had several mills, he was primarily a city boy. Though he farmed and mined and milled on his various properties, he lived in Fredericksburg, where he worked hard at his many civic responsibilities and had his finger in many commercial pies: he was a merchant, a shipping magnate, a land speculator, an investor in mining, a mill owner, and a real estate developer. His enterprises were not always successful, but he was one of Fredericksburg's primary citizens, as his fine brick dwelling attested.

An exchange of letters between George Washington and his sister Betty Lewis in 1793 is corroborating evidence that the Lewises considered themselves town-dwellers. Their brother Samuel had died, leaving three children as wards of his brother George. George had sent the boys away to school at his own expense, but his niece Hariot had come to live as a member of his family at Mount Vernon. In 1793, he and Martha had to go to Philadelphia for an extended stay. He didn't think it would be suitable for Hariot to remain unchaperoned at Mount Vernon, so he packed her off to Fredericksburg to stay with Betty, who had been a widow for twelve years and was struggling to make ends meet. In his letters to Betty, George Washington took responsibility for Hariot's expenses, but he cautioned his sister to be careful with his money and to keep an careful eye on his niece, whom he considered irresponsible and flighty. Betty answered as follows:

January 29, 1793

My Dear Brother,

Your letters of January the 6th and 14th of this month came duly to hand, the enclosed letter to my son Robert met with a speedy conveyance the same day, the other with the money for Hariot, which I shall see that no part of it shall be laid out but in those things that is really necessary, it is unfortunate for her my living in town, for many things that could be wore to the last string in a country place, will not do here where we see so much company and I must say less would be more agreeable to me.

I must in justice to Hariot say she Payes the strictest regard to the advice I give her, and really she is very ingenius in making her clothes, and altering them to the best advantage. . . . Hariot desires me to thank you for your kindness to her, and joins me in returning your compliment by wishing you many happy New Years.

I am with sincere love to you and my sister,
Your affectionate sister
Betty Lewis[3]

There are no records of Betty Lewis's garden, except for a local tradition that there were terraces on the river side of the house. There was a terraced garden at the old house on Lewis Street, and Mann Page had put in a large one at Mannsfield. These are certainly not proof that the Lewises' new garden was terraced, but at the time it was a fashionable style for a sloping terrain. There was a considerable lag between the planning and the building of the new house. In the planning stage, in the late 1760s, Fielding Lewis's finances were in good order, but by the time the house came to be built he had suffered some reverses. Particularly in the last stages of the building process, money was very tight. Lewis had taken a large mortgage on his Royston patent land, probably to pay for the building materials and furnishings for the new house. Paula Felder, a Fredericksburg historian, notes that the dependencies at the house John Lewis built for the young Fielding and his first bride were built of brick, but that at the elegant new dwelling they were built of wood. Moreover, by the summer and autumn of 1775, when the Lewises moved into the new house, Fredericksburg had once again become a depot and staging area, but this time for a much bigger war.

Fielding Lewis's wartime responsibilities were heavy, and he was also in failing health. In August, Fielding went for his annual cure to the hot springs at Berkeley (now West Virginia), and when he returned, he plunged into his multiple and demanding wartime duties. Thus, when it came time to organize the household and move, the job fell to Betty. With young children still at home, her widowed mother down the street, and the burden of moving on her shoulders, plus the entire responsibility of settling her household once she got there, it is hard to see how Betty could have had time to think about enjoying any sort of a pleasure garden. She would certainly have had a vegetable garden, though. Indeed, there is a May 1785 entry in George Washington's diary in which he notes that he has "planted filbert and Cobb Nuts given to me by my sister Lewis."[4] But there is no mention of where Betty's trees were—of whether she had an orchard or whether the nuts had come from trees planted about the house or in a garden.

Fielding Lewis died in late December 1781 or early January 1782, and his will was probated on January 17, 1782. Betty stayed at Kenmore until 1795, under increasingly difficult circumstances. Fielding's oldest son, John, was far from generous to his step-

mother, and her life was a constant financial struggle. She moved finally to Millbrook, where she died in 1797. Her beautiful house then passed from hand to hand, some more respectful or capable than others, until 1922.

BY THE EARLY TWENTIETH CENTURY, WHEN THE INTREPID LADIES OF FREDericksburg first donned their hats and gloves for the battle to save what was left of the Kenmore property, residential development had already crept along the Winchester Street side and partway up both Lewis and Fauquier Streets. There was a house at the corner of Fauquier and Washington Streets that they were able to buy, but it took longer to acquire the five houses along Winchester Street. All five had been built on deep, narrow lots on the reputed site of the Lewises' terraced garden. In the building of these houses, and then in tearing them down and clearing the land, many archaeological clues to the design of any original garden were lost, but it is hoped that new surveys and testing, utilizing modern technology, may be able to recover details about the garden and the rest of the Lewis properties.

Kenmore is the only one of the Garden Club of Virginia's restored gardens that has had three master plans, the second one of which (the Alden Hopkins plan) was commissioned by the Kenmore Association and not the GCV. This was a departure from precedent, to say the least. In the 1975 predecessor to this volume, Dorothy Hunt

KENMORE

1920s
Pre-Gillette

1920s
Gillette/Greenleaf Proposal

1930s
Gillette Proposal

1940s
Gillette Plan, Implemented

1984
Historic American Buildings Survey

1994
Addition of Wilderness Walk
Rudy J. Favretti

not recognize itself unless carriages could drive up either to the front or the back door. That is the only point in question. You know how women are— we listen and comment and then think of objections afterwards. I hope you had a satisfactory trip to Alexandria, and that you will come to see me again.

Yours faithfully,
Emily W. Fleming[7]

In the end, consensus was somehow reached and the driveway disappeared from the plans, in favor of a brick walk leading from the sidewalk to the front door.

Other additions and changes to the garden occurred in subsequent years. In 1937, the Kenmore Association asked the GCV for a "doing over of the grounds on the side of Kenmore toward the Mary Washington House."[8] By 1941, two "bowers," or arbors, had been built on the upper terrace.[9] A board fence, picket gate, and tool house were added during the 1940s, and a smokehouse was requested in 1955. And in 1958 a flurry of landscape activity began that lasted until 1964.

The second master plan was developed in 1960 under the direction of the Kenmore Association, who hired Alden Hopkins to create it. Since Hopkins also did work for the GCV, he insisted on checking with Charles Gillette, who had developed the first master plan under the GCV's auspices, before he would agree to accept the Kenmore commission. Then, in 1962, Hopkins retired, so subsequent work on the Kenmore garden was done under the direction of Ralph Griswold, working under contract to the GCV. In that capacity, Griswold drew a sketch for an additional service walk from the kitchen to the work shed, and one for new planting in the lower garden. Finally, in 1964, matters between the board of the Kenmore Association and the Restoration Committee of the GCV seem to have come to a head; the result was a joint meeting and the signing of a new agreement between the two organizations that detailed the responsibilities of each.[10]

In 1973–74, the need for a visitors' center and museum resulted in the building of the Crowninshield Gallery. It is sited below grade, next to Fauquier Street, and is separated by a brick wall from the front yard of the house. The GCV commissioned Ralph Griswold to design and plant a screen of evergreens to hide the wall.

In 1991, a "third master plan of revisions" was drawn up by Rudy J. Favretti, who had become the GCV's landscape architect in 1978. In this plan, new plantings refer indirectly to the old driveway circle in the front: Griswold's planting, which hid the wall of the Crowninshield building, was thickened into a curve more or less following the curve of the lost driveway. On the Lewis Street side, the curve was repeated in a "wilderness walk," which screened out the houses along Lewis Street and simulated the edge of a forest. This woodland was composed of native plants, and was used in Kenmore's educational program. It also, incidentally, created a tidy solution to a pedestrian traffic problem, providing an exit route for visitors leaving the house and avoiding congestion on the front walk.

Favretti's 1991 master plan also addressed the complete renovation of the lower garden. The Kenmore management requested that the boxwood edging along the brick walk be removed, since it had grown to a height of nearly twelve feet, making the walks almost impassable. Vernon Edenfield, Kenmore's then director, asked for perennial borders to line the walks, and the Restoration Committee agreed. Favretti also removed one of the "bowers" for which there was no documentation, although the similarly undocumented one on the north side of the garden was allowed to remain. It too has since disappeared.

Recent exploration of the area covered by the woodland walk shows that there had been a row of small houses there, probably a "street" of slave quarters. There is also evidence of oyster-shell paths, and of a picket fence from the corner of the kitchen, which would have separated the front from the garden side. This, incidentally, is apparent in one of the Gillette plans that was not adopted; it became the basis for a small formal garden in yet another of his suggested solutions, however. A magnificent restoration is planned for the interior of the house, which will result in the need for a new way for visitors to enter and exit.

Given the long history of the Garden Club's work with the Kenmore organization, and the fact that the 1932 restoration of that garden is so closely associated with the beginnings of "Garden Week in Virginia" (see Appendix A: The Beginnings of Garden Week), there has always been an emotional chain binding the Garden Club of Virginia to Kenmore. That chain has been tested from time to time by jurisdictional disputes, but it is still holding strong. There will be other opportunities for George Washington's Fredericksburg Foundation, née the Kenmore Association, and the Garden Club of Virginia to extend that chain.

Kent-Valentine House

RICHMOND

*Headquarters for the Garden Club of Virginia
and Historic Garden Week*

THE KENT-VALENTINE HOUSE, AT 12 EAST FRANKLIN STREET IN DOWN-
town Richmond, was designed by Isaiah Rogers for Mr. and Mrs. Horace Kent in 1845.
Kent had moved from Connecticut in 1828 to establish Kent, Paine, and Company,
which would become the largest wholesale importer and jobber of dry goods in Virginia.[1] The Massachusetts-born Rogers was primarily a hotel architect, and few of his
residential buildings remain.[2] For Kent, Rogers designed "a three-bay Italianate dwelling skirted by an intricate cast-iron veranda."[3] The house was sold in 1875 to Charles
Talbott, a successful manufacturer, and in 1904 to Mr. and Mrs. Granville Gray Valentine. The new owners modified and enlarged it significantly. They replaced the cast-
iron veranda with Ionic columns, using the original railings between them, and added
a two-story wing on the west side of the house. Their son, Granville Valentine Jr., taking advantage of historic preservation laws enacted by the Virginia General Assembly
in 1966 as part of the Virginia Outdoors Plan, placed the property under historic easement in 1971.

The Garden Club of Virginia bought the Kent-Valentine House shortly after it
received its historic designation. It is currently used as the Club's headquarters and to
house the offices for Historic Garden Week. Downstairs, the house is furnished with
eighteenth- and nineteenth-century antiques, some of which came with the house and
some of which were bequeathed or donated by Garden Club members and generous
friends. Among these items is one of Virginia's largest collections of bird and plant
prints by the eighteenth-century naturalist Mark Catesby. In the library, a growing collection of books on horticulture, garden history and design, and flower arranging is
useful to the members.

In 1973, the grounds were renovated under the direction of Ralph Griswold, of
Griswold, Winters and Swain. The carriage house at the back, converted to an architect's office, required a driveway, and the Club needed parking for staff and visitors.

81

Front entrance and portico with cast-iron railing

Griswold arranged the limited space to include an in-and-out drive that enters from First Street and exits to the alley, and six parking spaces tucked in between existing large trees. Additional trees, shrubbery, and groundcover provide a park-like, rather than parking-lot, setting. The surrounding brick walls, iron fences, and gates were repaired as needed, and brick walks laid. A wood fence was built along the west property line and faced with a row of 'Nellie Stevens' hollies running the length of the fence. A yellowwood tree thrives by the carriage house. New gates at the alley exit match those at the First Street entrance.

Except for the Executive Mansion in Capitol Square, this is the last house in downtown Richmond surrounded by trees. Southern magnolias shade the house, and gingkos line the sidewalk along Franklin Street. There are crape myrtles, dogwood, boxwood, hydrangeas, and beds of English ivy around the house. Two massive iron urns flanking the front door are planted with seasonal displays of boxwood, pansies, and summer-flowering annuals.

A complete structural renovation of the house was staved off for twenty-five years, but had to be faced in 1996–98. A two-story wing was added to the east side of the house, which provided handicapped access, elevators to the third floor, and other needed amenities. At the same time, Rudy J. Favretti drew up a new landscape plan for the back garden. Outside the new wing, in the back, he added an entirely new brick-paved entrance court, miraculously sparing five of the parking spaces and carefully preserving the existing trees. Besides serving as an entrance to the new wing, the space functions as a patio. Decorative urns flank a bench given in honor of Mrs. Gordon Leggett, who was president of the Garden Club during this renovation, to make an inviting garden seat.

In 2004, it was necessary to revisit the garden again. The venerable hollies along the brick wall separating the Kent-Valentine property from the alley on the north were causing the wall to buckle ominously. The first plan, to save

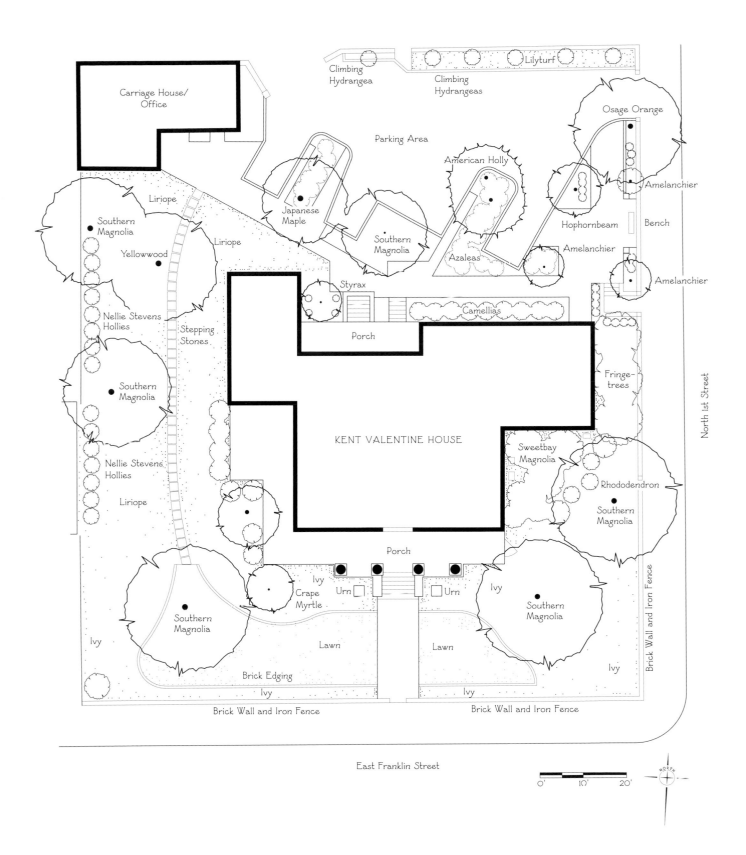

Carriage House/
Office

Climbing
Hydrangea

Climbing
Hydrangeas

Lilyturf

Osage Orange

Parking Area

American Holly

Amelanchier

Liriope

Southern
Magnolia

Japanese
Maple

Hophornbeam

Bench

Yellowwood

Liriope

Southern
Magnolia

Azaleas

Amelanchier

Amelanchier

Nellie Stevens
Hollies

Styrax

Camellias

Porch

Stepping
Stones

Southern
Magnolia

Fringe-
trees

North 1st Street

Nellie Stevens
Hollies

KENT VALENTINE HOUSE

Sweetbay
Magnolia

Liriope

Rhododendron

Southern
Magnolia

Porch

Southern
Magnolia

Ivy
Crape
Myrtle

Urn

Urn

Ivy

Southern
Magnolia

Ivy

Lawn

Lawn

Brick Wall and Iron Fence

Southern
Magnolia

Brick Edging

Ivy

Ivy

Ivy

Brick Wall and Iron Fence

Brick Wall and Iron Fence

East Franklin Street

0'   10'   20'

NORTH

KENT-VALENTINE HOUSE

the trees by bridging their roots, proved impractical; the roots had compromised the footing of the wall. Very reluctantly, it was agreed that the hollies had to go; now nobody misses them. After much discussion, the city granted a variance so that the wall could be rebuilt to its original height, and the space gained by the absence of the hollies accommodates extra parking. Climbing hydrangeas, flat against the wall, will soon clothe the bare bricks. In the same renovation, William D. Rieley redesigned the front walk and the ivy beds on the south side of the house, planted rhododendrons to hide the air-conditioning units, and added a row of camellias along the porch at the back of the house to shield the area at the base of the basement steps. Young fringetrees flower over the east wall, replacing a big one that was lost to the 1996 construction.

In this rescue of a threatened landmark and its transformation from family residence to organization headquarters, the Garden Club of Virginia demonstrated its commitment to the principle of adaptive reuse as a lynchpin of historic preservation. The adaptation of the Kent-Valentine House helps to promote the continuing vibrancy of downtown Richmond, while at the same time giving new life to a grand old lady.

Ker Place

ONANCOCK

A Federal-style house with a long garden walk and arbor

VIRGINIA'S EASTERN SHORE SEEMS REMOTE TODAY; THE DRIVE ACROSS THE Bay Bridge-Tunnel emphasizes the separation from the mainland, and sailing across the bay and back can be a two-day adventure if the weather turns. But in the seventeenth and eighteenth centuries, the Chesapeake Bay was the interstate highway, and the Eastern Shore was more easily reached from Jamestown and Williamsburg than were the overland settlements to the west. The Indians too were relatively friendly: the first royal grant issued in the New World was from an Indian king to an English boy. A highway marker in Northumberland County reads, in part: "Here, in Savage's Neck, was the home of Ensign Thomas Savage, who came to Virginia in 1608. Granted a tract of land by Debedeavon, the 'laughing king' of the Indians, in 1619, Savage became the first permanent English Settler on the Eastern Shore." Savage's descendants are still there.

The town of Onancock has a long history: John Smith first navigated its now tricky deepwater creek in 1608 on his exploratory voyage to map the Chesapeake Bay.[1] The site of the present town of Onancock was the stronghold of Eekeeks, king of the Onancocks, a tribe that on occasion traded valuable grain to the Jamestown settlers. In the mid-seventeenth century, Onancock was known as Port Scarborough, or Scarburgh, named for and controlled by the influential and autocratic Edmund Scarborough, whose brother, Sir Charles Scarborough, was physician to the king. This relationship was a great protection for Edmund, a man of legendary and ruthless high-handedness. Sometimes called the first developer of the Eastern Shore, he patented large tracts of land there and on the mainland, and took full advantage of the lucrative trade up and down the Chesapeake Bay. Indeed, one of his most successful ventures was in slave trading to provide hands for Virginia's tobacco fields.

The 1680 Virginia Act of Cohabitation required each of the colony's nineteen settled areas to set aside fifty acres for a port and market town. One of these set-aside

85

Crape myrtle allée

areas was Port Scarborough, which later became Onancock; along with Norfolk, it is one of Virginia's two surviving original ports of entry. During the seventeenth and eighteenth centuries, Onancock was a bustling community and port of trade. One of the community's late eighteenth-century citizens, John Shepherd Ker, was a prosperous merchant of Scottish descent with broad financial interests and investments in grain, wharves, and storehouses. His wife, Agnes Corbin Ker, had inherited her father's plantation at Onancock. In 1799, John Ker was able to establish by deed his reversion interest in the property, and he began building the fine Federal dwelling at what is now 69 Market Street in Onancock, which was completed by the time of his death in 1806.

Ker Place, a Virginia Historic Landmark, is also listed on the National Register of Historic Places. The house is unusual for the Eastern Shore, which has a prevalent architectural style, known as "big house, little house, colonnade and kitchen," that appears rarely in other parts of Virginia. On the Eastern Shore, a young couple would typically build a small, story-and-a-half house attached to an outside kitchen by a covered, colonnaded passage; as fortunes and families increased, a larger, two-story addition would be built on the other end of the little house. But the already successful Ker started with the big house, a two-story, seven-bay Federal mansion with a three-bay, pedimented central pavilion. Following local custom, the house was attached on the east side to a one-story colonnade leading to an outside kitchen. At some point, however, the outside kitchen was removed and the colonnade was enclosed and raised to a two-story wing. When the Eastern Shore Historical Society bought the property in 1960, that wing was reserved for the use of the last private owner.

In its nearly two-hundred-year history, Ker Place, as it is now known, was handed down in only two families until it was sold to the Eastern Shore Historical Society in 1960. It stayed in the Ker/Snead family until 1875, when George W. Powell bought the house and seven acres. Powell, a successful and well-respected ship's merchant and maritime agent, added a glass cupola on top of the roof, from which he could watch the harbor and the comings and goings of his ships. The cupola was later damaged by a hurricane and never replaced. A third generation of Powell owners sold Ker Place, with two acres of land, to the Eastern Shore Historical Society to serve as its headquarters.

WHEN IT WAS BUILT, KER PLACE WAS IN THE COUNTRY. The town of Onancock has since grown up around it, but skillful landscaping of its two remaining acres gives it the privacy of a much larger property. In 1981, the Board of the Eastern Shore Historical Society applied to the Restoration Committee of the Garden Club of Virginia for help with the landscape. Since there was no historical record or archaeological evidence of an original garden, in 1982 Rudy J. Favretti, landscape architect to the Club, designed the landscape to make a gracious and appropriate setting for the historic dwelling. The mature sycamores around the house became the focus of the restoration. As Favretti noted, "The idea of growing a mixture of high-branched trees to shade a house was popular at the time."[2] A later planting of Virginia redcedars, along Market Street, shielded the house from traffic. Flanking the straight driveway, shrubberies screen the adjoining properties and channel the eye toward the imposing façade, often sunlit, at the end of

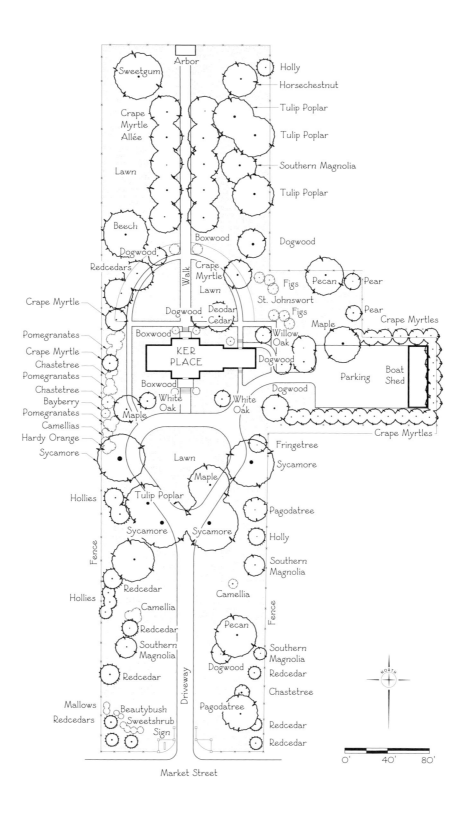

Sweetgum

Arbor

Holly

Horsechestnut

Crape
Myrtle
Allée

Tulip Poplar

Tulip Poplar

Lawn

Southern Magnolia

Tulip Poplar

Beech

Boxwood

Dogwood

Dogwood

Redcedars

Crape
Myrtle
Lawn

Walk

Pecan

Figs

Pear

Crape Myrtle

St. Johnswort

Pear

Figs

Crape Myrtles

Pomegranates

Dogwood

Deodar
Cedar

Maple

Crape Myrtle

Boxwood

KER
PLACE

Willow
Oak

Chastetree

Pomegranates

Chastetree

Boxwood

Dogwood

Boat
Shed

Bayberry

White
Oak

White
Oak

Parking

Pomegranates

Maple

Camellias

Dogwood

Hardy Orange

Crape Myrtles

Sycamore

Fringetree

Lawn

Sycamore

Maple

Hollies

Tulip Poplar

Pagodatree

Sycamore

Sycamore

Holly

Southern
Magnolia

Hollies

Camellia

Redcedar

Camellia

Fence

Pecan

Southern
Magnolia

Hollies

Redcedar

Dogwood

Southern
Magnolia

Redcedar

Fence

Redcedar

Chastetree

Mallows

Beautybush

Redcedar

Redcedars

Sweetshrub

Pagodatree

Sign

Driveway

Redcedar

Market Street

NORTH

0'   40'   80'

the shady drive. In front of the house, curved beds of periwinkle and daylilies suggest the more elaborate flower beds that might once have been there. Behind the house, a bed of periwinkle and daylilies survives in the hot summer sun, and a double row of pink crape myrtles flanks the long axial walk leading to an arbor against the fence that marks the northern boundary of the property. In Favretti's original plan, the walk was flanked by cherry trees, but these soon succumbed, "victims of the many diseases that attack cherries in the southern climate."[3] A variety of specimen trees, planted in the lawn on either side of the long walk, complete the design for the back of the house.

The plant palette is largely native: redcedar, flourishing clumps of bayberry, fringetree, summersweet, and sweetshrub. All provide variety and summer fragrance in the shrubberies and along the peripheries. Existing fig trees were moved to the east side of the house. Lilacs, honeysuckle, flame azaleas, and rhododendron bloom in the spring, while the crape myrtles, sourwood, and sweetgum blaze in the fall.

The Eastern Shore Historical Society is the custodian of a distinguished history, and John Shepherd Ker's elegant house is a fitting headquarters. The Garden Club of Virginia is proud to have had a part in preserving this important heritage for the citizens of the Eastern Shore of Virginia and all its visitors.

*Lee Hall from outside
the curtilage*

Lee Hall Mansion

NEWPORT NEWS

Period landscape for an 1850s Italianate plantation house

THERE SEEMS TO BE NO CONNECTION BETWEEN THE FAMILY OF RICHARD Decatur Lee, the builder of Lee Hall, in Warwick County, and the Lees of Westmoreland County, but the Warwick County Lees have a longer history in Virginia. The founder of this line was Dr. Henry Lee (1623–1657), who immigrated to Jamestown and served in the House of Burgesses in 1652.[1] Henry Lee's descendants were prolific, spreading out into York and Warwick Counties. (Warwick River Shire was among the first group of political subdivisions established in the colony, in 1634; the eight original shires were later divided into counties.)

Henry Lee's great, great, great-grandson, Richard Decatur Lee, was born in 1821. "Decatur" was the surname of Stephen Decatur, a great naval hero of the Barbary Wars and of the War of 1812, who had been killed in a Maryland duel shortly before Lee's birth. The Barbary Wars, fought between the United States and the Barbary states of North Africa—Morocco, Algiers, Tunis, and Tripoli—had put an end to international piracy, proved the strength of the fledgling U.S. Navy (to the surprise of the international community), and ended the murderous system of piracy and blackmail that had menaced ships in the Mediterranean for centuries. Stephen Decatur's heroism in the Battle of Tripoli was widely celebrated in the years leading up to Richard Decatur Lee's birth, and this was said to be the origin of the latter's middle name. The Lee Hall literature uses a different spelling—"Decauter"—but research shows that this spelling is merely a variant of "Decatur."[2] This bears on the history of Lee Hall only in that it gives the modern visitor to the house a sense of the attitudes of Lee's own time, before the sky fell in.

The current interpretation of Lee Hall Mansion dwells on the history of the bitter 1862 Peninsula Campaign, which destroyed Richard Lee's world. But it is also true that the builder of Lee Hall was born at a time when America had just solidified its position as a military and political force to be reckoned with, when its naval heroes engendered the kind of adulation we give today to rock stars or great athletes. However you spelled it, Decatur was a proud name to give to a little boy who was meant to grow up to make his family proud. And Richard Decatur Lee did just that.

Richard Decatur Lee was nineteen when his father died and he inherited the Lee estate, his father's two sons from a first marriage having died without issue. The young Lee married one of his distant cousins, Martha Lee Young, a widow with two young sons, and he then set about enlarging his property. Under his care, the farm grew and his fortunes flourished. In 1856, he bought thirty acres of land on the Warwick River and built a gristmill, a lucrative investment that further strengthened his financial situation.[3]

Sometime during the 1850s, Richard Lee built the grand house that his political position and prosperity, as well as his progeny, required: he had been appointed a justice of the peace, he was one of the richest men in Warwick County, and he had six children and assorted relatives to house.[4] Lee Hall, set on a rise, is an imposing Italianate plantation house. To find the house these days, you have to get off Interstate 64 and look for it; but when it was built, the narrow country road onto which it now faces was a main county thoroughfare, the "Great Warwick Road." It was clearly a house meant to be handed down through the generations.

But that would not be possible for the Lees. Richard Lee had less than ten years in his new home before the Civil War ended the pleasant life of a successful gentleman farmer for him and for his generation of Virginians. Lee Hall's elevated site and

Bachelder sketch

LEE HALL MANSION

strategically valuable location attracted the attention of a succession of military commanders, on both sides of the war. There is an undocumented yet persistent story that while Lee Hall was in Confederate hands, at least one reconnaissance balloon was sent up from its redoubts. The Confederate Generals John B. Magruder and Joseph E. Johnston both headquartered there at different times, but it was Union General George B. McClellan's forces who took firm possession of Lee Hall early in the war, at the beginning of May, 1862. McClellan's taking of the mansion is memorialized in a haunting pencil-and-watercolor sketch drawn by John B. Bachelder (1825–1894), a Union soldier from New Hampshire who later became a leading historian of the Battle of Gettysburg (the sketch is now in the collection of the Gilder Lehrman Institute of American History in New York).

Lee Hall from the west

Richard Lee was never able to recover financially after the war, and he was forced to sell Lee Hall in 1870. The country around Newport News, consisting of swaths of open, undeveloped land with proximity to shipping, was ripe plucking for northern investors, who descended like locusts on the battered South. Lee Hall was bought first by one William Henry Aspinall of New York, who never saw it. After he died, the mansion was acquired by the Old Dominion Land Company, whose lawyer, Robert Bickford, bought it next and fixed it up as a country retreat. Bickford was divorced from his wife when he died, in 1925, and he left Lee Hall, along with most of the rest of his estate, to his secretary, Pearl Yost. Miss Yost was quite a remarkable woman; she lived at Lee Hall and kept it going as a dairy farm for thirty-five years. But after struggling through the Depression, she too finally had to sell it, to her lawyer, William Carleton. (Pearl Yost died in 1963, shortly after she sold Lee Hall, and she is buried beside Robert Bickford at Greenland Cemetery in Newport News.) The Carletons did considerable remodeling to the house during the time they owned the property. In 1996, they sold it to the city of Newport News, after which it was restored to its original antebellum appearance. Lee Hall Mansion was opened to the public in 1998 as a house-museum.

In 1999 the city of Newport News asked the Garden Club of Virginia for assistance in the restoration of the Lee Hall landscape. While there is no evidence that the property ever had a formal garden, landscape architect William D. Rieley employed maps from before and during the Civil War, the Bachelder sketch, a detailed survey of the site from 1916, and post–Civil War documents to glean important clues about an appropriate landscape strategy for the site. He began with the

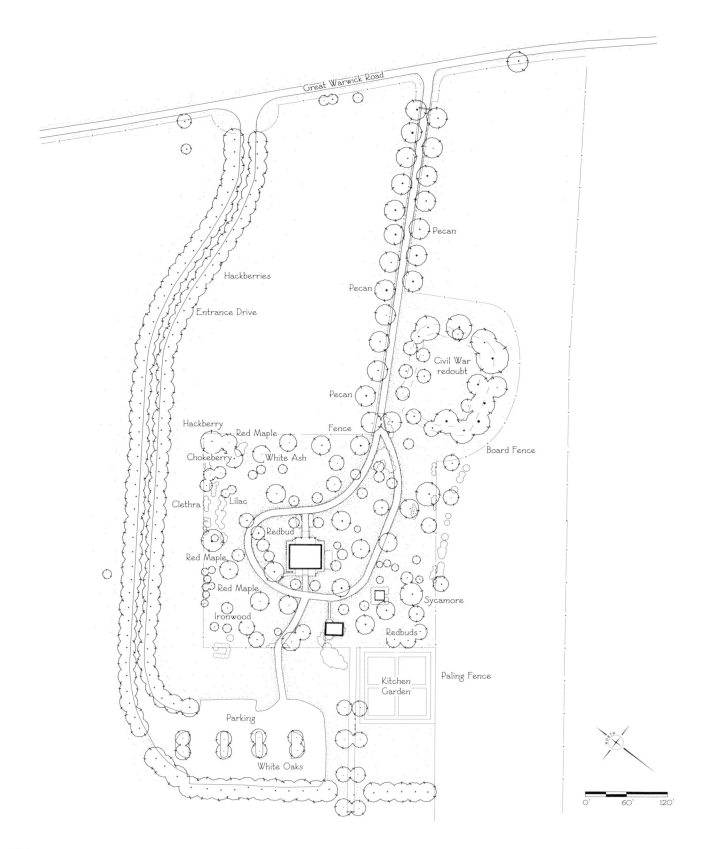

Great Warwick Road

Hackberries

Entrance Drive

Pecan

Pecan

Civil War
redoubt

Pecan

Hackberry   Red Maple   Fence

Chokeberry   White Ash

Clethra   Lilac

Board Fence

Redbud

Red Maple

Red Maple

Sycamore

Ironwood

Redbuds

Kitchen
Garden

Paling Fence

Parking

White Oaks

NORTH

0'   60'   120'

framework of fencing that had organized the land. Several Civil War–era maps show Lee Hall within a rectangular "curtilage," or fenced-in yard, that surrounded the house. Field observations confirmed such a pattern. By the mid-nineteenth century, the circular saw had been invented, which would have made it economically feasible to produce boards at a cost low enough to use them for board fencing. The curtilage, then, was designed to enclose the house yard with a three-board fence in a rectangular shape. The 1916 survey showed that the original entrance drive and back alley had also been fenced, and that the Civil War redoubt to the north of the house was also enclosed. A document uncovered by Sarah Goldberger and Michael Moore, of the Lee Hall staff, indicates that Mr. Lee had sought reimbursement for fences that had been destroyed by the hostilities. An amazingly detailed accounting shows that a post-and-rail fence (with cedar posts and four chestnut rails) had been run along Warwick Road, and that the internal farm fences were pine snake, or worm, fencing, with ten rails per panel. So Rieley's plan was designed with post-and-rail fencing along the Warwick Road in

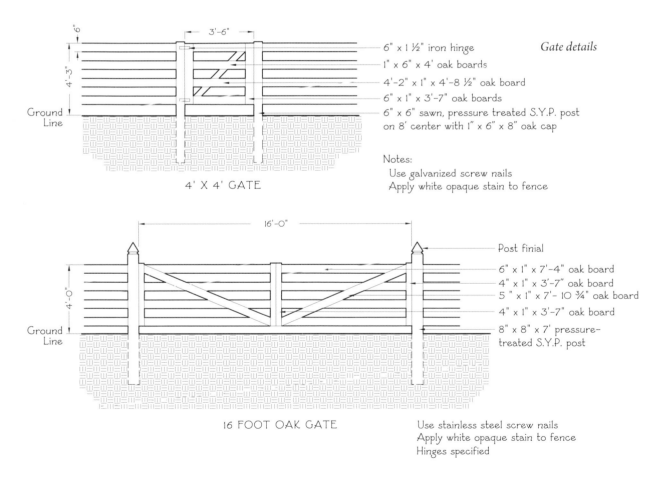

Gate details

6" x 1 ½" iron hinge
1" x 6" x 4' oak boards
4'-2" x 1" x 4'-8 ½" oak board
6" x 1" x 3'-7" oak boards
6" x 6" sawn, pressure treated S.Y.P. post
on 8' center with 1" x 6" x 8" oak cap

Ground Line

4' X 4' GATE

Notes:
Use galvanized screw nails
Apply white opaque stain to fence

16'-0"

Post finial
6" x 1" x 7'-4" oak board
4" x 1" x 3'-7" oak board
5 " x 1" x 7'- 10 ¾" oak board
4" x 1" x 3'-7" oak board
8" x 8" x 7' pressure-treated S.Y.P. post

Ground Line

4'-0"

16 FOOT OAK GATE

Use stainless steel screw nails
Apply white opaque stain to fence
Hinges specified

front of the house, and pine snake-rail fencing on both sides of the new entrance road, to illustrate the fencing that had been used for the internal farm roads.

Outside of the curtilage, agricultural fields ran right up to the fencing. The plan developed by the Garden Club of Virginia strongly recommended keeping as much land as possible around Lee Hall in agricultural use. Within the curtilage, the grounds are embellished in a manner typical of the mid-nineteenth century, which is to say, they are planted with large shade trees, as maps and the Bachelder sketch suggest. As this was the period in American landscape design when flowering shrubs were coming into wide use as a landscape element, Rieley added shrubs of the period to the supplementary planting of shade trees. A kitchen garden would have been essential for a house like Lee Hall, and a location was chosen for a demonstration garden that is plausible, from the perspective of proximity and topography. Taller and tighter fencing typical of vegetable garden fencing of the period was designed for this enclosure.

The first phase of the work consisted in the building of the board fence, the planting of selected trees and shrubs within the curtilage, and tree planting along the margins of the new entrance road. Future work will include the vegetable garden fencing, rail fencing for the Warwick Road and the entrance road, and stabilization of the redoubt. Recently, the city of Newport News requested additional professional assistance from the Restoration Committee for the design of new pathways around the house, a new exterior lighting plan, and a new design for the entrance to the property off of Yorktown Road. Mr. Rieley and his associates have developed plans for these improvements, which will be implemented by the city using grants and its own funds. They will include new stone-dust paths edged in brick, a plan for low-key lighting suitable to a historic site, and a new entrance area with simple and appropriate signage.

The completed landscape will represent more of a conjectural historic setting for this very interesting house than a re-creation of the plantings at any point in the past. Nevertheless, it is a setting that evokes the aesthetics of the period and is an appropriate backdrop for the elegant dwelling that Richard D. Lee so proudly built.

Mary Washington House

The home and cottage garden of
George Washington's mother

THIS GARDEN WAS FULLY DESCRIBED IN THE GARDEN CLUB'S EARLIER VOL-ume, *Historic Virginia Gardens,* by Dorothy Hunt Williams, but it reappears here both because it has since been twice refurbished and because the full history of the 1761 house that George Washington bought for his mother in 1772 was not included in the 1975 volume.

In 1752, George Washington, at the behest of his sister's husband, Fielding Lewis, surveyed the 861 remaining acres of a 1671 patent, part of which had been taken by eminent domain in 1728 to establish the original town of Fredericksburg.[1] Lewis subsequently bought the land for £861 and laid out a new suburb, divided into square two-acre blocks, which were then further subdivided into four half-acre lots. It was an optimistic venture because some of the lots of the original town had not yet been sold. This enlargement of the town was incorporated in 1759, and by the end of 1760 Lewis had realized a tidy profit of £1,100. He set aside lots 107 and 108 for Washington, who planned to move his widowed mother into town to be nearer to her daughter. However, Lewis never registered the deed.

In 1761, Lewis built a cottage on lot 107, at the corner of Charles and Lewis Streets, presumably for Mrs. Washington, but she then announced that she was not ready to move. To recoup his investment, Lewis sold lot 107 along with the house, as well as lot 108, to Michael Robinson for £250. He then set aside another couple of lots, 111 and 113, for George Washington. But Lewis didn't register that deed either, and he subsequently resold those lots to James Mercer. When, in 1772, Mrs. Washington decided that she was ready to leave Ferry Farm, her son came to inspect his lots, only to find James Mercer's house occupying them. At the same time, Mrs. Washington expressed her desire to live in the cottage on lot 107, the one she had originally been promised. Obligingly, Michael Robinson agreed to sell lots 107 and 108 back to George Washington for £275 and the problem was solved.

The garden and lawn with Aquia-stone gnomon and sundial

When Mary Ball Washington moved to Fredericksburg, her property consisted of two half-acre lots on the north side of Lewis Street, between Charles and Prince Edward. Her house fronted on Charles Street, at the corner of Lewis and Charles. The back lot, fronting on Prince Edward, was presumably used for stables, slave quarters, a garden for fruits and vegetables, and possibly some crops to feed the animals.

By 1968, WHEN THE GARDEN CLUB OF VIRGINIA WAS ASKED FOR HELP WITH a garden for the Mary Washington House, the back lot (108, fronting on Prince Edward Street) had long since been sold off and developed. The original cottage had been extended north along Charles Street in several additions, the first of them built by George Washington for his mother in 1772. Behind the house, the original outside kitchen was still standing, as well as another outbuilding of a later date. There was no archaeological or documentary evidence of an original garden;[2] the only trace of the eighteenth-century landscape was a double row of overgrown English box bordering an old brick walk. According to local legend, Mary Washington herself had ordered

MARY WASHINGTON HOUSE

this walkway laid for her daily visits to her daughter's new house, now known as Kenmore, which was under construction in 1772. Furthermore, tradition says that George Washington himself planted thirteen chestnut trees along this walkway between his mother's and his sister's houses, one for each of the original colonies. The trees were actually along Fauquier Street and they were probably planted by James Mercer, but somehow their location got transposed to the walk on Mary Washington's property and the erroneous idea was later perpetuated in the design of the new garden. Given what we now know about the layout of the town in 1772, it is more likely that the walkway from Mary Washington's house led to the stable and vegetable garden in the back lot.

Behind the house there was also an old Aquia-stone gnomon, or shaft, with a sundial plate on top, also said to have belonged to Mary Washington.[3] As it turns out, the metal sundial plate could not have been hers, as evidenced in the following letter from Ralph Griswold to the Restoration Committee of the Garden Club of Virginia:

> Reluctantly, I have had to accept the statement of the Maryland Historical Society that "F.W.&R. King, manufacturers of survey and daguerreotype instruments, was first noted in 1851, and disappeared in 1875." Since this, unmistakably incised identity of *Baltimore* is definite, I cannot see how we can call it her sundial. It is none-the-less a very distinguished garden ornament, probably of the early nineteenth century as far as the pedestal is concerned, [and] in my estimation, has lost none of its importance to garden art by loss of its identity with Mary Washington.[4]

Despite its shaky provenance, Griswold's drawing of the shaft and its nineteenth-century sundial plate graced the cover of the house's 1969 presentation program.

Griswold assumed that both the sundial plate and the shaft had been made during the late nineteenth century. Dorothy Hunt Williams was more respectful of the legend and uncovered the fact that the Aquia quarry had indeed operated during Mary Washington's lifetime, before going out of business in 1830. In *Historic Virginia Gardens,* Williams also noted the presence of a second set of anchor holes in the top of the shaft, and she surmised that the original sundial plate had undoubtedly been changed, but that the shaft itself could have belonged to Mary Washington.[5]

Mary Washington's garden was a countrywoman's garden. When George Washington's mother finally agreed to leave her beloved Ferry Farm, she brought along not only her furniture but as much as she could of her previous life. With her own animals, and with the plants from her old garden transplanted to the new one, she could begin to feel at home in the cottage she had rejected eleven years earlier. W. Thomas Borellis, an associate with the firm of Griswold, Winters and Swain, described the conceptual basis for the design of the restored garden:

I have gathered together all of the facts immediately made available to me on the life of Mary Washington and, in particular, her life in Fredericksburg between 1772–1789. This information is, by far, incomplete, but it gave some understanding of her habits, her likes, and her needs in a garden. These facts and findings were then used in restoring a garden which best fits the character of the mother of George Washington.

Mary Washington was an ardent gardener. Her interests in gardening were not only in the ornamentation of her home, but also a deep understanding and experimentation in the planting and growing habits of the plants in her garden. Her garden was also a practical one where food and herbs had a major place. Her years at Ferry Farm undoubtedly made her a very good farmer, and when she moved from Ferry Farm to Fredericksburg she certainly brought much of this knowledge with her. This knowledge and interest in gardening was applied again in Fredericksburg only at a much

smaller scale. It has been recorded that she brought "slips, and herbs, and simples [medicinal plants] from the Ferry Farm," also "two horses, a cow, and a dog" to build a garden in her new home. In the last years of her life, the nearness of Kenmore and her daughter and grandchildren must have brought much satisfaction. The pain caused by the illness in her later years was probably soothed by walks and meditation in her garden.

The garden restoration can be divided into three sections: (1) the Kitchen Garden; (2) the "brick boxwood-lined path" and; (3) the pleasure garden. This preliminary [sketch] shows proposed locations for various outbuildings which may or may not be included. If the latter is the case, an extension of the garden into that area will be the answer permanently or until such time when the structure can be built. This might be called historical master planning. The locations of the outbuildings, the stable, the privy, and the well, are not proven to be correct, but only

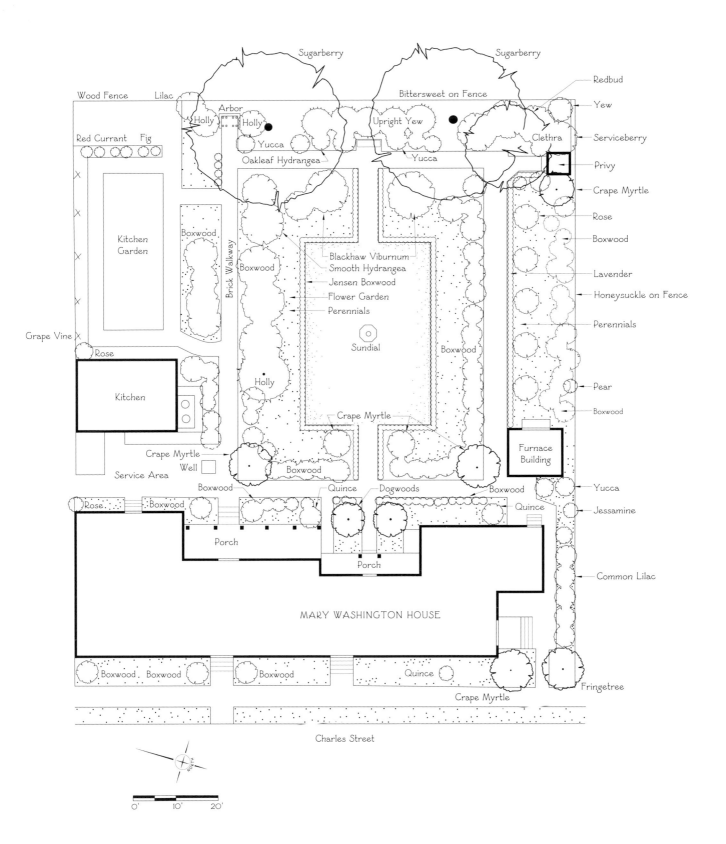

Sugarberry
Sugarberry
Wood Fence
Lilac
Arbor
Redbud
Yew
Bittersweet on Fence
Holly
Holly
Upright Yew
Servicerberry
Clethra
Red Currant
Fig
Yucca
Privy
Oakleaf Hydrangea
Yucca
Crape Myrtle
Rose
Boxwood
Kitchen
Garden
Boxwood
Boxwood
Lavender
Brick Walkway
Blackhaw Viburnum
Smooth Hydrangea
Honeysuckle on Fence
Jensen Boxwood
Flower Garden
Perennials
Perennials
Sundial
Boxwood
Grape Vine
Rose
Holly
Pear
Boxwood
Kitchen
Crape Myrtle
Crape Myrtle
Furnace
Building
Well
Boxwood
Service Area
Boxwood
Quince
Dogwoods
Boxwood
Yucca
Quince
Rose
Boxwood
Jessamine
Porch
Porch
Common Lilac
MARY WASHINGTON HOUSE
Boxwood
Boxwood
Boxwood
Quince
Fringetree
Crape Myrtle
Charles Street
NORTH
0'   10'   20'

typical in relation to existing site conditions. The existing building at the northeast corner could easily pass for a smoke house or other related out-buildings.

The Kitchen Garden would supply the food needs, the herb garden would give the spices, and the simples, the cures for various ailments in the family, these being all basics to a gardener in the 18th century. An orchard was, I am certain, a large item. Mary Washington must have brought many small trees from the orchards at Ferry Farm. However, because of the subdivision of the property to its present size, an orchard would be impossible to estab-lish and impractical to keep. The close relationship with the Lewis family justifies the "brick boxwood-lined path" to Kenmore and plays a dominate [sic] part in the garden restoration. The existing boxwood (some believed planted by Mary Washington) serves as an excellent basis for a section of the "brick boxwood-lined path" to be restored. As a terminating point for this walk, the construction of a simple simulated wood gate to match the character of the existing wood fence along the back of the property would be the answer; similar in idea to the gate at the end of the brick walk at Ken-more. Mary Washington undoubtedly had a small pleasure garden where her best annuals and perennials were displayed in the outdoors and created a setting for the sundial existing even today in the garden. It was here she would have entertained out of doors.

I have elaborated somewhat on the thoughts of the design and have pur-posely omitted details such as: plant names, transplanting, pruning, etc. These details can be worked on after the design is reviewed. Please let me know the Committee's comments and I will work on a final presentation plan for Mr. Griswold to present in May.[6]

In its execution, Griswold's design carefully preserved remnants of the old gar-den while overlaying it with an orderly and beautifully proportioned new one appro-priate to the period of the house. Using a palette of outbuildings, paths, and ornamen-tal and vegetable plantings, the Griswold composition is an extraordinary blend of both preservation ethics and design skill. There is a generous rectangle of lawn out-lined by boxwoods and perennial beds, with a wide flower border along the north fence. A shrub border with flowers, also box-bordered, along the west fence, shields the garden from the neighbors. About a third of the garden area on the south side, behind the kitchen, is devoted to vegetables and herbs. This, and the service area in front of the kitchen, are hidden from the pleasure garden by the large boxwoods lining

the walkway. The disputed Aquia stone pedestal with its Baltimore gnomon sits in the middle of the lawn.

The Messrs. Griswold and Borellis knew their clients; the Restoration Committee commented at length and very specifically on the plan. Its members held strong opinions on every detail of the plan and planting, and their suggestions were incorporated into the final plan. The garden was presented to the Association for the Preservation of Virginia Antiquities in September 1969.

Since that time, the garden has been refurbished by two of the Garden Club's subsequent landscape architects, Rudy J. Favretti and William D. Rieley, both of them working within the framework of Griswold's elegant design. In each of the refurbishings, the planting scheme had to be updated because of changes in the pattern of shade in the garden. Favretti replaced the diseased English boxwood edging around the lawn with germander. As he wrote:

> My revisions were made as a result of a terrible hurricane, or tornado, [that] ripped through Fredericksburg in 1994. It leveled at least two large Pecans across the garden. When they were removed, what had been a shade garden was now in full sun. We had to draw plans for the entire ornamental portion of the garden and replace it. This was an expense that the Restoration Committee did not expect, hence the Germander instead of boxwood. Also the

boxwood that had been there was not doing well, thought to have a nematode problem. Therefore it was felt that using Germander for a period of years might help alleviate the problem.[7]

Since then, new, more hardy box cultivars have been developed, and so, under William D. Rieley's watch, Jensen box has been substituted for the germander and is thriving. Rieley also addressed problems of privacy along the back and designed a new arbor, replacing the gate that led to nowhere with a lattice-framed garden seat.

Of all the Garden Club's restorations, this is perhaps the one that is most evocative of the eighteenth century. Though Fredericksburg's historic downtown, in good weather, is usually full to overflowing with tourists, most of the time Mary Washington's garden is quiet and removed from the hullabaloo of the twenty-first century. If you are lucky, you see the garden by yourself. You come through the house, which is dark in the hall, onto the porch and into the light of the garden, just as she would have done, and you find yourself transported in time in a way that none of the bigger and more heavily visited gardens can match.

Maymont

RICHMOND

A landscape that expresses the splendor
of America's Gilded Age

SITUATED ON A STEEP BLUFF OVERLOOKING THE RAPIDS AT THE FALL LINE of the James River, Maymont is Richmond's prime example of a suburban estate of the Gilded Age, the period from about 1890 to 1910 when great, untaxed fortunes were made and palatial houses were built on grand urban avenues or on large, newly acquired suburban acreages. The Maymont house was built by Major and Mrs. James H. Dooley from 1890 to 1893, during the heyday of this era. From the beginning, Maymont has had an unusual relationship with Richmond because the Dooleys wanted people to enjoy it. They treated Maymont as if it were the park of a great English estate and opened its gates for visitors to stroll the grounds and gardens.

James Henry Dooley (1841–1922) was a first-generation Irish-American native of Richmond.[1] He served in the Confederate Army as a private and was wounded, but after the war his admirers promoted him to "Major" and he was called by this honorific title from then on. Dooley studied law, practiced for a time, and served three terms in the Virginia legislature, from 1871 to 1877. But his real talent was as a financier and industrialist who devoted himself to rebuilding and developing the city of Richmond. His primary interest was in the expansion of railway systems in the South. He became one of Richmond's most successful businessmen, and by 1892 he was one of only four thousand known millionaires in the country, nationally recognized and respected.

In 1869, Dooley married Sallie May, of Lunenburg County. She came from an old Virginia family who traced its lineage to the very early days of the colony; one of her ancestors had served on the governing council at Jamestown. She became the first regent of the first chapter in Virginia of the Daughters of the American Revolution, and a charter member of the Colonial Dames in Virginia. She was proud of her heritage and close to her relatives. Her husband was proud of her, supportive of her many interests, and very generous to her family as well as to his own.

Major and Mrs. Dooley first came across the Maymont site one day in 1886, on

Rose-colored serpentine walk

an afternoon ride in the country just outside the Richmond city limits. She was entranced with its views of the river and could see the potential for a splendid new home with wonderful and extensive gardens. Major Dooley bought a hundred acres of this Henrico County farmland on the dramatic bluff and gave it to his wife. When they were ready to build, a few years later, the Dooleys hired a fashionable young architect, Edgerton Stewart Rogers (1860–1901), son of the neoclassical sculptor Randolph Rogers, whose wife, Rosa Ignatia Gibson, was from Richmond. Born and educated in Rome, the young architect came to Richmond in 1887, where his family connections gave him an entrée, both socially and professionally.

The house Rogers designed combines Romanesque Revival sobriety with Queen Anne decorative flourishes, which pretty well describes Major and Mrs. Dooley. The Dooleys christened their new home May Mont, combining Mrs. Dooley's maiden name with a description of the setting high above the river.

Mrs. Dooley was a passionate and serious horticulturist, as Major Dooley testified:

> Ever since this [his purchase of the site] Mrs. Dooley has been devoting her time and energies and her studies to making this place beautiful. We do not cultivate it for profit; we tried to get it in grass, and make it as beautiful as possible, and to that end she put out six hundred rose bushes and thousands of other flowers, and purchased the most costly evergreens from all parts of the world, and all those beautiful cherry trees they have in Japan, at great cost, and set them out in this place. She has covered it with the work of her own hands and some twenty men we have there, and I have made cement walks to all points of interest and beauty, put up summer houses, four in number, and made various other improvements to beautify the place.[2]

The hearing from which this quote is taken was held as a result of Major Dooley's objections to the city's plan to annex the Maymont acreage. He argued that he had no need of city services: he'd built his own road, he had his own spring, he had installed equipment to manufacture his own gas, and the ravine which separated his property from that of his neighbors made any development out of the question. Major Dooley won the day, and Maymont was not annexed.

In the fashion of the day, the Dooleys incorporated ideas they had gleaned from their own travels, utilizing various architectural styles in the designs of both the gardens and the various outbuildings. Garden historian Denise Otis has written: "American tolerance of variety and lack of interest in theoretical correctness made American landscape design particularly susceptible to the collecting instincts of turn-of-the-

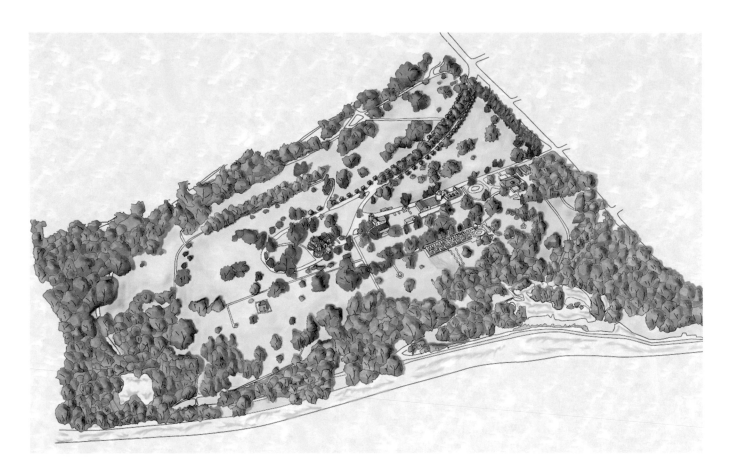

century Americans and to Beaux-Arts eclecticism. The country estate became an anthology of gardens, which might include a French flower parterre, an old-fashioned American garden, an Italianate pergola and terraces, a Japanese tea garden, an arboretum, a rock garden, and a fernery, plus herb, cutting and vegetable gardens, all set into a landscaped park."[3] Such, almost exactly, is Maymont: the larger landscape is a naturalistic English park; the granite barn, water tower, and carriage house show a strong Norman influence; the scalloped stone fountain was inspired by one at the Villa Torlonia outside Rome; and one of the gazebos was bought in Venice and shipped home. There is a terraced Italian garden with parterres and pergola, designed by the Richmond architectural firm of Noland and Baskervil; there is a grotto; and there is a Japanese garden designed and constructed by a master Japanese gardener. According to Dale Wheary, Maymont's curator: "Research suggests that the Japanese garden was the work of Y. Muto, who also developed estate gardens in Philadelphia and at Tuxedo Park during the same period."[4] Mrs. Dooley was well aware of the best designers of the day. She also kept up with the latest horticultural introductions. From the size and age of many of the exotic trees and shrubs on the Maymont grounds, it seems possible that these specimens were among the first of their kind to be introduced into the United States—among them, the false larch, from Japan; the white enkianthus, from China; and the Persian parrotia.

Major Dooley lived out the remainder of his days at Maymont, and when his widow too died, in November 1925, she left their beloved estate to the city of Richmond as a public park and museum, something they had decided together she would do. The house and grounds were closed for six months after Mrs. Dooley's death. On the day the estate reopened as a city park, in 1926, there were five thousand visitors. For several years during the Great Depression, a Saturday column in the *Richmond News Leader* entitled "Maymont Week by Week, by The Stroller" related what was then in bloom at the estate. Maymont remains a place of beauty and escape for all the citizens of Richmond.

IN 1971, MAYMONT WAS LISTED ON THE VIRGINIA LANDMARKS REGISTER and the National Register of Historic Places. As Mrs. Dooley's bequest had not included an endowment, the maintenance of such a sizable estate eventually became too much for the city. In 1975, the nonprofit Maymont Foundation took over the estate's operation and preservation. Building on the Dooley legacy of generosity to Richmond, the foundation has restored the mansion and opened it to visitors, and it has added a Nature and Visitors' Center accessible from Byrd Park. Adjacent to the Visitors' Center is a Children's Farm, which introduces children and adults alike to domestic livestock typical of the farms in the area. Along the ravine walk leading from the Nature Center to the Japanese garden, there is a series of habitats for the many wild animals native to the area along the fall line of the James.

The park around the mansion not only provided space for an arboretum, but it frames and enhances the house. This six-acre expanse of ornamental lawn, with its specimen trees, gazebos, rose bowers, sculpture, and a labyrinth for displaying the most popular shrubs of the time was restored in 1996–98 by the Garden Club of Virginia. The restoration plan was based on old photographic evidence, a series of 1903 watercolors of the grounds, invoices for plants and trees that had been ordered by the Dooleys, and other early maps and blueprints found in the Maymont archives.

The restoration was designed and supervised by Rudy J. Favretti, then landscape architect to the Garden Club. It was done in several phases, the first being the restoration of the lawn area surrounding the mansion. Mrs. Dooley's collection of twenty-eight different species of trees was replanted, the locations determined from observing changes in turf color in the spring as well as depressions or humps in the ground made by rotted or rotting stumps. Contemporary paintings and photographs, both

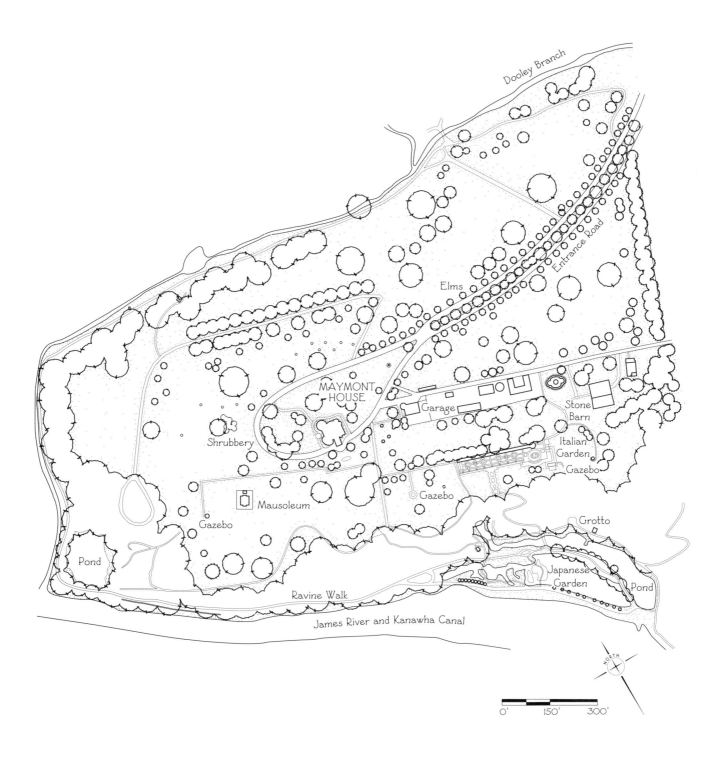

Dooley Branch

Entrance Road

Elms

MAYMONT
HOUSE

Garage

Stone
Barn

Italian
Garden
Gazebo

Shrubbery

Mausoleum

Gazebo

Grotto

Gazebo

Japanese
Garden

Pond

Pond

Ravine Walk

James River and Kanawha Canal

NORTH

0'   150'   300'

Rose arbors with roses in full bloom

aerial and ground, verified the placements. Three rose arbors on the sloping south lawn, shown in a watercolor hanging in the mansion, were re-created from fragments and placed in their original beds, and are now covered with climbing roses of the period.

According to Favretti:

The front walks had been replaced several years ago with another concrete walk in which coal had been used as an aggregate (similar to the one that currently exists under the *porte cochere*). The staff (Wheary, Peggy Single-mann, Director of Horticulture, and Fred Murray, Superintendent) knew that these walks were not correct, based on documentary research. So I drew plans for their authentic replacement using the same textured pattern that appears in other original walks on the property. We even had a jig made up in order to achieve the patterning. When the "wrong walks" were

New elms along drive
from main gate

removed, fragments of the old walk were discovered, and these fragments showed that the original pavement had been tinted a rose color in order to match other masonry that was part of the mansion. We stopped the process, and had the contractor tint the concrete that he planned to install.[5]

Another phase of the restoration was the replanting of the shrubbery that was mentioned in documents and that showed up clearly in an early aerial photograph. Favretti made a special trip to Richmond in the spring of 1997 to see if evidence of the shrubbery would show up in the new grass. "Sure enough," he reported, "the grass was greener where the labyrinth had stood and this gave us the dimensions for it." A contemporary newspaper clipping mentioned that the shrubbery had originally been planted to spirea, but since the later aerial photograph showed a variety of shrubs, some of them evergreen, Favretti decided to vary the planting. "Shrub labyrinths," he wrote, "were popular landscape features in early times: Jefferson had several at Monticello in his grove. They were an effective and entertaining way to display a collection of shrubs."[6]

Along with the rose-colored serpentine walk, all the plants around the house now have been chosen to harmonize with the rosy colors of the exterior marble and trim, and to provide the mansion with a suitable setting. A bed of 'Seven Sisters,' or butterfly roses, blooms just east of the porte cochere, their color ranging from yellow through pink to rose. The house is once again the central hub of the estate, from which

Major Dooley's original walkways lead to the Italian garden and the Japanese garden, the shrubbery, or one of the four summerhouses, each sited to take advantage of a different spectacular view.

In the summer of 2003, Hurricane Isabel roared through Maymont, smashing and uprooting almost everything in its path. It was remarkable that anything survived, but the house and its immediate surroundings came through relatively unscathed. The shrubbery, however, was damaged, and its restoration was the occasion for some rethinking. Going back to the Depression-era *Richmond News Leader* column "Maymont Week by Week," Director of Horticulture Peggy Singlemann requested and the Restoration Committee approved a redesign that replaced most of the shrubs with Japanese white spirea, a very popular cultivar of the period. She removed some other, very overgrown plantings as well, retaining the trees.

The "via flora," the flowering border along the walk from the house to the Italian garden, has also been replanted by the Maymont staff according to the old photographs, and the Japanese garden has been refurbished. In 2006, the Garden Club of Virginia replaced an entire allée of elms that lined the driveway from the main gate. The original trees were long gone, victims of Dutch elm disease; they were replaced with the disease-resistant hybrid, the Princeton elm. The complete restoration of the arboretum is progressing, and the grotto is presently being repaired, thanks to a grant from the 1772 Foundation. Today's blue-jeaned, twenty-first-century visitors to Maymont have an experience of the garden that is nearly comparable to that of the Dooleys' elegant fin de siècle guests.

Flower border on
Monticello West Lawn

Monticello

The restoration of Thomas Jefferson's landscape

LOOKING NORTHEAST FROM THE TOP OF MONTALTO DOWN TOWARD MONticello, imagine that you are seeing Monticello just as Thomas Jefferson did from that same spot. If he could stand there now, he would see that the picture in his mind's eye, so carefully recorded in his sketches, letters, and garden book, has been restored by the Thomas Jefferson Foundation to a perfection he could only dream of. The house, guarded by its great tulip poplars and sugar maples, and the West Lawn, with its oval beds overflowing with flowers three seasons of the year, many of them the same species forms Jefferson knew, fit so naturally into the landscape that they might have grown up of their own accord. The neat rows of the vegetable garden, seen from this angle, make it appear that part of the picture has spilled out into the frame. This optical illusion, a very modern artistic device, jolts the viewer back to the present, to marvel again that the man who could envision the Monticello landscape was also the man who planted many of the seeds and recorded the appearance of each green shoot.[1]

All Virginians think they know Thomas Jefferson. We are teethed on Jefferson. To borrow a phrase from Wendell Garrett, he stands out in our imagination, like "a perfect Doric column."[2] But the Doric is among the simplest and purest of the architectural orders, and Thomas Jefferson was a very complex man.

In 1976 William Howard Adams assembled an exhibition, "The Eye of Thomas Jefferson," at the National Gallery of Art in Washington, D.C. Brilliantly conceived, the exhibition was a catalogue of Jefferson's visual education, from the red clay of Shadwell to the elegant interior detail of Tuckahoe, from the magnificence of the William and Mary Wren Building and the Palladian layout (never completed) of Rosewell, to the classicism of France and the romanticism of the English landscape. It all came together at Monticello.

The extent of Jefferson's political, intellectual, and architectural influence on American history and culture is well known. The difference he made to America's horticultural history is at least as great, although that fact is not widely discussed now in our suburbanized, industrialized society. But for Jefferson, it was paramount. As he wrote from Poplar Forest, in his much quoted letter of August 20, 1811, to Charles Willson Peale:

> I have often thought that if heaven had given me choice of my position and calling, it should have been on a rich spot of earth, well watered, and near a good market for the productions of the garden. No occupation is so delightful to me as the culture of the earth, and no culture comparable to that of the garden. Such a variety of subjects, some one always coming to perfection, the failure of one thing repaired by the success of another, and instead of one harvest a continued one through the year. Under a total want of demand except for our family table, I am still devoted to the garden. But though an old man, I am but a young gardener.[3]

Jefferson began his garden book at Shadwell, his boyhood home, on March 30, 1766, when he was not quite twenty-three. On that day, according to the diary, the purple hyacinth had begun to bloom. A week later, Jefferson would note that the "Narcissus and Puckoon" (bloodroot) had opened; and a week after that (on April 13, his birthday): "Puckoon flowers fallen." On April 16: "a bluish colored, funnel-formed flower [Virginia bluebell] in low-grounds in bloom. April 30: "purple flag blooms. Hyacinth & Narcissus gone." May 4: "Wild honeysuckle in our woods open.—also the Dwarf flag & Violets." May 7: "blue flower in low grounds vanished." And then on May 11, the last entry that year: "the purple flag, Dwarf flag, Violet & wild Honeysuckle still in bloom. went journey to Maryland, Pennsylvᵃ, New York. so observations cease."[4]

Shadwell burned in February 1770. That November, Jefferson moved to Monticello; the top of the mountain had already been leveled—by hand, in 1768—in preparation for a new house. The first mention of Monticello in any of Jefferson's writings is a notation in the garden book for August 3, 1767: "inoculated common cherry buds into stocks of large kind at Monticello."[5] There are numerous lists of flowering plants and native shrubs in the garden book, and various memoranda mention tree planting. Later, letters written both during Jefferson's time in France and during his presidency, contain fulsome descriptions of America's native trees. Jefferson also wrote careful descriptions of his plans for landscaping in his account book of 1771.

The actual building of the house began in 1769; the first structure to be built was the south pavilion. There was frenzied activity on the mountaintop in 1771, though Jefferson spent much of that year in Williamsburg. One of Williamsburg's attractions was its proximity to "The Forest," a plantation in Charles City County which was the

home of the attractive young widow Martha Wayles Skelton. She and Jefferson were married on New Year's Day 1772, and the newlyweds reached Monticello by a leisurely route late on the night of January 25. The last miles of the journey were on horseback, as the weather was so bad the carriage couldn't make it up the hill. Jefferson's garden book entry for January 26 reads: "the deepest snow we have ever seen. in Albemarle it was about 3.f. deep."[6]

Reading the garden book today, one is awed by the energy of the man and the constant attention to, and fascination with, the smallest detail. From 1792 on, and almost every year until the end of his life, Jefferson continued to make notes in the garden book. The gaps occur when he was away from home for extended periods, usually when his professional or political life kept him on the road: the decade of the 1780s, when he was first governor of Virginia and then American minister to Paris; and from 1796 to 1808, the years of his service as vice president and then president. But during all that time, he continued to make entries in his farm book and his account book, some of which concerned his gardening interests. With Jefferson's retirement from the presidency, in March 1809, and his return home to Monticello that April, the entries in the garden book once again become as numerous as the seeds he was planting, and they continue through 1824. The year 1825 was the last year in which he ordered seeds. He died on July 4, 1826.

Even during the years in which he made no entries in the garden book, his letters were full of his interest in gardening, and there were also entries pertaining to gardens and gardening in the farm book. In 1781, for example, a M. de Marbois, of the French legation at Philadelphia, wrote Jefferson with a request for statistical information about the state of Virginia, including a question about the plants that grew there. Jefferson wrote that "a complete catalogue is probably not desired," and he then proceeded to make a comprehensive list of native plants "which would attract notice as being 1. Medicinal, 2. Esculent, 3. Ornamental, or 4. Useful for fabrication..."[7] Indeed, his responses to M. de Marbois were so comprehensive that Jefferson was urged to publish them; they soon appeared as *Notes on the State of Virginia.*

In March 1786 Jefferson traveled to London at the invitation of John Adams. He had been invited to help with negotiating a treaty with Portugal and to attend to other important state affairs, but when the business was done, he and Adams took off on a tour of English gardens. Jefferson noted in a memorandum: "My inquiries were directed chiefly to such practical things as might enable me to estimate the expense of making and maintaining a garden in that style. My journey was in the months of March and April, 1786."[8] His grand tour included the gardens of Chiswick, Hampton Court, Twickenham, Esher Place, Claremont ("nothing remarkable"), Paynshill, Woburn, Caversham, Wotton, Stowe, Leasowes, Hagley, Blenheim, Enfield Chase, Moor Park, and Kew. This trip was Jefferson's first introduction to the English naturalistic style of landscape design, and it had a lasting effect on his own ideas about the landscape at Monticello. Back in Paris, he wrote to John Page: "The gardening in that country [England] is the article in which it surpasses all the earth. I mean their pleasure gardening. This, indeed, went far beyond my ideas."[9]

Late in 1785, Jefferson had been elected an honorary member of the South Carolina Society for Promoting Agriculture, an honor which pleased him greatly and that opened a correspondence with other members of the society about their mutual interests. Now, from Europe, he sent rice seeds and olive trees to South Carolina and Georgia (the rice flourished; the olives failed). He also sent French plants home to John Bartram and Richard Cary. And he wrote to John Banister Jr. with a long list of native American trees and shrubs that Banister should send to Jefferson's great friend, "Madame la Comtesse de Tessé a Paris," along with detailed instructions about when to collect them and how to pack them so that they would survive the transatlantic voyage. He also wrote more generally to friends about the fruit and fruit trees of France, and he described the gardens he had visited. His passion for gardening was never far from his mind.

Jefferson arrived back in America in 1790 to find his mountaintop greatly in need of his attention. But he was soon invited to become President Washington's secretary of state—an invitation that, after much soul-searching, he accepted. In 1791, he and James Madison set out on a month's journey north. From Vermont, Jefferson wrote to Thomas Mann Randolph about his pleasure in "the botanical objects which continually presented themselves," among which was a "vast abundance" of the sugar maple. He then bought over a hundred sugar maples from William Prince, a nurseryman on Long Island, hoping to establish a maple sugar plantation at Monticello, following his own dictum that "the greatest service which can be rendered any country is to add a useful plant." Unfortunately, the experiment failed.

In 1792, the American Philosophical Society honored him by naming a woodland wildflower, the twinleaf (*Jeffersonia diphylla*), for him. At that meeting, Benjamin Smith Barton, professor of botany and natural history at the University of Pennsylvania, said of the wildflower, "I take the liberty of making it known to the botanists by the name of JEFFERSONIA in honour of Thomas Jefferson, Esq. Secretary of State to the United States," adding "My business [is] with his knowledge of natural history. In the various departments of this science, but especially in botany and in zoology, the information of this gentleman is equalled by that of few persons in the United-States."[10]

After Jefferson was elected president, in 1800, he had little time at Monticello, but he found ample ways to apply his horticultural interests. The president traded plants and seeds with Bernard McMahon, the distinguished nurseryman of Philadelphia who became the curator for the plants collected by the Lewis and Clark expedition and who would later author *The American Gardener's Calendar*. But it was Jefferson who imported many of the new plants, from the Jardin des Plantes in Paris, that would later appear in American nursery catalogues. Jefferson also experimented with different varieties of vegetables, carefully recording the results. As Peter Hatch, the current director of gardens and grounds at Monticello, has written, "Monticello was a botanic garden, an experimental station, [and] an Ellis Island of new and unusual introductions from around the world."[11] Jefferson planted at Monticello many of the specimens sent back from the Lewis and Clark expedition, to see how western prairie and mountain plants would survive in Virginia's red clay. Some did (the snow-

berry, or flowering currant), others did not. The president also met with Alexander von Humboldt—on his way home from a year of collecting scientific information about the flora and fauna of New Spain, of which Jefferson's Louisiana Purchase had been part—entertaining him at the White House and at Monticello, "where they had long discussions ranging over meteorology, agriculture, astronomy, and other shared scientific interests."[12]

After his retirement from the presidency, when his alterations and improvements to Monticello were more or less completed, Jefferson's garden again became his passion. He grew 330 varieties of vegetables and 170 varieties of fruit trees, leading Peter Hatch to wonder if any man had ever grown so many different vegetables in one place before. Jefferson was our first and only epicurean president, and though his experiments in winemaking were never as successful as he had hoped, he was nonetheless the father of American viticulture. He introduced many exotic plants into his own garden before they were brought into commercial production: one example, which has had a lasting influence on American street-tree planting, is the goldenraintree. Jefferson's life was not in many ways an easy one, but few men have had both the ability and the opportunity to wield such wide and lasting influence in so many spheres.

THE THOMAS JEFFERSON MEMORIAL FOUNDATION WAS ESTABLISHED ON April 13, 1923—Jefferson's 180th birthday. Its initial purpose was the purchase of Monticello from the estate of its last private owners, the Levy family. By December 1, 1923, Monticello and 600 acres belonged to the foundation, and the process of restoration could begin. The chairman of the Restoration Committee was Sidney Fiske Kimball, professor of architecture at the University of Virginia, and he was assisted by Edwin Morris Betts, professor of biology. One cannot help noting that it took two distinguished professors from entirely separate disciplines to cope with the restoration of one man's creation.

In 1927, the president of the Garden Club of Virginia was Mrs. William R. Massie, one of its founding members. Concerned by the deterioration of Jefferson's trees, she prodded the club to sponsor a three-day fair at Monticello, during which $7,000 was raised, to be used to preserve the few remaining trees on the lawn. In 1938, the Thomas Jefferson Foundation formally asked the Garden Club of Virginia to restore the gardens at Monticello following Jefferson's original design. At its annual meeting that year, the Club voted to devote the proceeds of Garden Week 1939 to the restoration of the West Lawn flower gardens at Monticello.

There were two main problems: in the 115 years since Jefferson's death, his gardens had vanished entirely; and it was not yet established which of his many drawings were experimental sketches and which had actually been executed. By that time, Mrs. Thomas S. Wheelwright was president of the GCV; her committee, which included a knowledgeable authority and Monticello neighbor, Hazelhurst B. Perkins, was determined to proceed with a restoration. Mrs. Perkins kept a record of the discussions leading up to the laying out of the West Lawn and its flower beds. As she wrote, on March 9, 1939, "In reporting on research for the restoration of the planting at Monticello, we had to consider five different schemes, any one of which has the original manuscript to refer to."[13]

The plan she described as number "1" was discovered by Edwin Betts at the Philadelphia Historical Society. It had been drawn by Jefferson in 1807. On it, the third president had written, "planted and sowed flower beds as above April 15, 16, 18 and 20." That must have been a Eureka moment: at last the club had a basis for the restoration of the Monticello garden. Later, a letter from Jefferson to his granddaughter, Anne Cary Randolph, turned up in the collection of the Massachusetts Historical Society. On the back of that letter, in Jefferson's hand, was a sketch depicting some new thoughts he had about the West Lawn.[14]

In the plan Betts found in Philadelphia, Jefferson had drawn the round and oval beds set in the angles made by the intersection of the terraces and the house and the shrub circles at each corner of the house. The later sketch, on the back of the letter to Anne, showed the serpentine walk around the West Lawn and the beds bordering the walk. The beds in the corners of the house were planted in 1807, but the serpentine walk and its accompanying beds were not established until later.

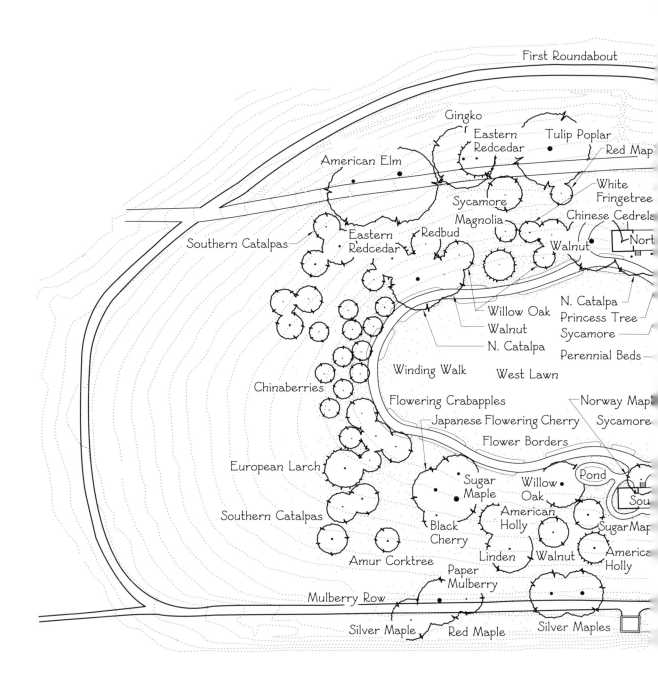

First Roundabout

Gingko

Eastern Redcedar

Tulip Poplar

Red Map

American Elm

White Fringetree

Sycamore

Chinese Cedrela

Magnolia

Southern Catalpas

Eastern Redcedar

Redbud

Walnut

Nort

Willow Oak

N. Catalpa
Princess Tree
Sycamore

Walnut

N. Catalpa

Perennial Beds

Winding Walk

West Lawn

Chinaberries

Flowering Crabapples

Norway Map

Japanese Flowering Cherry

Sycamore

Flower Borders

European Larch

Pond

Sugar Maple

Willow Oak

Sou

Southern Catalpas

Black Cherry

American Holly

SugarMap

Amur Corktree

Linden

Walnut

America Holly

Paper Mulberry

Mulberry Row

Silver Maple

Red Maple

Silver Maples

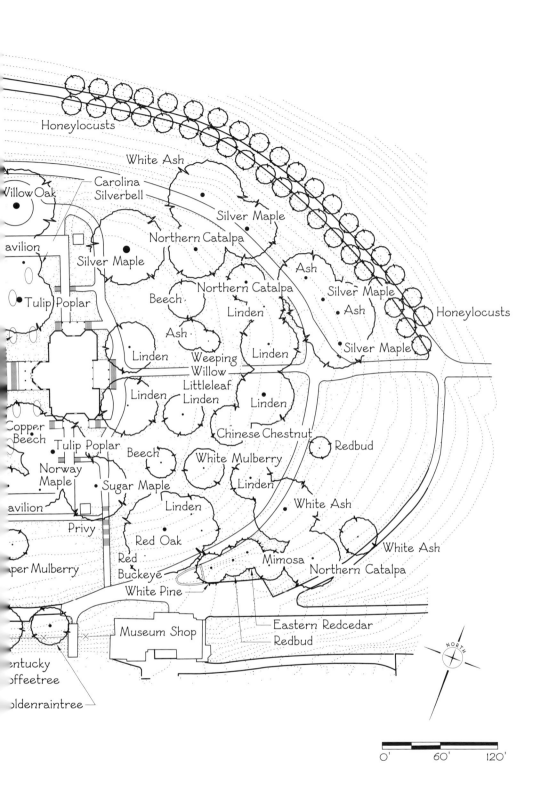

Honeylocusts

White Ash

Carolina
Silverbell

Willow Oak

Silver Maple

Pavilion

Northern Catalpa

Silver Maple

Tulip Poplar

Beech

Northern Catalpa

Ash

Silver Maple

Ash

Honeylocusts

Silver Maple

Ash

Linden

Silver Maple

Linden

Linden

Weeping
Willow

Littleleaf
Linden

Linden

Linden

Chinese Chestnut

Redbud

Copper
Beech

Tulip Poplar

Beech

White Mulberry

Norway
Maple

Linden

Sugar Maple

White Ash

Pavilion

Linden

Privy

White Ash

Red Oak

per Mulberry

Red
Buckeye

Mimosa

Northern Catalpa

White Pine

Museum Shop

Eastern Redcedar

Redbud

NORTH

entucky
offeetree

oldenraintree

0'   60'   120'

MONTICELLO   123

In the 1930s, archaeological techniques of landscape restoration were undeveloped, so it was still not quite clear exactly where everything had been. The plan ultimately chosen, according to Mrs. Perkins, was "approved by Kimball, Grigg and Betts (signatures on it). Shown by me to Restoration committee as tentative plan and casually approved by them in January 1939." Mrs. Perkins added, "On this photostatic copy I note in Mr. Kimball's handwriting that 'there is no evidence that this plan was ever carried out by Mr. Jefferson.'"[15]

Ignoring Mr. Kimball's opinion, and with Morley Williams to guide them, the resourceful ladies of the committee drove up to Monticello one night to shine their headlights across the West Lawn. They were able to see the ghosts of a path and beds visible in the moonlit grass, and Mr. Williams's survey duly reported these "depressions." The documentation for the garden having been verified by these ad hoc methods, the planting plan for the restoration was then drawn up by Garland A. Wood Jr., of T. W. Wood & Sons, a garden supply company in Richmond. "Very intelligent

MONTICELLO

young man," Mrs. Perkins commented. "Studied at Harvard and V.P.I. [sic] worked in landscaping firm in New York also employed by Morley Williams at Mt. Vernon."[16]

The Garden Club of Virginia only planted the first seeds. During the next fifty-odd years, the whole of Jefferson's landscape was re-created on top of his little mountain; but this was the work of the Thomas Jefferson Foundation and its directors. The current board of the Foundation, led by the management team of Director Daniel P. Jordan, Director of Gardens and Grounds Peter Hatch, and William L. Beiswanger, the Robert H. Smith Director of Restoration, has made possible the unobstructed view of Monticello from Montalto. According to the *Bulletin of the Virginia Outdoors Foundation*: "In 2004, Monticello placed 214 acres under easement with the [Virginia] Department of Historic Resources and 1,060 acres with the Virginia Outdoors Foundation."[17] Currently, a team of archaeologists, led in the beginning by Dr. William M. Kelso and more recently by Dr. Frasier D. Neiman, continues to uncover new facts about the landscape of Monticello. The discoveries are as never ending as were Mr. Jefferson's alterations and improvements to Monticello.

The Garden Club of Virginia, while keeping an eye on the flower gardens of the West Lawn, had no further involvement in the ongoing restoration until 1991, when the Thomas Jefferson Foundation applied for a grant to map the trees in the first roundabout, the topmost of a series of four roads laid out by Jefferson that ring the mountain at different levels.[18] The Restoration Committee approved the grant, and the Foundation hired the Charlottesville firm of Rieley and Associates to map and undertake a reverse-perspective analysis of the trees using old photographs. In 1998, the principal of that firm, William D. Rieley, succeeded Rudy J. Favretti as landscape architect to the Garden Club of Virginia.

The Garden Club of Virginia takes pride in having played a formative part in this miracle play in which the Thomas Jefferson Foundation is the star.

Restored gateway entrance
to Montpelier's garden

Montpelier

*Restoration of the duPont-era garden on the site of
James Madison's original terraced garden*

SIGNS DIRECTING THE TOURIST TO "JAMES MADISON'S MONTPELIER" TELL the approaching visitor that change is afoot. Until recently, the signs said simply "Montpelier." The house, built by President Madison's father, was sold by Dolley Madison in 1844, and it subsequently had a succession of owners, until 1901, when William duPont transformed it into a Gilded Age country estate. When duPont died in 1928, his daughter, Marion duPont Scott, established her famous horse farm and racetrack there, familiar to all Virginia steeplechase fans. After her death, in 1983, Montpelier was transferred to the National Trust, which for nearly twenty years interpreted both its Madison and duPont histories.

Montpelier's history arguably begins with a 1716 expedition of Virginia's then lieutenant governor Alexander Spotswood and his Knights of the Golden Horseshoe.[1] That year, Spotswood led a band of pioneering intimates on an exploratory trek from the settlement of Germanna westward to the Blue Ridge, which resulted in the discovery of both iron deposits that could be mined and a wide belt of deep, fertile soil that could be planted.[2] One of Spotswood's band was James Taylor II of Caroline. Taken by what he had seen, in 1722 Taylor registered the first of several patents and began amassing a large acreage in what is now Orange County. He then presented parcels of that land to his two sons-in-law, Ambrose Madison and Thomas Chew. An Act of Assembly of 1720 required new patent holders to submit accounts and appraisals of improvements made to their tracts within three years. In 1726, Ambrose Madison reported a valuation of £340 on "Mount Pleasant," a domestic complex which he had built somewhere near the present Madison family cemetery.

In the early 1760s, Ambrose Madison's son James, named for his grandfather Taylor, built a new, Georgian-style brick house at the top of the hill; this was Montpelier. James Madison and Nelly Conway, whom he married in 1749, ultimately had twelve children. The oldest, James Madison Jr., who would become the fourth president of

the United States, was born in 1751. Among his early memories were the building of the new house, which would take several years, and his carrying of light furniture at moving time. From beginning to end, Madison's life would be bound up with Montpelier.

James Madison Jr. and Dolley Payne Todd were married in Philadelphia in 1794. Forty-three years old, he was a Virginia representative in the U.S. Congress; she was a fetching young widow of twenty-six. In 1797 they returned to Montpelier, and they lived there for the next four years. It was to meet their needs that Montpelier underwent its first expansion, consisting of a thirty-foot addition to the north side of the house and a portico to tie the new and old sections together. Each section had it's own entrance; with no interior door to connect them, essentially, the bride and groom had their own separate house.

But the couple's full-time residence at Montpelier was to be short-lived. In 1801, Thomas Jefferson appointed James Madison secretary of state and the Madisons moved to Washington. Dolley—pretty, gregarious, and full of charm—was soon the center of the social life of the capital. In 1809, Madison succeeded Jefferson as president, which meant eight more years in Washington. For sixteen years, the arduous trip to the Montpelier estate in Orange became a regular part of their annual schedule. For James Madison, Montpelier was home, a lodestar, just as Monticello was for Jefferson, or Mount Vernon for Washington—and Madison's improvements to his property were almost as extensive as theirs, too.

To escape the pressures of the presidency and the heat of Washington summers, modern presidents have retreated to Camp David or to a summer White House air-conditioned by electricity or sea breezes. Shielded by advance men, Secret Service agents, and aides, cocooned in presidential helicopters and Air Force One, they are transported in comfortable certainty, well insulated from the vicissitudes of ordinary travel. Compare that mode of travel to Dolley Madison's description of a trip from the White House to Montpelier in May 1808:

> You ware very kind to me my dear friend to write the acceptable letter which I recc^d. this day—& for which I shall repay you but very sadly—In truth my limbs yet tremble with the terrow's & fatigue of our journey—from the little falls to this place replete with difficulties & danger. At the end of one week we had the Carriage taken to peices & in order to get us over the last river, the little boat sail'd six times across—our Horses had no chance but

to swim & then the Roads that to the Great Falls is beautiful in comparison to ours.

we passed 3 rainy days with my Aunt & Unkle, they enquired after you with affection & interest . . .

—We found all our fruit & good things retarded by the cold rains but now the Cheries are blushing & the peas ripening, around us.[3]

Mrs. Madison's spelling was questionable, but her spunk was not, nor was her pleasure in the garden. The trips to Orange were long and difficult, but there was no question but that the Madisons would go—for a few weeks in the spring, anywhere from two to four months in the summer, and sometimes again for a short stay in the fall.

Nor were these home visits quiet vacations or pastoral retreats, as is evidenced in this 1809 missive, written to Dolley in the first summer of Madison's presidency:

My dear M[rs] Madison,

As I understand that you are overwhelmed with Company, I fear my letter may be an intrusion. . . . I fear I cannot even afford you any information that you have not had already, for all the little news of our place I suppose you receive regularly, and you are at the fountainhead of great & public news, so I fear I can have no chance of entertaining you for a moment, and write only to remind you of one who wou'd be much hurt at a discontinuance of your remembrance & good will . . .[4]

Two years later, in August 1811, in a letter to her sister, Anna Cutts, Dolley would describe yet another exhausting hot journey from Washington to Orange, and end by saying, "I am busy fixing for 2 months housekeeping."[5] First Lady or no, she had work to do.

The summer of 1809 must have been a particularly busy one, since it was during this time that James Madison began the extensive changes to the house and landscape that would occupy him—along with his hired workmen and slaves—for the next several years. One-story wings were added to each end of the house, as was a rear colonnade with triple-hung windows that provided access from a remodeled drawing room. With Jefferson's blessing, Madison employed for the job three Monticello builders: the carpenters James Dinsmore and John Neilson and the brick mason Hugh Chisholm. John Neilson was also a gifted gardener. When the three men came to Montpelier in April 1809, Neilson carried a note from Jefferson to Madison: "If mrs. Madison has anything there which interests her in the gardening way, she cannot confide it better than to Neilson. He is a gardener by nature & extremely attached to it."[6]

Archaeology has shown that the present flat lawn on the east, or garden, side of Montpelier was originally hilly and uneven, and that Madison had it leveled, by hand, during this period. Sometime around 1817, a semicircular terraced garden and an orchard were laid out on the steep hill to the south of the newly leveled lawn. The fence separating the lawn from the garden originally repeated the semicircle of the terraces but was later straightened by the Madisons. There are no letters from James Madison himself describing any of this, but by piecing together the garden references in Dolley Madison's letters and in one letter to Madison from the Liverpool forwarding agent William Maury, it is clear that the garden was very important to both of them. Sprinkled among the political correspondence of Madison's retirement papers there are also references to ornamental plants and trees, as well as to agricultural crops. According to one of Dolley's nieces (Mary Cutts?), "Every rare plant and fruit was sent to him by his admiring friends, who knew his taste."[7]

A picture emerges of a combination orchard and garden with vegetables, small fruits, and flowers fenced from marauding animals within this large, terraced enclosure. Figs and cherries seem to have been the favorite fruit trees. Maury advises at length on the best way to plant the two kinds of strawberries he is sending from Liverpool "in a hamper": "I will send to Mrs. M. some flower seeds this autumn, & if I can [ ] it [ ] of the *Lupinus mutabilis,* the most beautiful of that tribe of plants which has ever been seen & possessing a perfume as strong and fragrant as the Orange Flower; it also continues in Flower from June until the Frost."[8]

Although documentation about the Madisons' garden before the 1817 renovation is scarce, there is a weather journal that James Madison began in 1784 and kept into the mid-1790s, and in which his father and brothers also made entries. In addition to the records of wind, temperature, and general weather conditions, there are notes on garden vegetables, flowering plants, the blossom times of fruit trees, and other observations. The journal also documents the following plants in the garden: blue and white hyacinths, March pinks, jonquils, daffodils and narcissus, "pionys," sweet William, primroses (probably *Primula veris*), bells (*Campanula persifolia,* or would it have been the Virginia bluebell, *Mertensia virginicus*?), tulips, monthly honeysuckle, snowdrops, woodbine, damask rose, red-and-white double pink, "Lilly," and hollyhock. The journal also mentions asparagus, cimblings, cucumbers, "Windsor beans," garden peas, strawberries, gooseberry, mulberry, plum tree, Duke cherries, peach trees, cherry trees, wheat, tobacco, and locust and poplar trees, and it notes the first budding of hickories on the tops of the Southwest Mountains.[9]

In terms of the location of the earlier garden, it is known that Dolley Madison's mother-in-law, whom the former first lady referred to as "the old lady," lived in the

south end of the house and that she continued to keep her garden as it always had been.[10] It is logical to assume that the elder Mrs. Madison would have been able to easily get from her living quarters to her garden. It is also known that her husband's first cousin, Colonel Francis Taylor, lived about five miles away; Taylor recorded in his own diary the vegetables and fruits that were grown in his garden, which was laid out in squares. So it is not too much of a stretch logically to infer that James Madison Sr. would have laid out the first Montpelier garden similarly, according to local and family custom.

The question then arises: Where did the design for James Madison Jr.'s terraced garden, so different from the ones he had grown up with, come from? There have been, and are, various theories, one of which—that the garden was "located by Mr. Madison, and was designed to represent the plan of the hall in Philadelphia where the Continental Congress met"—was published in the *Orange Observer* sometime in the 1880s. According to the newspaper, "The upper end, which was formerly circular, has been squared, and the boundaries of the garden are now straight lines. Within the enclosure are the fig trees which are always mentioned in connection with Montpe-

A formal request to the Garden Club of Virginia for help with the restoration of the walled duPont garden was made on February 20, 1989, and on January 4, 1990, the Restoration Committee authorized Favretti to prepare a conceptual master plan. At that time, the committee also sent a written request to the National Trust in which it asked for a letter to confirm "that no archaeological work involving disturbance of the ground will take place in the walled garden in the foreseeable future." The Trust assured the Restoration Committee that the restored garden would not be disturbed by future excavation.[16]

Favretti got to work, and he presented his plan for the garden in March 1990. In an earlier letter to Mrs. Robert Hopkins, dated October 24, 1989, he had described his approach to the project:

> It is clear that we cannot put back every detail of the garden. There are three parts of the garden that are critical and without them, it looks "bare." They are the gardens on the curved terraces (that have lately been planted with wildflowers); the lower most parterre gardens; and the upper most parterre gardens (now herbs).
>
> The curved terrace gardens are important because of their drama and the rhythmic effect they create in the garden. The lower parterre gardens are critical because with terraces such as those and steps such as the ones that exist—built to act as a belvedere—the garden cries for them.
>
> The topmost gardens, specifically created by Mr. Gillette, should be put back because they are the first "welcome" to the garden. The other gardens can be brought back through key shrubs, a few topiary, to suggest the garden without putting back every detail.[17]

Thus, it was the well-documented duPont garden that the Garden Club restored in 1992. The perennial beds inside the main entrance gate and Gillette's designs for the upper level were brought back to look as they did when Mrs. duPont enjoyed them. The platform at the top of the first set of steps was made bigger than it had been originally, to make a viewing platform for handicapped or less energetic visitors. The crescent perennial beds on the second level were also brought back to their former glory; the original plants had been moved to a nursery bed, where they had been well tended, and with the aid of contemporary photographs it was possible to replant the beds just as they had been in Mrs. duPont's day. Difficulty of maintenance, however, prevented the restoration of the original parterres on that level.

Restoration of the steps was a complicated process. The side flanks had fallen away from the steps, although the bricks and concrete work were sound. It was necessary to dig down around the flanks, jack them up, install a stainless-steel footing, push the flanks back into place, and anchor them. Also restored were Adirondack fences that had been installed along the edge of the terrace.[18]

The restored garden was presented to the National Trust in the fall of 1992. Only eight years later, however, the new century brought a call to look again at the interpretation of Montpelier. In 2001, a Mellon Foundation grant made possible a feasibility study for the restoration of the house. Upon the study's completion, in 2003, a monumental project to restore the house and surrounding grounds as nearly as possible to their early nineteenth-century appearance was undertaken, funded in large part by a bequest from Paul Mellon's estate.

The restoration process was continuing in 2005 when the Garden Club was asked to restore the garden's front gate. This included repointing the brick arch, sandblasting the wrought iron gate for repainting, and applying gold leaf. The Restoration Committee also hired a conservator to clean the lion sculptures situated at the top of the garden steps. At the conservator's recommendation the lions were conserved, but they retain some of the patina that reflects their long and loyal service.

Working with Montpelier horticulturist Sandy Mudrinich and the Garden Club's Restoration Committee, landscape architect William D. Rieley has recently developed plans to add summer color to the garden. Documentation for a 1791 seed order, placed with George Morris of Philadelphia, mentions Spanish thistle, sensitive plant, "Miginette," prince's feather, tricolor, ten-week stock, China pink, love-lies-bleeding, and Brunton stock. Though these plants hearken back to "the old lady's garden," the seed order is proof that summer annuals were commonly part of a Virginia garden early on, and it can be assumed that the custom carried over into the duPont garden as well.

As Rudy J. Favretti has pointed out, "Landscapes change rapidly [and] it is better to show a span of years rather than a frozen period."[19] The new restoration of James Madison's house to the period of his ownership and occupancy, of course, does tend to "freeze" the details of the house in place and time. But because no letters from either James or Dolley Madison have been discovered so far which describe the laying out of their garden or all the changes they made to the landscape, the Garden Club of Virginia has been assured that the restoration of the duPont garden will not be disturbed.

*East façade of Moses
Myers House, facing
Bank Street*

Moses Myers House

*The garden setting for the fine Federal-period
house of a prominent early-Norfolk family*

THE REVOLUTIONARY WAR PLAYED HAVOC WITH THE TOWN OF NORFOLK;
it was seriously hurt by Britain's naval blockade and almost leveled by bombardment
and the resulting fires. With the signing of the Treaty of Paris in 1783, foreign mer-
chantmen began to enter the Capes again, and it was not long before Norfolk resumed
its place as the chief port of entry and export for Virginia. In this period, the British
Navigation Acts forbade the importation of commodities into British dependencies
in "other than British bottoms," but after the French Revolution (1789–99) the British
navy was largely preoccupied by events in Europe. The British islands of the West In-
dies, therefore, in desperate straits, sensibly disregarded the Navigation Acts and welcomed the ships of the Norfolk merchants.

In 1787, a young Moses Myers, on his honeymoon, chartered a vessel to move
him and his new wife from New York to Norfolk to seek their fortune.[1] Within five
years, Myers owned a fleet of five ships and had a successful shipping business. In 1792,
his business flourishing, he set about building a new house—some say with bricks
made from English ballast—on the then outskirts of town, at the corner of East Freemason and Bank Streets. In 1796, three rooms were added, this time with American
bricks (the difference between the two forms of bricks is clearly visible today). Fire
insurance records show that the house was completed by 1797. Moses Myers was one
of Norfolk's first Jewish residents, and it is thought that one of the new rooms (the
one with an outside entrance) was used as Norfolk's first synagogue. The house was
home to five successive generations of the Myers family. In 1931, it was sold along with
many of its furnishings to a private foundation; it is now owned by the city of Norfolk
and the Chrysler Museum of Art.

Myers, highly respected in the community, became president of the city council. He also served as the local consul for Denmark and the Netherlands, and as mer-
cantile agent to the French Republic. According to the Norfolk-born historian Hugh

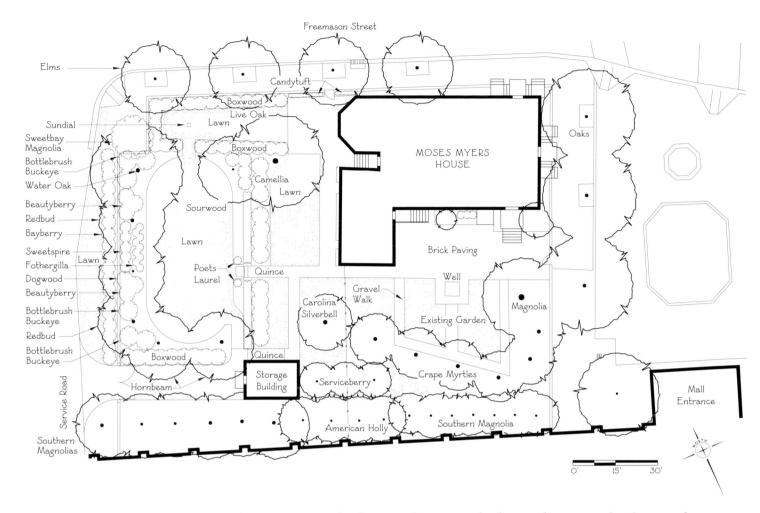

Freemason Street

Elms

Candytuft

Boxwood

Live Oak

Sundial

Lawn

Oaks

Sweetbay
Magnolia

Boxwood

Bottlebrush
Buckeye

Camellia
Lawn

MOSES MYERS
HOUSE

Water Oak

Beautyberry

Sourwood

Redbud

Lawn

Bayberry

Brick Paving

Sweetspire
Fothergilla

Lawn

Well

Dogwood

Poets
Laurel

Beautyberry

Quince

Gravel
Walk

Bottlebrush
Buckeye

Carolina
Silverbell

Magnolia

Existing Garden

Redbud

Bottlebrush
Buckeye

Quince

Boxwood

Storage
Building

Serviceberry

Crape Myrtles

Service Road

Hornbeam

Mall
Entrance

Southern
Magnolias

American Holly

Southern Magnolia

NORTH

0'   15'   30'

Blair Grigsby, Myers was the last gentleman in the borough to wear his hair in the eighteenth-century fashion, with a ribbon-tied queue at the nape of his neck.

The Moses Myers House was one of the first brick houses built in Norfolk after the Revolutionary War. It was first situated facing one street, but the front door was later moved to another side, supposedly to give it a more prestigious address. An elegant example of Federal architecture, its plasterwork is unusually ornate. This was the home of a man of consequence.

Today, nearly 70 percent of the furnishings are original to the house. The paintings include Gilbert Stuart's companion portraits of Moses Myers and his wife Eliza, as well as works by Thomas Sully and John Wesley Jarvis. The furniture is American, English, and French, as is an impressive array of glass, silver, and ceramics. Thanks to an extensive and recently completed renovation, dark and inauthentic colors have been replaced with historically accurate lighter ones. The elaborate and fanciful ceiling details in the downstairs front hall—plaster ribbons, tassels, individually set pearls and feather fans—which had been obscured by decades of whitewash and dark green paint, are now illuminated by white walls and light blue-green woodwork.

The Garden Club of Virginia, at the invitation of the Garden Club of Norfolk, undertook the restoration of the Moses Myers House garden in 2003. In a plat from the period when Moses Myers occupied the house, the land to the east of the house is annotated as the "Garden" and a small stable is shown on the southwest corner of the property. This may have doubled as a carriage house, as it is known that Myers was the owner of a fine carriage. There are also some late nineteenth-century photographs showing possible remnants from the earlier landscape. These were the only scraps of information about the location and configuration of the original garden.

In designing the new garden, landscape architect William D. Rieley worked with those scraps, also taking into account the desire of the property's owners to have a grassy area large enough to be tented for events. Rieley used landscape devices and plants typical of the Federal period and era. The lawn area was created within a hemicycle, or rectangle with semi-circular ends. A slight angular difference between the street and the house was utilized to create a forced perspective on the center line of

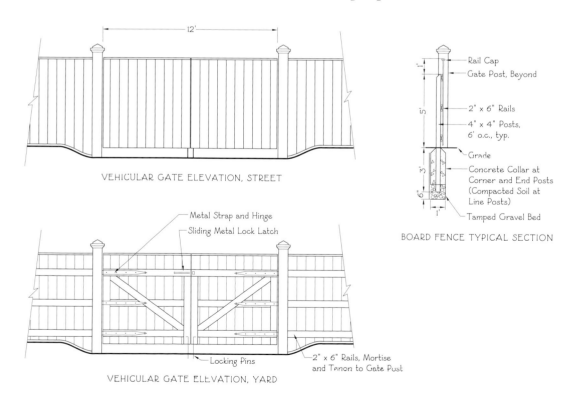

VEHICULAR GATE ELEVATION, STREET

VEHICULAR GATE ELEVATION, YARD

Metal Strap and Hinge
Sliding Metal Lock Latch
Locking Pins
2" x 6" Rails, Mortise and Tenon to Gate Post

Rail Cap
Gate Post, Beyond
2" x 6" Rails
4" x 4" Posts, 6' o.c., typ.
Grade
Concrete Collar at Corner and End Posts (Compacted Soil at Line Posts)
Tamped Gravel Bed

BOARD FENCE TYPICAL SECTION

Gate detail

Detail of restored fence

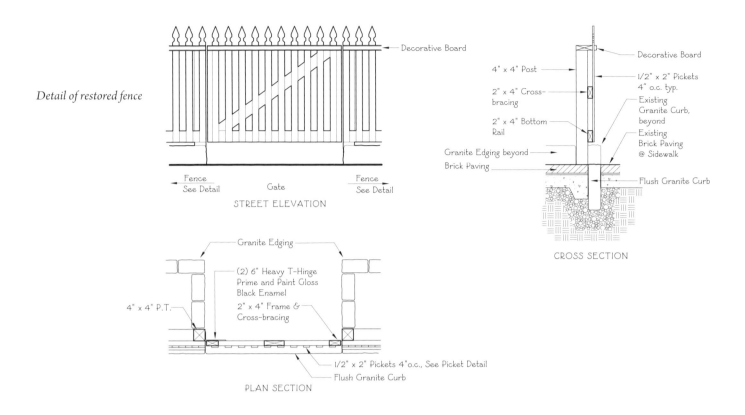

Decorative Board

Fence
See Detail

Gate

Fence
See Detail

STREET ELEVATION

4" x 4" Post

2" x 4" Cross-bracing

2" x 4" Bottom Rail

Granite Edging beyond

Brick Paving

Decorative Board

1/2" x 2" Pickets
4" o.c. typ.

Existing
Granite Curb,
beyond

Existing
Brick Paving
@ Sidewalk

Flush Granite Curb

CROSS SECTION

Granite Edging

(2) 6" Heavy T-Hinge
Prime and Paint Gloss
Black Enamel

2" x 4" Frame &
Cross-bracing

4" x 4" P.T.

1/2" x 2" Pickets 4"o.c., See Picket Detail
Flush Granite Curb

PLAN SECTION

Restored fence and crape myrtles

MOSES MYERS HOUSE

the dining room, punctuated by a sundial that had been donated to the Myers House as part of an earlier renovation. The fences were reproduced through the use of computer-enhanced photographs from the nineteenth century.

A possible future phase of the restoration will install a small, formal, four-square vegetable and herb garden off the kitchen, to the left of the walk as visitors enter the property. The garden will be bordered by an unusual lattice fence carefully replicated from old photographs. Though there was no contemporary documentation on which to base a plan for this garden, the suitability of Rieley's design has been verified by a recent, unrelated discovery: the plat of a very similar four-square vegetable garden at another early nineteenth-century house just up the street. Scientific study is the first choice, but on occasion serendipity comes in very handy. The Myers House garden forms a useful, beautiful, and appropriate setting for this remarkable remnant of Norfolk's rich design history.

Mount Vernon from across
the Bowling Green

Mount Vernon

ON THE POTOMAC RIVER, SOUTH OF ALEXANDRIA

Restoration of George Washington's Bowling Green
and the planting along the serpentine road

GEORGE WASHINGTON'S IMAGE IS A FAMILIAR ONE, BUT THE MAN BEHIND the image is not so well known. To find him, you have to go to Mount Vernon, where he worked for forty-five years, off and on, to perfect his world along the Potomac. It is in Washington's gardens and in the story of his involvement in everything from seed-gathering to transplanting, grafting, pruning, designing, and propagating that he comes alive. Here, he is not the enigmatic, regal statesman of portrait and statue, but the energetic, down-to-earth landowner managing his property, the gardener embellishing his grounds, the paterfamilias at home. It was Washington who drew the plans and specifications for the house, the design for the grounds, and who did the survey of the roads and gardens. His early surveyor's training stood him in good stead, and his sense of scale and proportion is everywhere evident in the Mount Vernon landscape.

Scholars have interpreted the Mount Vernon landscape differently. According to garden historian Mac Griswold, for example, Mount Vernon "wordlessly portrays Washington's hopes for his new nation. . . . Washington's carefully laid-out 'visto' [looks] westward to America's future. It is all as idyllic and prosperous as Washington so ardently wanted his new country to be."[1] But landscape architect Rudy J. Favretti does not agree with Griswold's metaphorical view. Favretti has argued that Mount Vernon is "an example of one of the earliest late-eighteenth-century English landscapes to be established on American soil . . . an incredibly well-planned site." He notes that Washington owned "two important books . . . Batty Langley's *New Principles of Gardening* [London, 1728] and Philip Miller's *Abridgement of the Gardener's Dictionary* [London, 1763], both of which were essential to every gentleman's library." According to Favretti: "Langley, in particular, urged the use of the informal serpentine walk or drive, and both authors suggested planting these walks with trees in order to provide shade for the user," although "there is no evidence that Washington copied plans for his landscape from these books. Instead, he used the ideas that he liked and adapted them to his own situation."[2] Like Griswold, Favretti believes that Washington was his own designer, but he insists that it was Washington's study of his English garden books rather than his celebration of his own young country's hard-won and incomplete conquest of the frontier that was the basis for the remarkable Mount Vernon complex.[3] He does not allow for the possibility that it could have been both.

In a 1997 paper written for the 11th Conference on Restoring Southern Gardens and Landscapes, Favretti said: "The first significant restoration and preservation effort involving national support was at Mount Vernon. . . . Prior to that time, there had been several individual efforts, but none of them had the planned national support of the project begun at Mount Vernon."[4] The organization responsible for that effort was the Mount Vernon Ladies' Association of the Union, founded by Ann Pamela Cunningham of South Carolina in 1853. Chartered by the Virginia legislature in 1858, the association purchased Mount Vernon from John Augustine Washington Jr. in 1858, paying the final installment for the purchase in December 1859 and taking possession of the buildings and grounds on February 22, 1860. The entire place had fallen into disrepair, so the task of restoration was monumental, as Favretti noted in his presentation to the conferees: "Over the years since the nineteenth century, the gardens have gone through several transformations as new knowledge and resources have been acquired. For example, the Orangery was reconstructed according to old images in 1951, 116 years after it was destroyed by fire."[5]

As his last commission for the Garden Club of Virginia before his retirement in 1998, Favretti designed and implemented the restoration of Mount Vernon's Bowling Green and its fringe of trees and shrubs that shade both sides of the "serpentine road," as Washington called it. Scheduled for completion in the fall of 1998, it was not formally presented until 2001. As part of his extensive research, Favretti found an earlier study, executed by Charles Sprague Sargent, of the trees and planting around the Bowling Green.[6] That study was done in 1914, 115 years after Washington's death, at which time several of the original trees and shrubs still remained. It became the "baseline" for Favretti's restoration. Nearly every tree or shrub in the restoration is a species that Washington cultivated at Mount Vernon, and most of them are native plants that he might have transplanted from his own woods and fields. The year-round display in the garden is spectacular. The redbud and mountain laurel that Washington loved are in full bloom every spring, and sweetshrub and sweetbay magnolia perfume the air. In the fall, sourwood and black gum blaze alongside the dogwood in the evening light. In the winter, there is color from the holly berries and beautyberries, and in February the yellow witchhazel begins a new cycle.

WHICHEVER THEORY ONE PREFERS, THE MORE SCHOLARLY OR THE MORE intuitive, it is clear George Washington brought more than a surveyor's experience or a soldier's sense of order to the realization of his vision at Mount Vernon. He also brought a sense of taste and elegance (one result of his introduction into the Fairfax household, with all its appurtenances of wealth and high social position, after the marriage of his brother Lawrence to Anne Fairfax); the country man's understanding of the way things grew; the general's grasp of the importance of planning and detail; and the gentleman's pride of place.

By the time George Washington brought his bride to Mount Vernon, he undoubtedly had begun to know exactly how he wanted his beloved place to be. He certainly knew what he wanted the visitor to see on the mile-long approach to the house: tantalizing glimpses through the woods as the long driveway wound toward the house, the underbrush cleared on either side—and then the house itself, almost obscured by the trees lining the Bowling Green as the road veered around it. He envisioned how the house was to be set off by its frame of greenery; how the repetitive curves of the Bowling Green, the carriage roundabout, and the semicircular arcades would emphasize the rectangular solidity of the building. It took some trial and error before he got it right. As he enlarged and reconfigured his dwelling, he moved service buildings to their own quarter and changed the shape of the walled gardens, making space for the expansive entrance courtyard and open lawn of the bell-shaped Bowling Green framed by the shady undulations of the driveway.

MOUNT VERNON

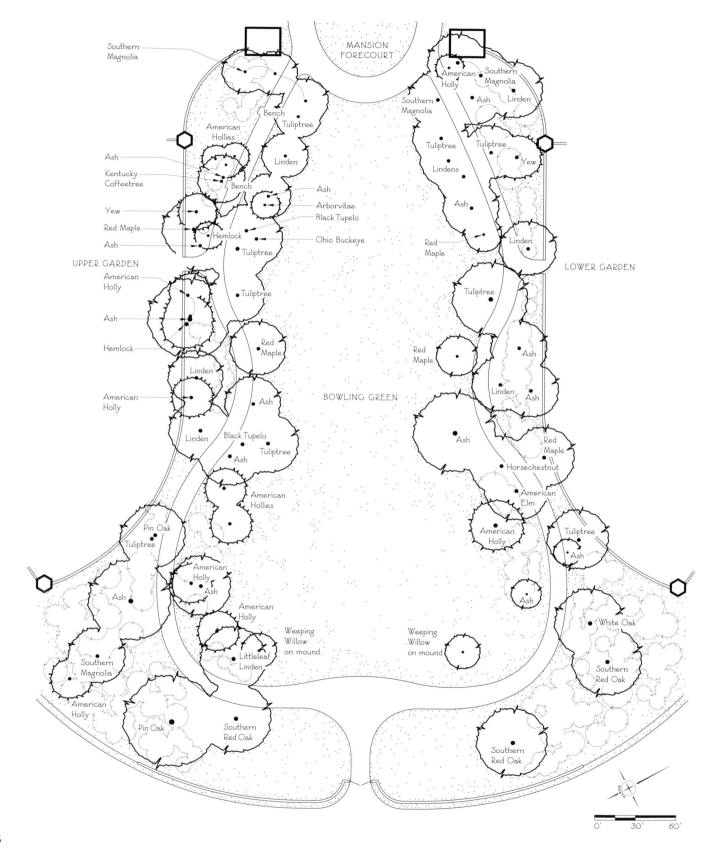

Southern
Magnolia

MANSION
FORECOURT

American
Holly

Southern
Magnolia

Ash   Linden

Bench

American
Hollies

Tuliptree

Southern
Magnolia

Tuliptree

Tuliptree

Ash   Linden

Tuliptree

Lindens

Yew

Ash   Bench

Kentucky
Coffeetree

Ash

Ash

Arborvitae

Yew   Black Tupelo

Red Maple

Hemlock

Ash   Ohio Buckeye

Red
Maple

Linden

UPPER GARDEN

Tuliptree

LOWER GARDEN

American
Holly

Tuliptree

Ash

Tuliptree

Hemlock

Red
Maple

Red
Maple

Ash

Linden

Linden

Ash

Red
Maple

American
Holly

Ash   BOWLING GREEN

Ash

Horsechestnut

Linden

Black Tupelo

Ash

Tuliptree

American
Elm

American
Hollies

American
Holly

Tuliptree

Pin Oak

Ash

Tuliptree

Ash

American
Holly   Ash

American
Holly

Southern
Magnolia

Littleleaf
Linden

Weeping
Willow
on mound

Weeping
Willow
on mound

White Oak

American
Holly

Pin Oak

Southern
Red Oak

Southern
Red Oak

Southern
Red Oak

146

George Washington was born in 1732 at Pope's Creek Plantation, in Westmoreland County, on the Potomac River.[7] His great-grandfather, John Washington, had emigrated from Sulgrave, England, in 1657. His father, Augustine, a slave-owning planter who also tried his luck at iron-mining ventures, died when young George was only eleven. George was the oldest child of his father's second marriage; there were three older and four younger siblings. It is said that his relationship with his mother was strained at times, although his love of gardening must have come from her. He was probably a lot like her: strong and capable, with an iron determination. It is easy to see how she would have frustrated him in her old age.

Bowling Green from upstairs window

The property that is Mount Vernon was originally known as Hunting Creek and was part of a 1674 grant from Lord Culpeper to Nicholas Spencer and John Washington. In 1743, it descended to John Washington's oldest great-grandson, Lawrence, George's half-brother, to whom he was very attached. Lawrence called the house he built there "Mount Vernon," in honor of Admiral Edward Vernon, on whose flagship he had served during the 1741 British expedition against Cartagena (in present-day Colombia). Lawrence married Anne Fairfax, whose father, William Fairfax, was cousin and land agent to Lord Culpeper's grandson and heir, Sir Thomas Fairfax. The propitious match also brought Lawrence's younger brother, George, into this privileged orbit.

In 1752, just nine years after inheriting the property, Lawrence Washington died without issue, and with the death of Lawrence's wife, Anne, in 1761, the 2,500-acre Mount Vernon estate passed into the hands of Lawrence's twenty-year-old half-brother. Seven years earlier, in 1754, young George had arranged to lease the farm lands on the estate from his widowed sister-in-law. In 1759, he had married Martha Dandridge Custis, a wealthy young widow with two small children, and when Anne Washington died, two years later, George moved his new family to Mount Vernon. His marriage had greatly increased his landholdings and his social status—he had acquired one-third of the Custis family holdings of 18,000 acres upon his marriage, and he managed the remainder on behalf of his wife's children. By 1775, he had increased his holdings in Mount Vernon to nearly 6,500 acres, which made him one of the wealthiest planters and landowners in Virginia. Washington spent years trying to reassemble the acreage in the original patent awarded to John Washington and Nicholas Spencer, and in 1786 he finally managed to acquire the last piece.

George Washington is portrayed in the history books as an unsmiling statesman, with silver-buckled shoes and black silk stockings, white hair pulled back severely, and

MOUNT VERNON

formally dressed in the velvet and ruffles of the day. But it was a tall, raw-boned, young George Washington, with deep-brown hair and a sunburned face, who brought his new family to Mount Vernon. They arrived to see a landscape that gently sloped down to the thickly wooded banks of the Potomac, with the green fields of Maryland to the east and the American frontier to the west. Washington later described it as "a high healthy country, in a latitude between the extreme of heat and cold, on one of the finest rivers in the world, a river well stocked with various kinds of fish, at all seasons of the year, and in the spring the shad, herring, bass, carp, sturgeon, etc., in abundance. The borders of the estate are washed for more than ten miles by tidewater, several valuable fisheries appertaining to it, the whole shore, in fact, one entire fishery."[8]

Washington was always a careful observer of the landscape. Even at age sixteen, while on surveying trips west of the Blue Ridge Mountains, he took notice of the "sugar trees" he saw there. And his travels while he was president to the westernmost reaches of the American territories and to every state in the Union would provide him with a geographic perspective that few of his contemporaries could match.

Starting in the late 1750s, when he was still in his twenties, he began acquiring the English agricultural, gardening, and animal husbandry books that would fill his library. In Batty Langley's *New Principles of Gardening* (1728), he found a variety of garden designs, including a kitchen garden for medicinal, cooking, and herbal uses. In William Gibson's *A New Treatise on the Diseases of Horses* (1751), he learned about the external parts of the horse, including color, markings, and signs for determining the age of an animal. Jethro Tull's *The Horse-Hoeing Husbandry* (1751) provided descriptions of the four-coultered plow and the drill plow, and a comparison of old and new husbandry. Edward Lisle's *Observations in Husbandry* (1757) discussed manures, field implements, the sowing of grains and grasses, the plant nursery, and the care of farm animals. Thomas Hale's *A Compleat Body of Husbandry* (1758–59) examined soils, the uses and care of farm animals, and the cultivation of hops, hemp, and flax. And Philip Miller's *The Abridgement of the Gardener's Dictionary* (1763) advocated the underplanting of trees with shrubs, to create a "closed grove," an idea that Washington would use in the planting of his shady carriage drive around the Bowling Green. By 1760, Washington was already implementing Tull's horse-hoeing techniques and cross-plowing. He also conducted compost experiments with oats and barley, using river mud, horse dung, cow dung, marl, sheep dung, black mould, and clay.

Washington's first phase of development at Mount Vernon doubled the size of the house and established the symmetrical geometry of the ornamental landscape around the house. The second phase, consisting of improvements to the landscape, began in 1774 and lasted throughout the Revolution and until Washington left for the presidency in 1789. During the Revolutionary War, letters flowed from Washington to his manager and cousin, Lund Washington, often from battlefield encampments. On Christmas Day 1782, for example, Washington wrote to Lund from Newburgh, New York. In that letter, Washington was primarily concerned with land he was trying to buy, but in a paragraph toward the end, he wrote:

> I observe what you say respecting the Flowering Shrubs and other Ornamental Trees at the No. end of the House, and as the locusts by the goodness of their growth may lay claim to an establishment there, I wish that the afore-mentioned shrubs and ornamental and curious trees may be planted at both ends that I may determine hereafter from circumstances and appearances which shall be the grove and which the wilderness. It is easy to extirpate Trees from any spot but time only can bring them to maturity.[9]

In a postscript, Washington added:

> When the case will admit of it, The Trees and Flowering Shrubs that are transplanted to the ends of the House have a better chance of living if taken from the open fields than the woods. In the first case they have been more accustomed to bear drought and are hardier than those taken from the Woods, where sun, winds, frost, nor drought has had much power on them, and besides are handsomer.[10]

Washington kept copious notes about Mount Vernon. His gardeners kept weekly accounts, and he himself left streams of letters, directives, diaries, plant lists, plans, memos, and correspondence about the place. Only in the diaries does his emotional attachment to nature and the land shine through. In the winter of 1785, for example, Washington began work on his "walks, groves, & Wildernesses." The diary entries from January through February are full of descriptions of the work:

> Wednesday 12th [of January]. Road to my Mill Swamp, where my dogue Run hands were at work & to other places in search of the sort of Trees I shall want for my walks, groves, & Wildernesses.

> Wednesday 19th. Employed until dinner in laying out my Serpentine road & Shrubberies adjoining.

> Monday 24th. Renewed my labors on the Walks, Shrubberies &ca.—but was much interrupted by the unsettledness of the weather.

> Tuesday 8th [of February]. Finding that I should be very late in preparing

Trees and shrubs along serpentine road

my Walks & Shrubberies if I waited till the ground should be uncovered by the dissolution of the Snow—I had it removed Where necessary & began to Wheel dirt into the Ha! Haws &ca. tho' it was exceedingly miry—bad working.

Friday 11th [of February]. Employed all day in marking the ground for the reception of my Shrubs.

Saturday 26th [of February]. Finished laying out my Serpentine Roads. Dug most of the holes where the trees by the side of them are to stand and planted some of the Maple which were dug yesterday . . .[11]

All that winter and into March the planting continued, even on days when he reported the ground to be "hard froze." And then, on Saturday, April 16, "a great Hoar frost and Ice at least the ⅛ of an Inch thick" produced the following, troubled entry:

What injury this may have done to the fruit & vegetation, will soon be seen. The Buds of every kind of tree & Shrub are swelling. The tender leaves of many had unfolded. The Apricot blossoms were putting forth. The Peaches, & Cherries were upon the point of doing the same. The leaves of the Apple trees were coming out. Those of the weeping willow & Lilac had been out many days, and were the first to show themselves. The Sasafras was ready to open. The red bud had begun to open but not to make any show. The Dogwood had swelled into buttons. The Service tree was showing its leaf and the Maple had been full in bloom ten days or a fortnight. Of this tree I observed great difference in the colour of the blossoms; some being of a deep scarlet, bordering upon Crimson—others of a pale red, approaching yellow.[12]

This Washington does not appear in his portraits.

According to landscape architect Ralph Griswold, when Washington retired to Mount Vernon, "his private conduct had not been altered by the grinding circumstances of war. He had taken no pay but his expenses; he had held his divided forces together, gained independence for the colonies, and founded a new nation. His honor resplendent, he was highly sensible of the widespread love and admiration he had won along with the Revolution. Life's heroic endeavors were completed, and now he could plant trees and finish creating his own symbol of independence, Mount Vernon."[13]

The early Mount Vernon garden was more "regular": controlled and symmetrical, axial and geometric, productive and useful—in short, the garden one would have expected to find in colonial America. However, by the time Washington died, in 1799, the regimented landscape of Mount Vernon had evolved into a freer, much more personal landscape, its groves and wildernesses now hearkening westward toward the frontier and furnished largely with American plants.

Thomas Jefferson summed up Washington's character in a 1784 letter: "The moderation and virtue of a single character probably prevented this Revolution from being closed, as most others have been, by a subversion of that liberty it was intended to establish."[14] Washington himself was acutely aware of his responsibilities as a leader. "I walk on untrodden ground," he wrote in 1789. "There is scarcely any part of my conduct which may not hereafter be drawn into precedent."[15] He was referring to his presidential duties, but he might also have been speaking of his life's work at his beloved Mount Vernon.

THE MOUNT VERNON LADIES' ASSOCIATION OF THE UNION IS BLESSED TOday with a strong and committed group of members, with representatives from every state. Mount Vernon's director, James C. Rees IV, and its director of horticulture, Dean Norton, are men of talent, vision, and energy. The Garden Club of Virginia takes pride in its involvement with George Washington's Mount Vernon.

Oatlands house and garden

Oatlands

Restoration of details in the terraced gardens
of George Carter's fine Federal complex

OATLANDS IS ONE OF THE LAST OF THE STRING OF GREAT HOUSES BUILT BY the descendants of Robert ("King") Carter of Corotoman. Two earlier Carter-related houses, Rosewell and Sabine Hall, have been documented by the Rudy J. Favretti Fellows (see appendix B). Oatlands was built by George Carter, fifteenth of the seventeen children of King Carter's grandson, Councillor Robert Carter of Nomini Hall, on land purchased by Councillor Carter in 1776 from the estate of Thomas, sixth Lord Fairfax, Baron of Cameron and Proprietor of the Northern Neck. Lord Fairfax owned all the land between the headwaters of the Potomac and the Rappahannock Rivers to the Chesapeake Bay. This enormous tract had been granted to his grandfather, Lord Culpeper, by Charles II. Since the headwaters of the Potomac were ultimately judged to be the spring that fed the Shenandoah River, Lord Fairfax's domain extended into what is now West Virginia, which essentially meant that his landholdings surpassed those of the colonial government. King Carter was his factor, and one of his surveyors was a very young George Washington. As a result, both King Carter's descendants and George Washington's relatives would acquire choice pieces of real estate from the Northern Neck across the Valley of Virginia and into the Alleghenies.

The construction of Oatlands, in Loudoun County near Leesburg, was begun in 1804.[1] It was originally designed in late Georgian style, and was altered in 1827 to reflect the new Federal style. George Carter himself "developed the mansion's design from illustrations in William Chambers's *A Treatise on Civil Architecture* (1786)."[2] He also laid out the terraced gardens and designed the greenhouse and the forcing wall.

George Carter died in 1846; his widow remained at Oatlands with their two sons and managed the plantation through the Civil War years. After the war, having lost their fortune and their slave labor, the Carters operated Oatlands as a summer boarding house, but this venture did not produce enough income to support the place. In 1897, Oatlands was sold to Stilson Hitchins, a cofounder of the *Washington Post,* but he

never lived there. In 1903, he sold it to Mr. and Mrs. William Corcoran Eustis, a very fortunate occurrence. The Eustises made it their summer home for a long lifetime, and together they brought Oatlands back to its former glory, enhancing and enlarging the garden while remaining faithful to its original design.

In 1923, Mrs. Eustis wrote of the Oatlands garden:

When the present owners bought it—not from the Carters—but from one who had not sensed its beauties, the Oatlands garden was falling into ruins; bricks were crumbling, weeds crowding the flowers and yet the very moss-grown paths seemed to say, "we are still what we were." It was a thankful task to restore the old beauty, although the thoughts and conceptions were new, but they fitted it, and every stone vase or bench, every box-hedge planted, seemed to fall into its rightful place and become part of the whole. Certain improvements were made—improvements the old designer would have approved; fruit trees, hiding huge box and yew, were cut down, and a rosary laid out as a counterpart to the box-grove. It was not always easy to get the right effect.

More than one-half of the garden can be seen from several vantage points: from the upper balustrade, looking down; from the oak grove, looking up, and from each separate terrace. The things to be striven for—mystery, variety, the unexpected—were difficult of attainment; but in certain places they have been attained. The tall north wall with brick coping and its small beds above descending stone walls—just the same as in Carter days; a shady, almost neglected spot, where the grass grows too tall sometimes, is a thing apart from the rest. Then the rose garden with its background of tall box and pine, in an enclosure of dark green fencing, cedar posts and chains, over hung with Dorothy Perkins roses, cannot be seen until you turn a corner and are on it unawares. And the bowling green, a long stretch of greensward, bordered by euonymus, flowering shrubs and Oriental Biota [arborvitae], is nearly always shaded, giving that sense of stillness and remoteness which a hidden mass of green so often suggests. At one end of it, the tall north wall shields it from blustering winds; at the other, a sunny, white-pillared tea-house overlooks a grove of great oaks which, more than house or garden, is the living glory of Oatlands. The rest of the garden—the staircase, box-hedges and brick pilasters to one side, with a great ivy-clad wall to the other, a larch tree crowning the whole; and, looking down and southward, an old pink Venetian well head, protecting a deep, cool well. Then the terraces, bearing some vases, a sundial, many low box-hedges, and innumerable flowers—they finish the tale. But the brick walls and, in one place, a slender white fence, shut it all in and give it that sense of separateness, of a certain aloofness almost, befitting the guardian of treasures, the storehouse of old secrets.

The Oatlands garden should be visited in the springtime first, I believe, so as to see the peonies and iris, after the tulips have faded. . . . But, take it all in all, the best of the year is generally June, because the roses are in bloom then on every wall, and the colours of the other flowers—larkspurs, pinks, lilies, with hummingbirds among them—vie with each other against backgrounds of stone or brick, ivy or box.[3]

After Mrs. Eustis's death, her daughters conveyed Oatlands to the National Trust for Historic Preservation in 1965. The Trust first approached the Restoration Committee in 1978 with a request that the Garden Club of Virginia restore the greenhouse, an original early nineteenth-century structure badly in need of repair. The committee considered the proposal in detail but rejected it because of the cost. Nine years later, in 1987, the National Trust came back with two proposals to choose from: the greenhouse restoration or a native plant garden adjacent to the north wall. On that occasion, the committee turned down both requests: the greenhouse was judged to

Restored forcing wall

OATLANDS

English oak and new edging box

be a "departure from our traditional emphasis upon garden design and plant material," and the native planting adjacent to the wall, "a departure from our mandated emphasis upon garden design and plant material." Encouraged by GCV members, however, the Trust remained persistent and returned yet again, in 1988, with four choices: the restoration of the greenhouse; an adaptation of the greenhouse to some contemporary reuse; the repair of the garden wall (ca. 1820s or earlier), with a wildflower and native flower garden on the terraces next to the wall; or the restoration of the garden dependencies (ca. 1820s) for adaptive use. This time the Restoration Committee was receptive, agreeing to repair sixty-nine feet of the north wall, which was judged by the committee to have been a forcing wall.[4]

Although the Trust had requested the repair of the entire length of the wall, the expense to do that would have been too great. When, on a hot summer day, landscape architect Rudy J. Favretti went to inspect the project, he found a mortared stone base in good condition topped by a tumbled-down brick wall. The wall was so dilapidated that it was impossible to tell how high it had originally been. Favretti went back very early the next morning; the nighttime humidity still lingering in the air had left the faintest ghost outline of the capped wall at the end of an outbuilding that abutted the highest section of the wall. Because the still-sturdy base was stepped to follow the contours of the land, it was easy to determine where the wall had been stepped as well. Favretti designed a wooden cap based on some fragments that had been found on another segment of wall elsewhere; the square, hand-forged nails of the fragments were identified as belonging to the same period as the old wall. "These wood or thatched capped walls go way back in history, witness evidence in England," Favretti noted. "They are still used in Canada . . . and you will see them reproduced, based on documented sources, at Old Salem in North Carolina."[5] The restored section of the wall was presented to the National Trust for Historic Preservation on October 15, 1992.

Two years later, the English boxwood in the east parterres fell prey to nematodes and the boxwood decline that swept through Virginia gardens, and the Restoration Committee agreed to replant the affected terraces. Since then, the English box has been replaced with a new cultivar, *B. sempervirens* 'Justin Brouwer', which has proven resistant.

The Garden Club of Virginia is delighted to expand its list of partnerships with the National Trust, which also includes Belle Grove and Montpelier, and to contribute to the preservation of yet another distinguished Virginia garden.

Greek Revival portico of
Old Portsmouth Courthouse

Old Portsmouth Courthouse

A brick courtyard setting suitable
for the 1846 courthouse

THE OLD PORTSMOUTH COURTHOUSE IS NOW THE COURTHOUSE GALLERies, part of the Downtown Portsmouth Historic District, which was added to the National Register of Historic Places in 2004. The courthouse building itself was individually registered on both the National Register of Historic Places and the Virginia Landmark Register in 1970.

In the 1840s and 1850s, Norfolk and the Hampton Roads area, along with Petersburg and Lynchburg, were flexing their economic muscles, competing with Richmond for rail routes and shipping business. The courthouse was built during this time, in 1846, toward the end of the Greek Revival period, and was described by a local newspaper as "a beautiful structure, highly ornamental to the town, and proudly indicating the liberality and importance of the County."[1] It was designed by William Singleton, a St. Louis architect who happened to be a native of Portsmouth; the builder was Willoughby G. Butler.

Portsmouth became an independent city in 1858, but the voters of Norfolk County decided to continue to use the same courthouse, despite the fact that there were not separate courtrooms for the new city and the old county. It would take another ten years to remedy that situation, as the advent of the Civil War brought all construction activity in the area to a grinding halt. During the war, Norfolk County was occupied by Union forces, but the courthouse records were not destroyed. They were saved, so the story goes, by "a level-headed clerk, who in 1860 loaded his precious record books into a covered wagon and drove off into the Dismal Swamp, not to reappear until the fighting was safely over."[2]

After the war, most of Virginia slumped back into its primarily rural and agricultural status for at least another hundred years, during which time the Portsmouth courthouse continued to serve its original purpose. Then, in 1963, after Norfolk County merged with South Norfolk to become the city of Chesapeake, the courthouse was finally abandoned. It stood derelict for several years.

The architect John Paul C. Hanbury, FAIA, was the first to focus on the building's endangered status.[3] With the help of two of his University of Virginia professors, Frederick B. Nichols and William B. O'Neal, Hanbury secured both Virginia and National Landmark Registry status for the building in 1970. Two subsequent grants, funded over a period of years, were used to begin the restoration of the building's exterior. By 1982, according to Hanbury, "the city realized we were serious and threw its support and civic dollars for its interior restoration. More importantly, the city established an arts presence for the community where heretofore none existed."[4]

Hanbury spearheaded the 1982 renovation of the building; he also designed the large brick-paved courtyard, with large planting beds at the main entrance and deep, brick-curbed beds for trees and shrubs along the border. He asked that Rudy J. Favretti, landscape architect to the Garden Club of Virginia, design the planting plan. The understated planting of ivy and shrubs lines the perimeter fence and is one of the most elegant features of the courthouse's landscape. The six-foot-tall, round, hand-wrought iron pickets have flattened, spear-shaped termini; the fence is set on top of a granite base, and it has evenly spaced ornamental cast-iron posts supported by ogee-curved

Courtyard outside the museum entrance

OLD PORTSMOUTH COURTHOUSE

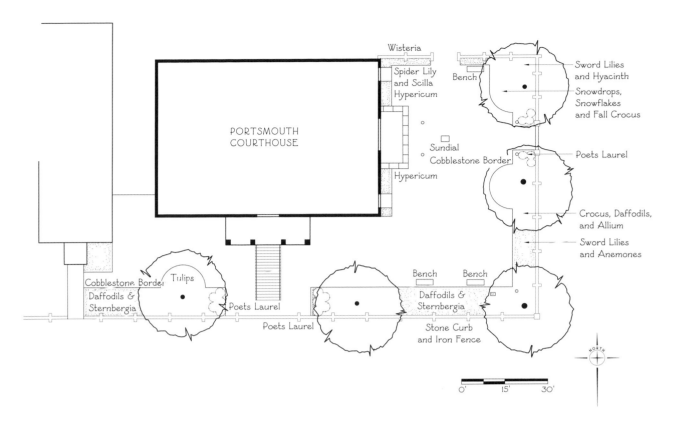

Wisteria
Spider Lily
and Scilla
Hypericum

PORTSMOUTH
COURTHOUSE

Bench

Sword Lilies
and Hyacinth

Snowdrops,
Snowflakes
and Fall Crocus

Sundial
Cobblestone Border

Hypericum

Poets Laurel

Crocus, Daffodils,
and Allium

Sword Lilies
and Anemones

Cobblestone Border
Daffodils &
Sternbergia

Tulips

Poets Laurel

Bench   Bench

Daffodils &
Sternbergia

Poets Laurel

Stone Curb
and Iron Fence

NORTH

0'   15'   30'

brackets set at right angles to the face of the fence. The evergreen border forms a perfect setting for the venerable live oaks that frame the building and shade the courtyard. In 2002, a request for more color led to the massing of crocus and daffodils and other spring-blooming bulbs in the ivy along the perimeter fence. Scraggly shrubs were also removed, so that for most of the year the classical purity of the building and the simplicity of its surroundings are left unadorned.

Although it took nearly twenty years to find the money to adapt the old Portsmouth Courthouse into an Arts Center and Children's Museum (it should be noted that the Children's Museum moved out of the ground floor in 1985, and that space has since become the Courthouse Galleries), today the stately old building is a center of cultural activity and tourism in Portsmouth's Historic Olde Towne.

*Restored entrance drive
at Point of Honor*

Point of Honor

A restored landscape for a Federal-period house

WILLIAM CABELL (1699–1774) ARRIVED IN VIRGINIA IN 1726, WHERE HE founded an influential and prolific clan that became known for two long-lasting family traditions: there were doctors in almost every generation of Cabells, and the various branches of the family peppered central Virginia with distinguished houses.[1] The family patriarch had emigrated from England when he was twenty-seven to settle his huge Henrico County patent. There, he took up the practice of medicine. He was apparently self-taught, since there seems to be no record of any prior medical training. In those days, training was not required: an aspiring doctor would buy medical books and supplies, study the books, and then use his newly acquired knowledge and supplies to practice what he had learned on ailing acquaintances, both slave and free.

William Cabell's part of Henrico County, which at the time stretched unbounded across Virginia to the west, eventually became first the County of Goochland, then Albemarle County, then Amherst County, and finally, after Cabell's death, Nelson County. Some of his acreage even ended up as part of Buckingham County, when, along with Amherst County, it was split off from Albemarle County. Shortly after his arrival, Cabell married Elizabeth Burks. They had six children, one of whom died in infancy. The four surviving sons all served in the Virginia Assembly; the older three were variously involved in the Revolutionary War.

Colonel John Cabell (1735–1815), the third of William Cabell's sons, produced fourteen children. His third son, George (1766–1823), carried on the family tradition, becoming the first Cabell to earn an official medical degree. He attended Hampden-Sydney Academy (later Hampden-Sydney College, the progenitor of the Medical College of Virginia, which is now the VCU Medical Center), before completing his medical training at the University of Pennsylvania in 1790. He then came home to set up his practice in Lynchburg, where, about 1815, on a promontory overlooking the James River, he built the beautiful Federal house called Point of Honor. (Dueling,

by that time, was outlawed in Virginia, so the name must have come down from an earlier legend.) Dr. George Cabell Sr., always so called to differentiate him from his cousin, namesake, and protégé, Dr. George Cabell Jr., became physician to his older friend, Patrick Henry, who had been governor of Virginia during the time that George Cabell's father, John, served in the General Assembly.

Dr. Cabell obviously had a very successful practice, if Point of Honor is any indication. The house is a worthy addition to the collection of elegant houses that were built by his uncles and cousins downstream along the James River in what is now Nelson County: Liberty Hall, Union Hill, Soldier's Joy, Edgewood, Bon Aire, Oak Ridge, Spring Hill (also called Montezuma, because of an American Indian cemetery on the property), and Norwood. The Cabells' homes were certainly their castles.

Point of Honor descended from the Cabell family to the Daniel family in 1830, after Dr. Cabell's son, William Lewis Cabell, and his bride, Eliza Daniel Cabell, both died. The house, which had been left to her, went to her father, Judge William Daniel Sr., who died in 1839, leaving it to his son and namesake, William Daniel Jr. The younger Daniel was also a judge, serving on the Virginia Court of Appeals from 1846 through the end of the Civil War. Sometime before the Civil War began, however, Judge Daniel sold Point of Honor to John S. Langhorne (whose son, Chiswell Dabney Langhorne, would later buy Mirador; see appendix B). During the Civil War, the house belonged to Robert Lathan Owen, president of the Virginia and Tennessee Railroad. His

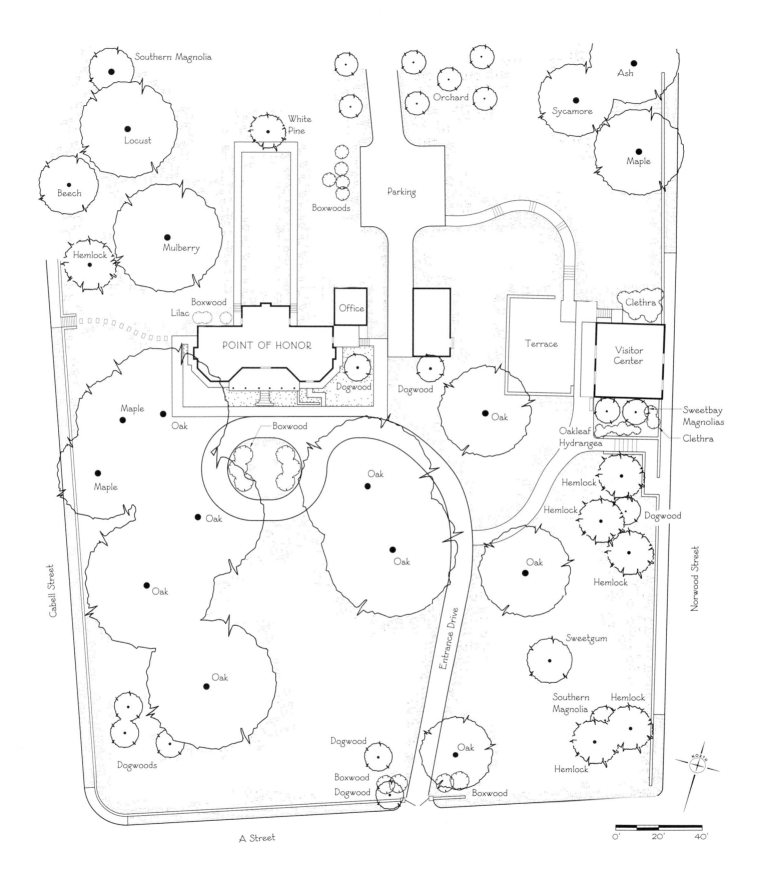

Southern Magnolia

Locust

Beech

Mulberry

Hemlock

White Pine

Boxwoods

Parking

Orchard

Sycamore

Ash

Maple

Boxwood

Lilac

Office

POINT OF HONOR

Dogwood

Dogwood

Terrace

Visitor Center

Clethra

Sweetbay Magnolias

Clethra

Maple

Oak

Boxwood

Oak

Maple

Oak

Oak

Oak

Oak

Oak

Oakleaf Hydrangea

Hemlock

Hemlock

Dogwood

Hemlock

Oak

Oak

Sweetgum

Southern Magnolia

Hemlock

Hemlock

Oak

Cabell Street

Entrance Drive

Norwood Street

Dogwoods

Dogwood

Boxwood

Dogwood

Oak

Boxwood

A Street

0'   20'   40'

NORTH

wife, Narcissa Chisholm, was the daughter of the Cherokee chief Thomas Chisholm. The Owens' son, Robert L. Owen Jr., would become Oklahoma's first United States Senator.

The founding charter for Lynchburg, where Point of Honor is located, was granted in October 1786. The town took its name from the village that had grown up around the site of John Lynch's ferry. Lynch, whose mother was a Quaker, established the ferry service in 1757, and by the end of the American Revolution the village around the ferry dock had become an important center of trade in tobacco and other goods. In the eighteenth century, Lynchburg had a devout Quaker population. They were the first religious group to settle in Lynchburg, but most of them left in the 1820s because of their opposition to slavery. Until the late 1840s, Lynchburg's main commercial artery

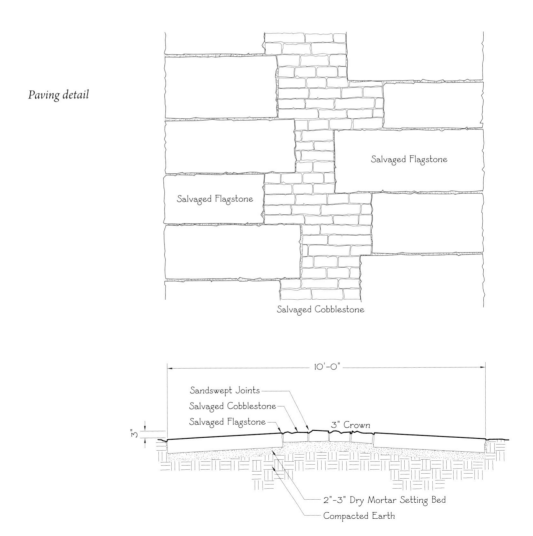

Paving detail

POINT OF HONOR

was the James River, upon which batteaux traveled regularly between Lynchburg and Richmond taking tobacco and other crops to market. The water craft were supplanted by the railroad after two disastrous floods in the 1840s.

THE GARDEN CLUB OF VIRGINIA FIRST ANSWERED a call for help with the landscape at Point of Honor in 1978; the landscape architect at that time was Meade Palmer. There was no original garden to restore, and the landscape that existed was inappropriate to the period. Palmer designed a long cobblestone driveway—edged with large, flat, rectangular stones—that ran from a new front gate up the hill to the turnaround circle in front of the house. Carriage wheels would have run smoothly on the large, flat-edge stones, and the horses would have had better traction on the cobbles. Palmer also managed to tuck a parking lot into the hillside, which, while convenient to the site, is almost entirely hidden from view. Large English boxwood flank the steps up to the front porch, and groves of trees appropriate to the period add interest to the steep front lawn.

View toward Lynchburg

In the 1990s, Point of Honor raised funds to build the Bertha Green Webster Carriage House, which serves as a visitors' center. Rudy J. Favretti, by then the Garden Club of Virginia's landscape architect, designed the landscape setting for the new building. A reception terrace for the visitors' center was defined by a seat-height wall, and trees and shrubs provided shade and interest for the new building. Favretti also designed, with the advice of Tom Burford, a demonstration apple orchard at the back of the house.

In 2006, the Garden Club of Virginia revisited Point of Honor once again. For this restoration, landscape architect William D. Rieley designed a new stone path to run from the parking lot at the rear of the property to the visitors' center.

Point of Honor is now part of the Lynchburg museum system. Its beautiful interior, with Adams-style designs by Owen Biddle of Philadelphia and the English craftsman William Paine, has been restored to its original elegance. The landscape, though simple, provides it with a suitable and becoming setting, and it sits proud on its hill above the river, a deserving addition to a long line of gracious Cabell homes.

Demonstration garden at Smithfield Plantation

Smithfield Plantation

Blacksburg

The frontier house of the Preston family, with a
Colonial Revival kitchen garden

IN THE EARLY 1700S, WHAT IS NOW SOUTHWEST VIRGINIA MARKED THE BE-ginning of the American frontier.[1] Into this wilderness, James Patton traveled with his surveying tools. With great foresight, he grasped the possibilities of the land he explored, and he urged his nephew, William Preston, also a surveyor, to purchase property there.

William Preston (who had immigrated as a young child with his parents from Ireland) was then living at Greenfields, near the town of Fincastle, with his wife, Susanna, and several of their children. He followed his uncle's advice, and in 1754 bought three parcels of land, totaling 1,010 acres, from William Ingles and John Draper. (Nearby Draper's Meadow was the first permanent English-speaking colony west of the Alleghenies and site of the notorious Draper's Meadow massacre, during which Mary Draper Ingles was captured by Indians.)

Years later, in 1773, William Preston began construction of a home on the property and purchased the adjoining 760 acres from Francis Smith. He moved his family there in 1774. Under his management, and with the help of as many as forty-two slaves, Smithfield developed into a thriving plantation.

The Preston dwelling was not a typical frontier house. Built in the Tidewater plantation style, it reflected a strong sense of elegance and refinement in its architecture and details. There were glass-paned transoms over the front and back hall doors for light and ventilation; transoms and doors could be opened to catch the summer breezes. A Chinese lattice banister graced the stair. Detailed woodwork in the parlor rivaled that found in the more sophisticated settlements to the east. Brightly colored fireplace mantels were highly glazed to catch the eyes of visitors. An end chimney was constructed flush with the outer siding of the house to conserve heat and create closet space on the interior—a progressive notion at the time.

Two years after the Prestons moved to Smithfield, Montgomery County was

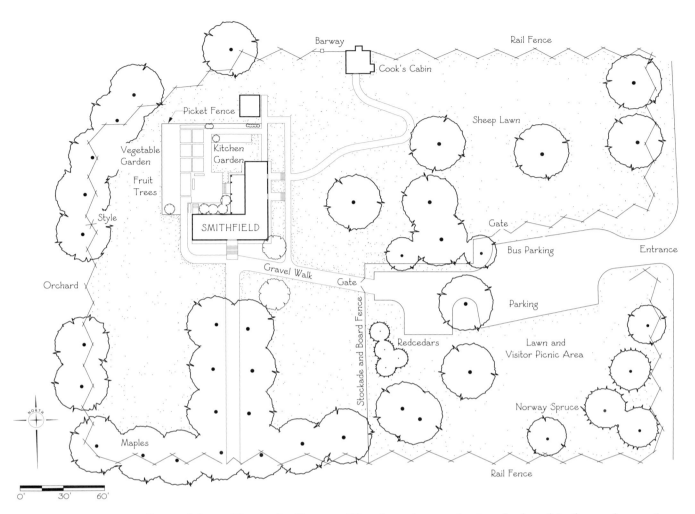

Barway   Rail Fence

Cook's Cabin

Picket Fence

Sheep Lawn

Vegetable Garden

Kitchen Garden

Fruit Trees

SMITHFIELD

Style

Gate

Bus Parking

Entrance

Orchard

Gravel Walk   Gate

Parking

Stockade and Board Fence

Redcedars

Lawn and Visitor Picnic Area

Norway Spruce

NORTH

Maples

Rail Fence

0'   30'   60'

formed from Fincastle County. The American colonies declared independence that same year, and William Preston, who had served in the House of Burgesses and held several county positions when he lived in Fincastle, was appointed County Lieutenant. Smithfield became known as a center of social and political activities.

Colonel William Preston died in 1783, and Susanna continued to run the plantation and raise their twelve children there. She remained at Smithfield for forty more years, managing it until her death in 1823. In that era it was exceptional for a woman to attend to the business of running a large plantation, and it should be noted that under Susanna's management the value of the enterprise more than doubled.

Five generations of Prestons lived at Smithfield. Over the years, four members of the family served as governor of Virginia: William's son, James Patton Preston (1816–19); two of his sons-in-law, John Floyd Jr. (1830–34) and James McDowell (1843–46); and a grandson, John Buchanan Floyd (1849–52). The first three generations lived at Smithfield year-round, but, later, Smithfield was used only as a summer home and changes were made to both the house and the land. Much of the land is now the site of Virginia Tech. Use of the remaining property by the family diminished further, and in 1959 Janie Preston Boulware Lamb, great-great-granddaughter of William Preston, presented the property to the Association for the Preservation of Virginia Antiquities, which undertook the restoration of the house. Smithfield Plantation was opened to the public in 1964.

IN 1982, THE GARDEN CLUB OF VIRGINIA VOTED TO TACKLE THE LAND-scaping of Smithfield. As there was no record of the original garden, the Smithfield staff requested a large garden for their educational program. They needed room to grow culinary, textile-dying, and medicinal herbs, as well as space for their classes and demonstrations. Rudy J. Favretti designed the landscape setting and kitchen garden with these requests in mind. He had no documentation to go by, except that the location of previous outbuildings was known. The garden was presented in 1984.

The yard, tightly enclosed by various forms of fencing, became the landscape focus. Acknowledging modern-day requirements, Favretti integrated the parking lot into the design. Periwinkle, azaleas, bulbs, and daylilies were planted to surround the large gravel lot. A mature linden tree was preserved to provide shade, and established dogwoods bloom in the neighboring family cemetery. A large picnic area occupies the slope down from the parking area to the field below.

A weathered wooden paling gate, encircled by violets, marks the entrance to the yard. Running southward from the gate and extending around the perimeter are three examples of fence styles that were used on the plantation. Favretti's design specified the materials as well as the styles. The first is the paling fence, designed to keep out predators and other animals and built of oak planks cut diagonally at the top to produce a sharp point on one side. This length of fence leads into the demonstration stockade fence, constructed of large, very sturdy, round locust posts honed to a point. A stockade fence originally provided Smithfield protection from the Shawnees and Cherokees in the area, as well as from Tories (at the beginning of the Revolution, a garrison of soldiers was sent to Smithfield by Governor Patrick Henry to provide further security). The next, and most prevalent form of fence, is the split-locust Virginia rail (or snake) fence. This type of fence served mainly to keep livestock separate from the house and out-buildings, and these fences were popular because they were easily moved to make different-size paddocks.

Wild mustard is allowed to grow outside the fence line. The maple is the dominant tree around the house; most are sugar maples. Some are old and large; some are newly planted in keeping with Favretti's plan. Two linden trees and a sweetgum grow near the house; oaks, walnuts, locusts, and dogwoods are on the periphery. A large Norway spruce anchors the southeast corner. Numerous more recently planted English boxwoods were removed to another site on the property.

The house was situated on a knoll, where it would be visually impressive and provide early sightings of visitors, friendly and otherwise. The landscape plan shows an avenue of maple trees marking the approach to the house. Janie Lamb recalls being told that in her grandmother's day, in the late nineteenth century, there was a circular drive between a double row of Virginia cedars leading to the square front porch. The current straight pea-gravel path begins at the fence line and is lined by rows of maples. According to Lamb, the fence and gate used to be of whitewashed boards. Evidence indicates that an overseer's cottage existed at what is now the intersection of Southgate Drive and Highway 460. The original approach to the house must have run through what is now a field owned and cultivated by Virginia Tech. Slave quarters were probably situated along this lane, but constant cultivation has destroyed any evidence of them.

In a concession to practicality, Favretti's plan delineated walkways, which would originally have been of swept dirt, to be laid with pea gravel. The front walkway leads past the main entrance of the home to the southwest garden entrance, then through the garden gate and down a few steps into the museum store where tickets are purchased; thus all visitors receive a visual introduction to the kitchen garden before their tour begins. Another walkway leads around the house to the second entrance to the kitchen garden and the reconstructed smokehouse (site of the restrooms).

Archaeological research was used to determine the existence and location of the smokehouse. Another similar-sized dependency existed a short distance away, but it has not yet been reconstructed. The kitchen garden was placed in the area between the house and these outbuildings. Both garden gates are paling-style and weighted with cannonballs to keep them closed.

The kitchen garden is divided into distinct plots. The main areas are separated by a running-bond brick walk leading to a brick terrace laid in a basketweave pattern. Two weathered wooden benches offer seating on the terrace. Moss is allowed to grow between the Old Virginia bricks. Favretti called for trodden paths to provide access to other parts of the garden. Each plot is designated for plant materials of similar purpose and use.

In subsequent years, the garden moved beyond the Favretti plan and included

wildflowers. Current efforts have reestablished plants in keeping with the original plan. The garden today essentially adheres to the perennial selection designated by Favretti's plan. The selection of annuals varies slightly from year to year.

Flower garden

Over the years, changes have been made in the placement of some plantings. Various fruits were to occupy the periphery. The row of currant bushes along the foundation of the house continues to produce fruit. The grapevine specified for the back fence still meanders over the oak boards. Some of the strawberries originally planted along the back fence remain, but the raspberries and gooseberries grew so profusely that their outreaching branches tended to snag visitors. The gooseberry now thrives in the opposite corner of the garden, away from foot traffic. The cherry trees failed after several years, and have been replaced with ornamental and textile plants, specifically, teasel, false indigo, black-eyed Susan, hollyhock, and flax.

Peas, cabbage, parsnips, beans, carrots, and corn grow in the vegetable plot, along with field crops such as corn, oats, wheat, and buckwheat, which are rotated for demonstration purposes. Two pole trellises bridging the path are covered with scarlet runner beans and gourds in summertime.

A corner of the grass-drying yard is occupied by a hop tower; in addition to their use in beverages, hops were used as a leavening agent in breads and pastries. A bed of medicinal herbs runs alongside the drying yard. Medicinal herbs include St. Johnswort, aconite, broom, bee balm, lady's mantle, feverfew, and elecampane, which was used for lung diseases and to treat skin problems in horses and sheep (hence its nickname, horseheal). Care is taken to separate medicinal and culinary herbs; some herbs of similar appearance may have toxic effects if confused and improperly used.

Favretti's plan did allow for the remnant of one English boxwood to be planted in the southwest corner of the kitchen garden where it is surrounded by periwinkle, lily of the valley, violets, and daffodils. Tansy, sweet Cecily, and peonies are well established. An area designated on one of the early drawings as a "wood pile location" is now a well-disguised heat-pump area, surrounded by paling fence. A demonstration wattle fence has been added. Lengthy branches interwoven horizontally from groundlevel up form a barrier to keep pests such as rabbits out of delectable plants like lettuce.

The landscape at Smithfield continues to evolve. In the fall of 2007, outside the rail fence on the western side of the property, an heirloom orchard was established. The orchard was a project of the Children of the American Revolution and the Garden Club of Virginia. Using documentation of an orchard from another part of the Preston property, the Smithfield orchard will contain heirloom apple, as well as peach, pear, and nut trees. A walkway gracefully curving to the weaver's cabin was designed by Will Rieley and laid in 1999. Millstones currently on site will be relocated to the western fence line to denote a pathway into the heirloom orchard, eventually leading to the ruined mill and the nearby miller's cabin.

Historic Smithfield, now twelve acres in size, sits on a knoll adjacent to the Virginia Tech campus and is surrounded by modern development. A path outside the split-rail fence in the front yard is used as a jogging trail. When the wind shifts, the rumble of Highway 460 can be heard. But visitors come regularly to enjoy the serenity of the site and to learn about life in the American colonies. The elegance and simplicity of the house and grounds are pleasing and representative of the circumstances and natural environment of the eighteenth century. The kitchen garden is a horticultural classroom. Its well-laid design and its groupings of fruits, vegetables, herbs both medicinal and culinary, field crops, and textile and ornamental plants are a living demonstration of how a colonial family provided for itself the needs of daily life.

St. Luke's Churchyard

SMITHFIELD

The grounds of the oldest existing church building
of English foundation in America

HISTORIC ST. LUKE'S CHURCH, IN ISLE OF WIGHT COUNTY, IS NOT ONLY THE oldest surviving Anglican parish church in Virginia, it is also "America's purest expression of original Gothic Architecture." According to the *Virginia Landmarks Register,* although the church is simple in design, "its buttressed walls, lancet side windows, and traceried east window have for more than three centuries formed one of the New World's most direct links with the architecture of the Middle Ages."[1] Although there is disagreement about the exact date of the church's construction, there is documentary proof that its ancestral parish, known as Warrosquyoake, was organized by the 1620s. Other documents demonstrate the parish's early vitality. In 1623, by order of the General Assembly of Virginia, it was named as one of four parishes outside of Jamestown where the General Court of the Colony was permitted to convene. Moreover, copies of the proceedings of the General Court show that in 1629, the Commissioners at Warrosquyoake delivered complete records of the monthly court proceedings, together with "the Register of Christenings, marriages and Burialls under the hand of the minister and churchwardens, and likewise a Coppie of their Levyes and disburstmts at *Warrosquyoake.*"[2]

By 1634, the Warrosquyoake parish had 522 members. In that year, an Act of Assembly created eight shires, or counties, one of which was Warrosquyoake. It was the only shire to be given an Indian name, which was short-lived; by 1637, it had become Isle of Wight. A period of relative peace with the Indian federation, which included the Warrosquyoakes, irrupted into bloody warfare sometime before 1640. A last, devastating attack on the plantations south of the James River resulted in the massacre of five hundred settlers, but also in the capture and subsequent murder of Opechancanough. Then, in 1643, the county was split into two parishes: the upper, which remained Warrosquyoake, and lower, which became Newport Parish. Historic St. Luke's was built as the Newport Parish church.

Seventeenth-century apse window

In this day of stringent separation of church and state, it is hard to understand that before the Revolution, in Virginia there was virtually no separation between these two entities. From 1619 until 1785, the Virginia General Assembly was responsible for the creation of ecclesiastical as well as civil entities: it defined parishes as well as shires, or counties. In other words, as in the mother country, the Assembly had two, complementary administrative agencies, to oversee the civil and religious life of the colony, and the two went hand in hand. Many of the functions of the civil administration were carried out through the parish vestries: the courts met in the churches until courthouses were built; upcoming elections were announced from the pulpit; and delegates to the Assembly were elected at meetings held in the parish church. Election to the church vestry was therefore also of political as well as ecclesiastical significance. The fact that Warrosquyoake not only became one of the first eight shires, but that it also had a population large enough to warrant division into two parishes by 1643, speaks to its importance in the early history of the colony.

There has been an ongoing controversy about the exact date of construction of the Newport Parish Church, which has also been known as the Old Brick Church and, by the nineteenth century, as St. Luke's. Opinions range from 1632 to 1685. No one has questioned the age of the parish, however, or that there was a church built in Warrosquyoake Parish following an Act of Assembly passed in February of 1631 or 1632. At issue has been the precise date of the existing seventeenth-century brick building now known as Historic St. Luke's. There is a long-standing tradition, backed by voluminous anecdotal and circumstantial evidence, for the 1632 date. However, the primary documentation in support of this claim is not conclusive. Two Acts of the Assembly, of March 1623, ordered that every plantation should offer a separate house or room for the worship of God, and that there should be a monthly court session held in Warrosquyoake. Another Act, passed in February 1631 or 1632, ordered that work toward the building of a parish church in Warrosquyoake should be started by December 1632, under penalty of a fine of £50.[3] It is clear, therefore, that the building of a church was begun that year. It is not clear that it was this particular brick church.

Architectural historians are agreed that the present church was standing in the 1680s, but only William H. Pierson Jr., in *American Buildings and their Architects* (1970), gives the 1632 building date the benefit of the doubt. More recent scholars have come to a different conclusion. Dell Upton, Richard Guy Wilson, Carl Lounsbury of Colonial Williamsburg, and Calder Loth, senior architectural historian of the Virginia Department of Historical Resources, are all in agreement on this point: without existing parish records earlier than 1734, or dendrochronological evidence, it is impossible to establish a precise building date for the Newport Parish Church. They have all reached the same conclusion as to the probable date of construction, however, which they unanimously place in the last quarter of the seventeenth century, which coincides with construction of two other comparable brick churches: the James City Parish Church at Jamestown, and the second Bruton Parish Church, which has been dated by documentary evidence to 1681–83.[4] Calder Loth adds that "the hard fact remains that the church is America's finest example of Gothic Survival architecture. It was built sometime in the seventeenth century; the exact date of construction has not been verified."[5]

On May 20, 2007, Robert S. Fulghum, of Greenville, North Carolina, addressed the participants of the 50th Annual Pilgrimage to Historic St. Luke's. Fulghum is descended from Captain Anthony Fulgeham, who recorded a patent in Isle of Wight County in 1642. At the gathering, he read from a deed of sale, recorded on September 6, 1683, "for one acre of land situate lying and being in the Forest Parrish whereon the Churchhouse now standeth by the Deepe Swampe."[6] The deed was signed by An-

Pine trees screening churchyard from neighboring development

thony Fulgeham's third son, Michall, and his wife, Ann Izard Fenneryear, who had inherited the acre of land from her first husband. The existence of this deed has been known for a long time, but proponents of the earlier building date have held that it was inconclusive evidence. Robert Fulgham believes that the vestry of the church obtained the deed upon the completion of the Old Brick Church. As proof, he cites a lengthy and confusing complex of genealogical and marital relationships that lead back to "an early, if not the first, rector of the Old Brick Church."[7]

Historic St. Luke's is no longer an active parish church, but as a historic site and nonprofit foundation, Historic St. Lukes, Inc., is much visited. The venerable church itself, as the old saying goes, is still much used for "weddings and funerals and feasts."[8]

THOUGH THERE WAS NO GARDEN TO BE RESTORED OR re-created, when the Restoration Committee of the Garden Club of Virginia was asked for a plan to enhance and protect the surroundings of this remarkable building— uniquely important both architecturally and historically— a favorable decision was the obvious outcome. As William D. Rieley's notes for the project indicate, there would be "no effort to attempt to portray what the churchyard looked like in the seventeenth or eighteenth centuries." Rather,

the charm of these sites [other churchyards that the Garden Club has worked on] is that they are ancient, and look it. Several generations of native trees have grown up, grown old, died and been replaced by succeeding generations. Generations of parishioners occupy the ground around the church. While there is evidence of how this landscape has evolved over time, such as the trace of the old road in front of the church leading to the west (replaced by modern Route 10) that runs through the site, the overriding quality of the site is that it has evolved within a very consistent pattern: large trees in a park-like setting and burial places for the families that sustained the church in their own times.

So the task is not to restore, so much as to preserve this rich layering of history that adds to our understanding of the antiquity and real significance

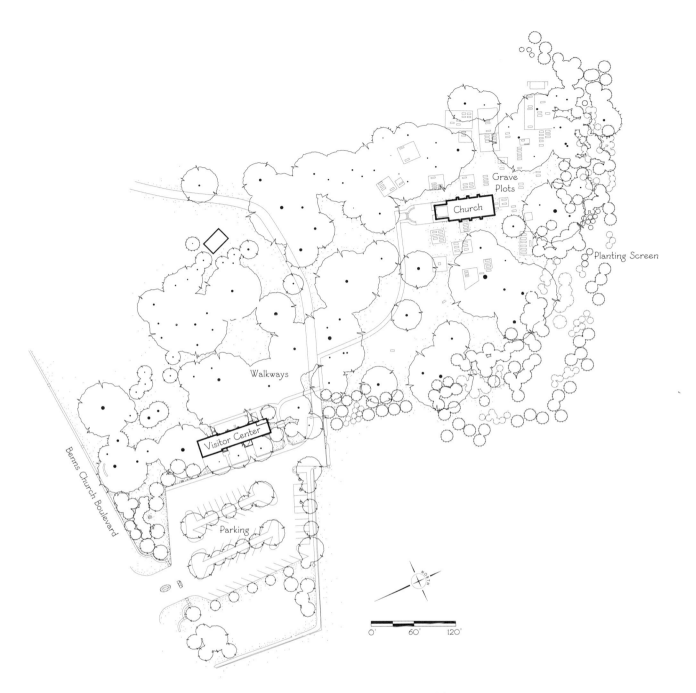

Grave Plots

Church

Planting Screen

Walkways

Visitor Center

Benns Church Boulevard

Parking

NORTH

0'   60'   120'

of the site. Our intervention is mostly on the perimeter: adding screening to diminish the impact of oncoming development on adjacent land, adding and improving walks to allow visitors to get to the site in a safe and aesthetically harmonious way; improving the visitors' experience from the time they enter the parking lot until they get to the church. A good bit of our work will focus in the arrival area and in screening for future protection of the churchyard scene.[9]

New walkway at dawn

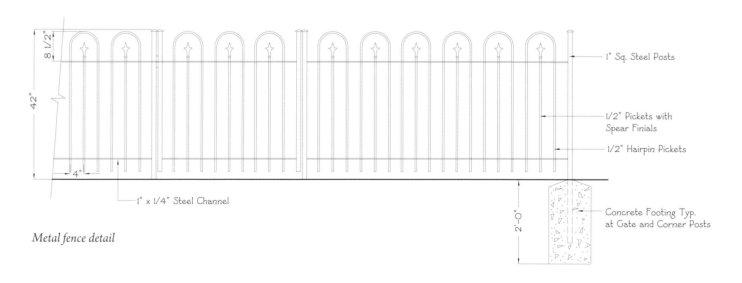

8 1/2"

42"

4"

1" Sq. Steel Posts

1/2" Pickets with
Spear Finials

1/2" Hairpin Pickets

1" x 1/4" Steel Channel

2'-0"

Concrete Footing Typ.
at Gate and Corner Posts

Metal fence detail

ST. LUKE'S CHURCHYARD

The screening Rieley refers to consists of native trees and shrubs that would have been available when the church was built: yaupon hollies, dogwoods, hornbeams, river birches, sweetbay magnolias, live and willow oaks. One special addition is a Franklinia tree, a species discovered by John Bartram in 1770 and named for Benjamin Franklin. It has not been seen in the wild since 1790, so all plants of this type sold today presumably descend from the seeds that Bartram collected.

In 2007, work began on reconstruction of the terrace area in front of the church. It soon became apparent that the storm-drainage pipe serving the terrace was clogged, due to its being too small, and that a new one would be necessary to carry the runoff safely from the building. A corridor was chosen that had no recorded burials or gravestones; it had already been crossed by modern utility lines. Nevertheless, after the work had begun, archaeologist Alain C. Outlaw and his crew ran into several burial sites. Work was immediately shut down until proper permits could be gotten from the Virginia Department of Historic Resources, after which the remains were carefully removed and re-interred in the churchyard. The new terrace is now complete; it was formally presented in September 2007.

Of all the historic buildings whose grounds have been conserved through the efforts of the Garden Club of Virginia, Historic St. Luke's Church is perhaps the most surprising, and certainly one of the most moving. In its buttressed solidity and still secluded Southside Virginia setting, Historic St. Luke's Church harks back to America's early beginnings, as well as to Virginia's long and varied architectural heritage, in a way that no other building or setting can match. It is very far removed from the raucous world of the twenty-first century, and it is the privilege as well as the responsibility of the Garden Club of Virginia to help to keep it so.

*Front façade of
Sutherlin House*

The Sutherlin House
(Danville Museum of Fine Arts and History)

Restoration of the nineteenth-century perimeter fence to its original appearance

IT WAS APRIL 3, 1865, AND ULYSSES S. GRANT WAS PREPARING TO SEND UNION troops into Richmond, Virginia, then the capital of the Confederacy.[1] Confederate president Jefferson Davis, accompanied by members of his cabinet with the exception of the secretary of the navy Stephen Mallory, escaped that day by train. Traveling on the Richmond and Danville Railroad, they arrived in Danville, a town to the southwest located along the Dan River. Davis would spend the final week of the Confederacy as the guest of one of the town's prominent citizens, Major William T. Sutherlin. The Sutherlins' handsome Italian-style villa, completed in 1858, was located on the outskirts of town amidst a mature grove of trees. It takes little stretch of the imagination to envision Davis pushing open the gently swinging gate of the house's lovely picket fence as he approached.

Before the war, Major Sutherlin had established himself as an influential and successful tobacco businessman, banker, and town leader. As a delegate to the Virginia Convention of 1861, he had resisted secession, but that changed when the first shot was fired at Fort Sumter. Afterward, on April 17, 1861, he signed the ordinance by which Virginia repealed its ratification of the U.S. Constitution, establishing itself as a "Free and Independent State." Poor health prevented Sutherlin from actively serving in the military forces of the Confederacy, but he nevertheless rose to the rank of major as the quartermaster of Danville, which was a vital supply depot and arsenal.

During the week that Jefferson Davis stayed at the Sutherlin house, he slept in the back bedroom, perhaps because it offered a means of escape through the rear of the property. It is believed that several six-pounder cannons were placed on the south lawn during Davis's occupancy, more for effect than for actual use.

It was on a black marble–topped table, which is still housed in the building, that Davis signed the last official proclamation of the Confederacy, which stated with assurance that the Confederacy would endure. On April 10, 1865, however, Robert E.

Lee, commander of the Army of Northern Virginia, signed the papers of surrender at Appomattox. With Lee's surrender, Davis and his cabinet left Danville by train. At Greensboro, North Carolina, they split up, going their separate ways so as to complicate any pursuit. Davis was captured in Georgia about a month later, and temporarily imprisoned there.

About two weeks after Davis's departure, the Federal Army marched into Danville and Mayor J. M. Walker officially surrendered. Although no battles had been fought in the town or in the area immediately surrounding it, the townspeople had suffered heavy losses, both personal and material, since many men of the community had fought and died in battle elsewhere.

Years passed, and other grand houses were built nearby the Sutherlin mansion. The road in front eventually became Danville's West Main Street, also known as Millionaire's Row. Members of the family continued to live in the home until 1911. A granddaughter, Janie, then inherited it. She lived in Mississippi, so the house was sold and the contents auctioned off. Mr. Pearman, who had been Major Sutherlin's secretary, purchased a number of the items, and many others were sold to families along Millionaire's Row. After the building became a museum, numerous pieces were donated back.

Picket fence

THE SUTHERLIN HOUSE

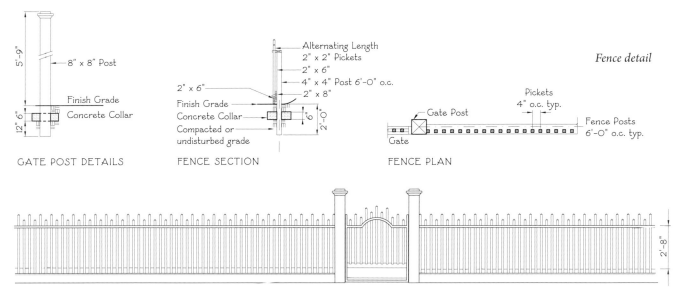

GATE POST DETAILS   FENCE SECTION   FENCE PLAN

Fence detail

FENCE AND GATE

When the house went on the market, a group of local women tried to raise enough money to buy it. They were unable to do so, and the mansion ended up in the hands of the city of Danville. It became a library in the 1930s, and remained such until 1974 when a new library was built. Throughout these changes, and continuing today, two of the mansion's upstairs rooms remained under the control of the United Daughters of the Confederacy.

While the house was a library, structural changes were made. The main staircase was moved; a secret stairway which ran to the upper floor from a downstairs bedroom was dismantled; and two wings were added. The ornate ceiling molding was covered when the ceilings were lowered to accommodate the library's needs. The molding was thus well preserved and easily restored when the lowered ceilings were later removed.

Following its years as a library, the house served as an art museum. A local group of citizens organized the art museum, and in 1984 they were recognized as a chapter of the Virginia Museum of Fine Arts. Today the Sutherlin Mansion is the home of the Danville Museum of Fine Arts and History.

IN 2000, THE GARDEN CLUB OF DANVILLE, UNDER THE LEADERSHIP OF MEG Clements, sought to have the grounds of the museum restored to their original design during the Sutherlins' tenure. The club approached the Restoration Committee of the Garden Club of Virginia with the request that they undertake the landscaping as one of the Garden Club's state projects.

William D. Rieley, landscape architect for the Club, produced two plans for consideration. The first would have restored the grounds to their appearance in the period 1860–80. This plan recognized that the Sutherlins' Italian-style villa in its parklike setting would have been on the cutting edge of fashion in its day, and that it had certainly been influenced by the ideas of Andrew Jackson Downing (1815–1852), who widely promoted the Romantic landscape. Originally set at the edge of town, with trees making up its predominant feature in an almost woodland setting, the Sutherlin house would have been a perfect example of Downing's theories. Under this plan, all plantings and other features that had been added to the garden since the 1860–80 period would be removed and the walkways reconfigured to their earlier, simpler pattern. In addition, a memorial garden would be established at the back of the house to contain the flags, pediments, statues, and other decorative objects that had been added to the front lawn since the 1860–80 period.

The second plan would have paid tribute to the various uses of the house over the years: as a home, a library, and a museum. It would have left in place such later elements as the boxwoods, a fountain, foundation plantings, more recently added trees, and what was thought to be a monument to the women of the Civil War (this turned out to be just the base of the monument, the statue itself having been mysteriously removed shortly after it was installed). But this plan, too, called for the relocation of some objects, including an obelisk that was topped by a Confederate flag, which stood by the front door, as well as the removal of a garden area in the southern section of the yard.

The Board of the Danville Garden Club favored the restoration to the earlier period, rather than an approach that celebrated the evolution of the property over the years. They did not feel, however, that it would be acceptable to remove all the memorials. The obelisk, with its Confederate flag, was a particularly problematic issue, since the land on which it stands had been deeded to a private organization. Without an agreement to pursue one of these two approaches, the Garden Club of Virginia elected instead to make a gift of one component of the garden that was common to both schemes: the replacement of the distinctive picket fence that was original to the house and that was well documented by late nineteenth-century photographs.

Bordering three sides of an entire city block, the restored fence is painted in the same polychromatic scheme as the house. It forms an elegant and suitable frame for the setting of this gracious building which has performed so many key roles in Danville's history. Along the east side of the property, posthole digging for the fence unearthed a six-pound solid-shot cannonball 3.67 inches in diameter. Balls of this kind required 1.25 pounds of black powder to be fired, and they were capable of traveling up to 1,523 yards. This particular ball was probably never fired, but it is evidence that cannons had been placed on the grounds during Davis's stay there.

The Danville Commission of Architectural Review approved the project, and P. L. Anderson and Son were contracted to construct the fence under Will Rieley's direction. The fence was completed and dedicated in October 2005 and is diligently maintained by the City of Danville.

Today, the gates gently swing open to welcome the museum's fourteen thousand annual visitors. They come for the art, and they come for the history, and they come to see where Jefferson Davis spent the last days of the Confederacy.

Sweet Briar house from
     entrance court

Sweet Briar College

SWEET BRIAR

*Eighteenth-century Sweet Briar House and grounds,
home to the college's president*

SWEET BRIAR COLLEGE FOR WOMEN WAS FOUNDED IN 1901 BY INDIANA Fletcher Williams in memory of her own daughter, Daisy.[1] Indiana was the daughter of a Vermont schoolmaster, Elijah Fletcher, who came to Virginia in 1810 to teach at Alexandria Academy. That first year, Fletcher boarded at nearby Hollin Hall, the home of George Mason's son, Thomson. The following year, he was offered a job as headmaster of a small academy in Amherst, and it was there that he met Maria Antoinette Crawford, of Tusculum, a nearby plantation. They were married in 1813. Two years later, the death of Maria's father occasioned a career change, as the schoolmaster found himself in charge of Tusculum and the seven other plantations that made up the Crawford estate. In 1818, the Fletchers moved to Lynchburg, where Elijah bought *The Virginian,* a Whig newspaper, and began a third career. Wearing this hat, he became a prominent civic leader, serving on the town council and being twice elected mayor of Lynchburg. In 1830, he bought a farm called Sweetbrier, which became part of an eventual landholding of eight thousand acres.

Sweetbrier was at first the Fletchers' summer home, but the estate and its plantations required supervision, so Elijah sold the newspaper in order to be able to attend to his other affairs. Some time later, the Fletcher family moved from Lynchburg to live full-time in the country. Their house was a two-story red-brick farmhouse, which the Fletchers altered and enlarged in 1851, adding the tower wings to transform the simple farmhouse into a very stylish Italian villa.

When the property eventually descended to their daughter Indiana, she changed the spelling of the name to two words, "Sweet Briar." Indiana married James Henry Williams, an Episcopal minister from New York, and they divided their time between New York and Sweet Briar. Their only daughter, Daisy, was born at Sweet Briar in 1867. She lived to be only sixteen, and when she died, her parents vowed to found a college for women in her memory. The result was Sweet Briar College, chartered by the Com-

Long-term plan

Earthen Terraces

Garage

Earthen Terraces

Arbor

Stone
Retaining Wall

Allée

Parking Terrace
Fence & Gate

Upper
Terrace

Pavilion

Garden
Cottage

Boxwood Room

SWEET BRIAR HOUSE

Boxwood
Circle

Brick Path

Retaining Wall

Parking Area

Overlook

Parking Area

NORTH

0'   15'   30'

monwealth of Virginia in 1901. The first class, made up of fifty-one students, entered in the fall of 1906. The five who graduated in 1910 received diplomas that were patterned after Elijah Fletcher's 1810 diploma from the University of Vermont. Sweet Briar has never changed that design.

Since its founding in 1906, Sweet Briar has had nine presidents, all of whom have chosen to live in Sweet Briar House. It is one of the state's finest expressions of the Italian villa style, listed on both the Virginia Historic Landmarks Register and the National Register of Historic Places. Its beautiful landscape is part of the Fletcher–Williams legacy. Their travels, coupled with their great interest in gardening, resulted in the introduction of exotic trees and plants into the original native planting around what was originally a simple country farmhouse. The boxwood circle and hedges, which by 2000 had grown big enough to obscure the house, were planted by the Fletchers. Daisy also had a garden of her own, though it was not the existing formal flower garden that is called "Daisy's Garden" in her honor. Daisy's Garden was designed in the 1990s by Mark Brimijoin, a landscape architect from the Amherst/Lynchburg area, and it replaced an earlier, smaller version designed by Elsetta Gilchrist Barnes, a graduate of the Cambridge School of Design.

IN 2001, ONE HUNDRED YEARS AFTER SWEET BRIAR College received its charter, its beautiful landscape was beginning to show signs of age, and the grounds around Sweet Briar House were faced with new needs. The college appealed to the Restoration Committee of the Garden Club of Virginia for a conceptual plan for the improvement and rearrangement of the entire grounds. The request was for a plan that would open up views of the mountains that had been obscured by overgrown box behind the house; add to the Fletchers' collection of trees, which had come to be a widely enjoyed arboretum; and create outdoor spaces around the house for the contemporary needs of a college president.

William D. Rieley's plan accomplished all these things, and the Restoration Committee concluded that its implementation should be a joint venture between Sweet Briar and the Garden Club of Virginia. Mrs. Robert Carter, the Restoration Committee chair, wrote to Dr. Elisabeth Muhlenfeld, Sweet Briar's president:

> We would like to collaborate on the landscaping of the front quadrant of the President's House. We would like the college to be responsible for the necessary grading, the removal of the existing roadway, and rebuilding the road. The Garden Club of Virginia would undertake the walls, paths, pruning and additional plantings. This would all be done according to our landscape architect, Will Rieley's plan. . . . If this appeals to the college, we will have an agreement drawn up, which will state what we will do, and commit the college to the maintenance of the landscape.[2]

The restoration of the front arrival court was formally presented to Sweet Briar on April 28, 2005, by Mrs. Robert C. Wood III, a Sweet Briar graduate, who had succeeded Mrs. Carter as chair of the Restoration Committee. In her remarks, Mrs. Wood described the collaboration:

> The GCV implemented the first stage of the plan with the new front arrival court and re-establishment of the arboretum. The bricked circle is bisected by a road and flanked by sorely needed parking areas, which the College installed. [The Garden Club of Virginia's] brick walls, walks and steps, which comprise a fairly complex masonry project, move up through an outer tier of huge American boxwoods and across the lawn approaching the house. [The walk] winds around the inside perimeter of a second tier of smaller boxwood that forms a circle, known to generations of students as the site of Sweet Briar's annual May Day tradition.[3]

The trees planted by the Fletcher–Williams family were more than a hundred years old. Some had had to be taken down; others were suffering the infirmities of old age. The Garden Club of Virginia's gift augmented and rejuvenated the arboretum by the addition of both native and exotic species: hackberry, yellowwood, cryptomeria, white ash, bougainvillea, goldenraintree, white oak, and parrot tree. Winter jasmine cascades over the brick wall.

The overgrown boxwood circle was successively pruned to open a vista, both toward and away from the house. The view from the house opens to a wide, rolling landscape, blocked off before by walls of boxwood. And if

New entrance court

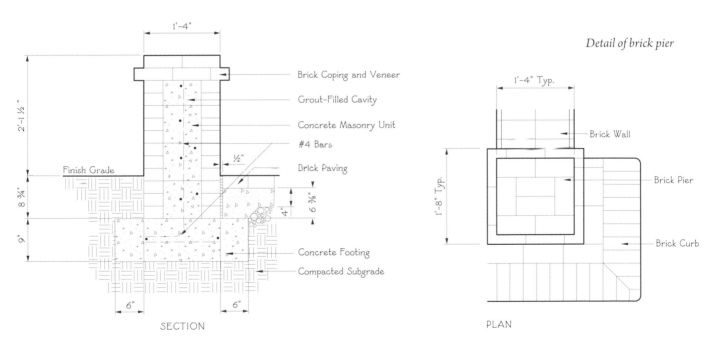

Detail of brick pier

SECTION

1'-4"

2'-1½"

Finish Grade

½"

8¾"

6⅜"

4"

9"

6"

6"

Brick Coping and Veneer

Grout-Filled Cavity

Concrete Masonry Unit

#4 Bars

Brick Paving

Concrete Footing

Compacted Subgrade

PLAN

1'-4" Typ.

1'-8" Typ.

Brick Wall

Brick Pier

Brick Curb

you look toward the house from the campus, the founders' Italian villa–style mansion is once again a focal point in the Sweet Briar landscape, beckoning both students and visitors to come in.

As Mrs. Carter wrote in her initial letter to Sweet Briar president Muhlenfeld, "Our members would be very happy to have a small part in the garden restoration at Sweet Briar." The members are very happy indeed.

University of Virginia Pavilions III and VI

Two pavilion gardens enclosed by serpentine walls

AFTER TWO TERMS AS PRESIDENT, THOMAS JEFFERSON CAME HOME TO CAM-
paign for a new institution of higher learning in Virginia. As he wrote to the French
architect Destutt Tracy, "This institution of my native State, the hobby of my old age,
will be based on the illimitable freedom of the human mind, to explore and to expose
every subject susceptible of its contemplation."[1]

On February 14, 1816, the Virginia legislature enacted into law a bill to establish
a college in the County of Albemarle. More than a year later, on May 5, 1817, a quo-
rum of visitors for the proposed college met to inspect a suitable tract of land that
was being offered for sale. Having examined the site, the visitors ratified a proposed
agreement to buy the land. Jefferson then wrote describing his project to his friends
William Thornton (who did the original designs for the U.S. Capitol) and Benjamin
Henry Latrobe (who as Architect of the Capitol had overseen the restoration of that
building after the War of 1812), asking them for suggestions. He had developed plans
for ten pavilions, or lodges—stately faculty houses with living quarters upstairs and
classrooms down, interspersed at regular intervals in two rows of student rooms, or
barracks, facing each other across a long, open, grassy space—the Lawn. Everything
would open onto inward-facing colonnades—covered walkways to give "dry commu-
nication between all the schools."[2]

Thornton answered right away with a lengthy and detailed letter that included
sketches of his ideas for columns instead of rectangular piers for the colonnade on
what would become the Lawn. Jefferson immediately accepted the suggestions, although he left the rectangular piers along the ranges. Latrobe was slower to respond,
but when he did, his main suggestion was an idea that had already occurred to Jefferson: close off the north end of the Lawn with a magnificent central building.[3] The
result was the Rotunda, a building inspired by the Pantheon in Rome, which was a

*Ionic capital in garden
of Pavilion III*

symbol of enlightenment. At the bottom of the Lawn, the vista was left open to the mountains.

On July 18, 1817, construction began on what is still affectionately known as "Mr. Jefferson's University." For the next seven years, until 1824, two years before he died, Jefferson made almost daily trips to supervise construction of his "academical village."

Taken as a whole, the Lawn is a textbook of classical architecture, since each pavilion façade employs a different version of the Roman classical orders. The space between each pavilion increases with its distance from the Rotunda. While Jefferson never explained this, some have theorized that the spacing was intended to compensate for the changing perspective as one looks south from the Rotunda; others have speculated that it was designed to exaggerate the perspective of the Rotunda when viewed from the south end of the Lawn, to make it appear larger and farther away; the less reverent say it was just dictated by the topography. An earlier design envisioned the landscape of the Lawn as an expanse of grass and trees. Today, a double row of shade trees lines each side in counterpoint to the architecture of the pavilions. Ash trees have been substituted for the black locusts Jefferson probably specified.

Behind the pavilions are garden spaces defined by serpentine walls. Two long alleys separate these walls from the West and East Ranges—additional rows of student rooms, facing outward and interspersed with a set of "hotels" where private families provided food for the students. Built later than the rooms and pavilions on the Lawn, they were nonetheless part of the original design. Cross-alleys give access to the Lawn. Jefferson saw the composition as a whole, in which buildings, layout, and landscape were one. The central quadrangle (200 feet by 600 feet) made up what was, and is still, the Lawn. The drawings showing the layout of the site, executed by Peter Maverick, a New York engraver whose services Jefferson engaged in 1822, are preserved at the University of Virginia Library. The serpentine garden walls were completed by 1824, but Jefferson left no specific plans for the gardens located between the Lawn and the Ranges, intending only that they should contain "embellishment of grounds by fancy"—his definition of gardening "as a fine art."[4] Pavilion residents were to design, plant, and maintain their own gardens.

Since Plato's time, if not before, gardens have been linked to the scholarly life. The pavilion gardens provided both a place to study and a subject of study, a typically Jeffersonian concept. He wrote that "such a plan would afford the quiet retirement so friendly to study."[5] Through the years, some of the pavilion gardens have seen smokehouses and sheds for small animals, but others were cultivated with great care and contained specimen plants significant to occupants of the day. Maximilian Schele de Vere, a Professor of Languages, cultivated a boxwood garden behind Pavilion IV. In 1826, the year of Jefferson's death, George Tucker, Professor of Moral Philosophy, planted an odd ash seedling he had brought down from the mountains in Pavilion IX. In 1845, when the Reverend William H. McGuffey moved in, he tended Tucker's tree, foregoing his own flower garden. Seated under the tree's sprawling branches, the Reverend would read his McGuffey readers to children. The McGuffey ash stood until 1989.

As residents came and went, the designs of the gardens changed. Small buildings were added; service roads were cut through the middle of all ten gardens; and new walls were built without respect for the original locations shown on the Maverick plan. The Garden Club of Virginia, in a departure from its usual precedent, recognized a need and offered to restore the gardens in the early 1950s. The challenge was to bring them back to their Jeffersonian character as historically accurately as possible. Alden Hopkins, then landscape architect for the Colonial Williamsburg

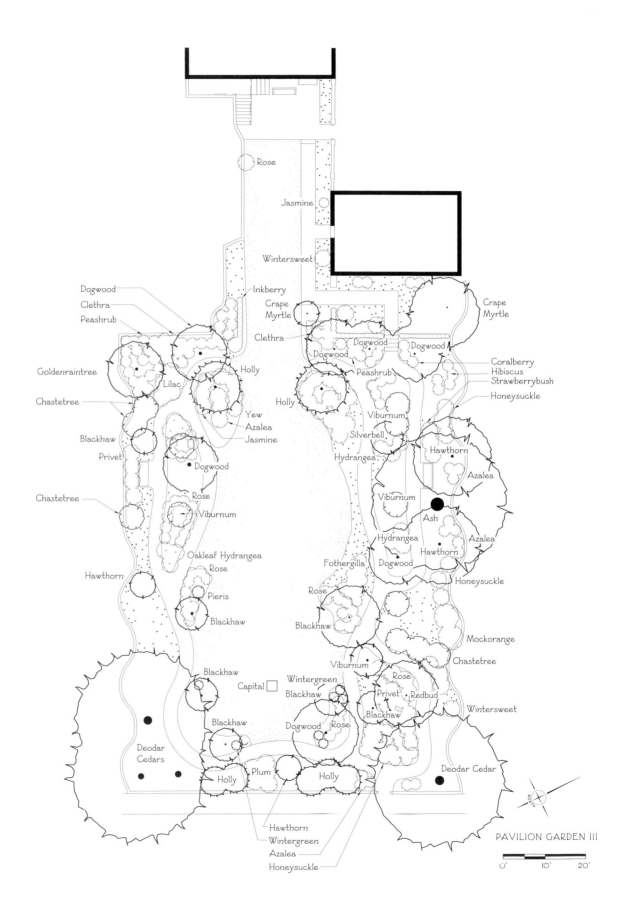

Rose

Jasmine

Wintersweet

Dogwood
Clethra
Peashrub

Inkberry
Crape
Myrtle

Crape
Myrtle

Clethra

Dogwood

Dogwood

Dogwood

Goldenraintree

Holly

Lilac

Peashrub

Coralberry
Hibiscus
Strawberrybush

Honeysuckle

Chastetree

Yew
Azalea
Jasmine

Holly

Viburnum

Silverbell

Hawthorn

Azalea

Blackhaw
Privet

Dogwood

Hydrangea

Chastetree

Rose

Viburnum

Viburnum

Ash

Azalea

Hawthorn

Oakleaf Hydrangea
Rose

Hawthorn

Hydrangea
Fothergilla

Dogwood

Hawthorn

Pieris

Rose

Honeysuckle

Blackhaw

Blackhaw

Mockorange

Blackhaw

Viburnum

Chastetree

Capital

Wintergreen
Blackhaw

Rose

Redbud

Privet
Blackhaw

Wintersweet

Blackhaw

Dogwood

Rose

Deodar
Cedars

Holly

Plum

Holly

Deodar Cedar

Hawthorn
Wintergreen
Azalea
Honeysuckle

PAVILION GARDEN III

0'   10'   20'

198

Foundation, was chosen to do the work. For archaeological excavations and research, his colleague James Knight was included in the restoration team. Hopkins developed conceptual plans for all the gardens, and he completed detailed construction documents for the West gardens. His approach was to reflect Jefferson's own design ideas.

Hopkins's plans followed the example of the pavilions on the Lawn: each garden distinct in its own right. He kept in mind the dual influences of classical French and naturalistic English landscape styles, using both in the plans for the ten gardens. Workmen reconstructed the garden walls using Peter Maverick's engravings from the 1820s, archaeological studies, and the surviving standing pieces. The graceful serpentine form of the walls is more than decorative; it makes possible a thickness of only one brick. "Necessary houses," or "privies," were reconstructed in six of the gardens, to serve as garden sheds.

Planted in the pavilion gardens are many of the flowers and shrubs that Jefferson grew in his gardens at Monticello, as well as those familiar to eighteenth-century gardeners and writers. Many of Jefferson's flowers were European (e.g., the Madonna lily), while others, like the Virginia bluebell, were the native plants he loved. Jefferson carried on a decades-long correspondence on the subject of horticulture with Bernard McMahon, the eighteenth-century nurseryman and one of Jefferson's great friends and admirers, much of which has been preserved. McMahon's introductions to American gardens include carnations, crown imperial lilies, and dwarf Persian irises. His snapdragons, double hyacinths, peonies, and African and French marigolds might have bloomed in pavilion flower beds. Dutch tulips, including parrot and striped varieties, were also wildly popular at that time.

The five West gardens had been restored by 1952 and were dedicated that year. When Hopkins died, his successor, Donald Parker, embarked on the preparation of detailed plans for the East gardens. Parker's drawings were based on Hopkins's conceptual plans and on his own consultations with Ralph Griswold. The East gardens were finally dedicated in 1965. Though different because of the topography—the West gardens are relatively flat and the East gardens are on a steep slope—the end result is equally impressive. True to Jefferson's vision, they are all beautiful settings for thought and study.

Native and exotic trees and shrubs beautify the restored pavilion gardens throughout the seasons—dogwood and redbud for spring and summer interest, maples for fall color, and hemlock and hollies in winter. Fruit trees, a utilitarian necessity on the nineteenth-century campus,

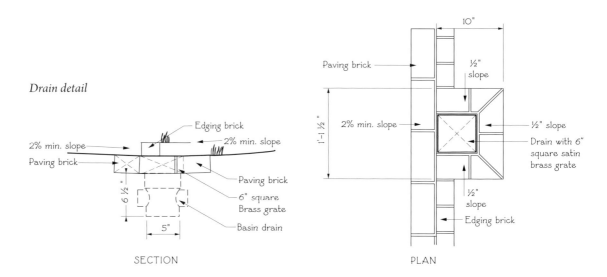

Drain detail

2% min. slope

Paving brick

Edging brick

2% min. slope

Paving brick

6" square
Brass grate

Basin drain

6 ½"

5"

SECTION

10"

Paving brick

½"
slope

2% min. slope

½" slope

Drain with 6"
square satin
brass grate

½"
slope

Edging brick

1'-1 ½"

PLAN

were also used extensively in the garden plans. The pavilion gardens include a young American sweetgum in the garden of Pavilion I; the native tulip poplar, Jefferson's "Juno of Our Groves," below the Pavilion IV garden;[6] and a spreading mimosa in the Pavilion VI garden.

In 1987, the University of Virginia and Monticello were named World Heritage Sites by the United Nations Educational, Scientific and Cultural Organization (UNESCO), joining the Taj Mahal, Versailles, and the Great Wall of China, among others.[7] In 1999, the American Society of Landscape Architects awarded its Centennial Medallion to the Academical Village, declaring it one of the nation's "most influential landscapes." In announcing the honor, the society cited the Jeffersonian precinct for its "enduring appeal" and its "perfectly proportioned balance between buildings and landscape."

From 1984 to 1989, the Garden Club and the University of Virginia undertook the first major repairs to the pavilion gardens. Because of the cost of the initial restoration, the original steps in the gardens had been made of railroad ties. In the revitalization of the 1980s, designed and directed by Rudy J. Favretti, the deteriorating railroad ties were replaced by cut-stone steps. The set of steps for each garden was different, so this was a complicated project. In addition, shade patterns had changed; some plants had died, while others had outgrown their allotted spaces. Constant use had made bare spots in the grass in many of the sunny gardens, and had completely worn away the turf in the shady woodland garden at the bottom of Pavilion VI. Gates were rotting, walls needed pointing-up, and some of the walks had drainage problems. These improvements were successfully completed, and the gardens were presentable again.

Pavilion III path and shrubberies

In 2003, the university asked for another revisitation. The garden restorations by now were more than fifty years old, and in the 1990s more problems had surfaced. Generations of gardeners and administrators had made incremental changes that had not been addressed in the refurbishments of the 1980s. The cumulative effect was that most of the original plants had disappeared or outgrown their intended role in the gardens. In many cases, the gardens had lost much of their original horticultural variety.

The Pavilion III garden was chosen as the first subject for revitalization. Alden Hopkins's original plans and his notes and correspondence were compared with the current state of the garden. It became clear that this garden had been transformed from a composition dominated by shrubs to one dominated by English ivy. In addition to the loss of original plants, the paths had sunk, resulting in drainage problems that caused further erosion and made the paths difficult to maintain. Garden Club of Virginia landscape architect William D. Rieley, working closely with University of Virginia landscape architect Mary Hughes, developed plans to replace the original plants

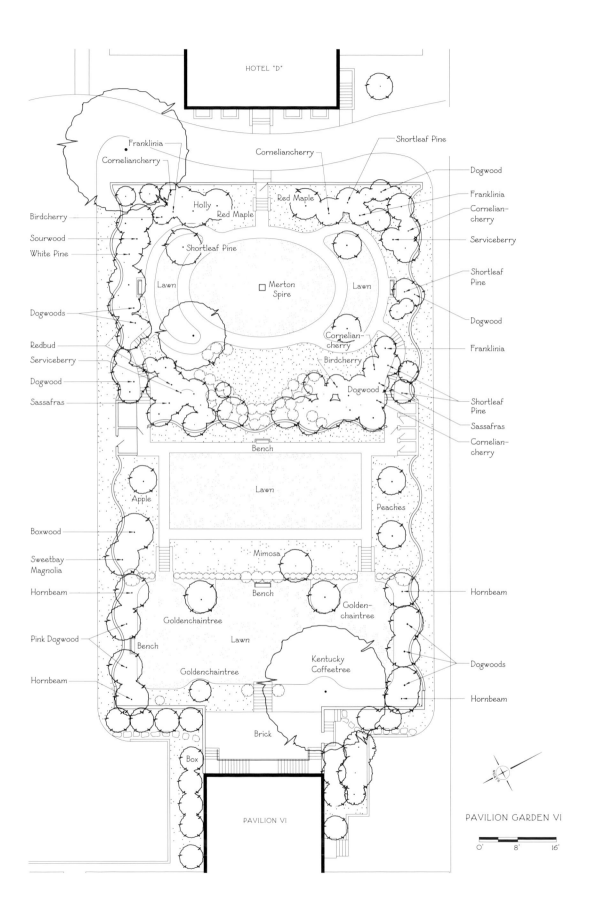

HOTEL "D"

Franklinia
Corneliancherry
Corneliancherry
Shortleaf Pine
Dogwood
Birdcherry
Holly
Red Maple
Red Maple
Franklinia
Cornelian-cherry
Sourwood
Shortleaf Pine
Serviceberry
White Pine
Shortleaf Pine
Lawn
Merton Spire
Lawn
Dogwoods
Dogwood
Redbud
Cornelian-cherry
Franklinia
Serviceberry
Birdcherry
Dogwood
Dogwood
Shortleaf Pine
Sassafras
Sassafras
Cornelian-cherry
Bench

Lawn

Apple
Peaches

Boxwood
Mimosa
Hornbeam
Sweetbay Magnolia
Bench
Hornbeam
Goldenchaintree
Golden-chaintree
Pink Dogwood
Lawn
Bench
Kentucky Coffeetree
Dogwoods
Hornbeam
Goldenchaintree
Hornbeam
Brick
Box

PAVILION VI

PAVILION GARDEN VI

0'   8'   16'

where possible, or make appropriate substitutions where current conditions made the use of the original plants impractical—where, for example, current shady conditions prevented the use of the original, sun-loving plants.

In addition to the horticultural adjustments, modern requirements dictated raising the grade at the entrance to the garden to eliminate steps (an obstacle to disabled access to the garden), and the elimination of an arch in the wall that had been built to accommodate a tree that had since died and been removed. These initiatives required the complete replacement of the west wall of the garden and the adjacent path.

Inside the garden, the paths were completely rebuilt, this time with a built-in drainage system, and were aligned as closely as possible to Hopkins's original plans. Rieley and Hughes have said that they feel the paths follow Hopkins's plan even more carefully than did the original construction. The resulting renovation of Hopkins's beautiful creation is now ready for the enjoyment and instruction of another generation of students, faculty, and visitors.

Having completed the renovation of the garden of Pavilion III, the Garden Club and the university turned their attention to the garden of Pavilion VI. In the summer of 2005, a severe storm had battered this garden. Several large trees had gone down in the lower garden, and the Merton Spire, given to the university by Oxford in 1928 in honor of Jefferson's educational ideals, had been damaged. The upper garden, directly behind Pavilion VI, was in generally good condition. The work there consisted of the replacement of brick edging and the addition of two trees that had been a part of the Hopkins-Parker-Griswold plan. The middle terrace had originally been conceived as an orchard of fruit trees planted in a quincunx, the pattern of the five dots on a die.

The lower garden was a woodland garden, its center punctuated by the Merton Spire. This garden had been the focus of too many gatherings, and the combination of shade and foot-traffic had turned the area around the spire into a surface of compacted dirt instead of the lawn proposed in the original plan. University landscape architect Mary Hughes suggested a solution to this problem: remove the fruit trees on the middle terrace and use that space for events; then the lower garden could return to being the quiet woodland envisioned by its original designers. The revitalization plan, which Rieley developed in association with Hughes, took this approach. Their plan shows replacement of the original species of trees and shrubs and reestablishment of the original configuration of the path. The Garden Club of Virginia and the University of Virginia are looking forward to the renewal of the vision of Griswold, Parker, and Hopkins.

*Washington and Lee
University chapel with brick
entrance terrace*

Washington and Lee University

The Lee Chapel landscape and the Lee House garden

THE INVOLVEMENT OF THE GARDEN CLUB OF VIRGINIA WITH THE RESTO-ration of the grounds of Washington and Lee University began in 1933, when the Blue Ridge Garden Club of Lexington approached the GCV for help. The request was "to consider the building of a Boxwood Memorial Garden to Robert E. Lee at his tomb on the grounds of Washington and Lee University."[1] This idea had the approval of both the Blue Ridge Garden Club and Dr. Francis P. Gaines, president of the college. A Ro-anoke landscape architect, Curtis Walton, had drawn a plan for an elaborate boxwood maze that would cover the hill to the side of the Lee Chapel. The trouble was that the maze would have been both expensive to install and impractical to maintain on such a steep slope. The Garden Club of Virginia, therefore, commissioned Charles F. Gillette to draw up an alternate plan; the plan he delivered was dated October 9, 1933. Exactly one year later, on October 9, 1934, Gillette also produced a second plan, "suggesting an Arrangement and Planting of Parking Areas for Washington and Lee University, made for the GCV." When *Historic Virginia Gardens,* by Dorothy Hunt Williams, was pub-lished by the Garden Club of Virginia in 1975, it was thought that these drawings had been lost, and so the record was incomplete. Since that time, both plans have come to light, and it is for this reason that Gillette's work is illustrated in the present volume.[2]

Washington and Lee University is the ninth-oldest institution of higher learn-ing in the nation.[3] It began as Augusta Academy, a small classical school for young men founded in 1749 by Scots-Irish settlers at Greenville, in Augusta County. After the Battle of Lexington, which occurred on on April 19, 1776, the school's trustees changed its name to Liberty Hall. The institution was kept alive through the Revolution by the support of the Presbyterian Church in the Shenandoah Valley. In 1780 it was moved to a ridge overlooking Lexington, and in 1782 the General Assembly of Virginia char-tered it as Liberty Hall Academy. The ruins of its major building, erected in 1793 and burned in 1803, are still preserved. After that fire, the school was moved a mile or so into town, where it put down permanent roots.

In 1796, Liberty Hall Academy was struggling with serious financial difficulties. George Washington came to the rescue with a gift of a hundred shares of stock in the James River Company, which the General Assembly of Virginia had voted him. Valued at $20,000, it was one of the largest gifts ever made to an educational institution up to that time; its dividends still make a contribution to the modern university's operating budget. As an expression of their gratitude, the trustees promptly renamed the school Washington Academy.

In 1865, at the end of the Civil War, the defeated Confederate general Robert E. Lee, homeless and virtually penniless, his world in shambles, retired along with his wife and family to Derwent, a modest cottage in Powhatan County, which had been offered to him by a generous friend. Lee's only thought was to retire quietly to the life of a farmer, and to somehow show by example how to rebuild both a life and a region. But, one day, according to Douglas Freeman, Lee's biographer,

> there came up to the road to Derwent, unannounced and unexpected, a tall and lanky gentleman with another summons to service to Virginia and the South.
>
> The visitor proved to be John W. Brockenbrough, rector of Washington College, Lexington, Va., and teacher of a private school of law in that town. To the complete surprise of General Lee, who had not been approached in any way, he stated that on August 4 the trustees of Washington College had unanimously elected the General president of the institution, and wished to know if he would accept.[4]

The story may be apocryphal, but it is said that the reason Mr. Brockenbrough came alone that day to Derwent, with no accompanying delegation, was that when the trustees had met to elect a new president, the state of their collective postwar wardrobes was such that it took the entire board to produce a single suit whole enough for a visit to their unanimously chosen candidate. It would not have been acceptable to call on General Lee in patches. Mr. Brockenbrough, as rector of the board, was thus equipped by the other members to represent them properly attired.

Almost three weeks later, General Lee wrote to the board with his conditional acceptance. His reservations had first to do with his own health: he did not feel strong enough to teach any classes along with his proposed duties as administrator. But, more important in his mind was the fact that, having been

> excluded from the terms of amnesty in the proclamation of the President of the U.S. of the 29th May last, and an object of censure to a portion of the

206   WASHINGTON AND LEE UNIVERSITY

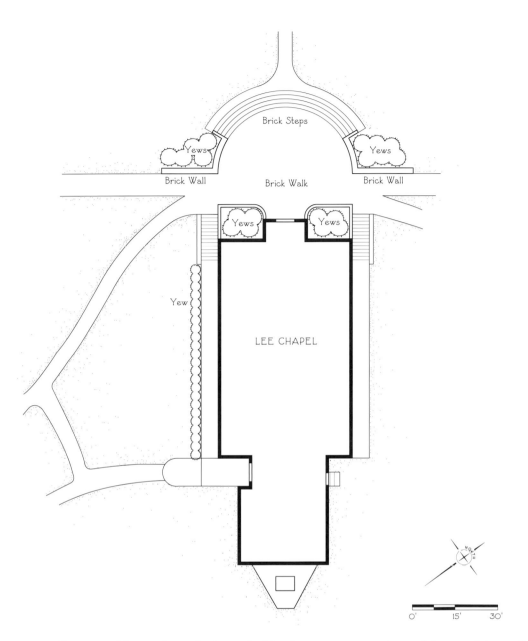

Country, I have thought it probable that my occupation of the position of president might draw upon the College a feeling of hostility; and I should, therefore, cause injury to an institution which it would be my highest desire to advance. . . .

Should you, however, take a different view, and think that my services in the position tendered to me by the Board will be advantageous to the College and Country, I will yield to your judgment and accept it; otherwise, I must most respectfully decline the office.[5]

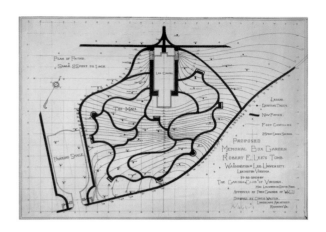

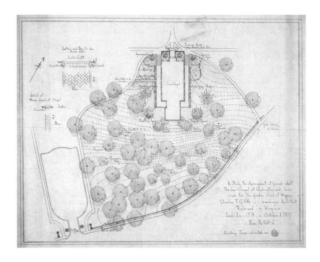

Above: *Plan for boxwood maze behind chapel, never executed*

Below: *Gillette plan for same hillside*

The Board, again unanimously, was delighted to rise above his reservations and announce his appointment. It was a decision, says Lee's biographer, "that symbolized not for himself only but likewise for the entire South a turning from war and politics to peace and education."[6]

The college opened its doors in September 1865 with four professors and "a thin platoon of students."[7] Lee's next two years were spent in putting the college on a sound financial footing; in doubling the curriculum; in establishing the first school of journalism in the country, as well as the schools of engineering and law; and in partially restoring the school's library.

As the college's endowment grew, the trustees went to work on improving the buildings and grounds. The first priority was the construction of new academic buildings to accommodate the burgeoning faculty and student body. In 1867, a new chapel was authorized, at a cost not to exceed $10,000, and the trustees also adopted a resolution for the construction of a new President's House (now called Lee House), as soon as the funds could be found. Lee took a great interest in the campus landscape, planting ash trees and planning the walk in front of the chapel, which he insisted should be simple and surrounded by trees. By May of 1869 the new President's House was ready, and the Lees moved in. General Lee died in that house sixteen months later, and was buried in the chapel which he had helped to design. After his death, the name of the college was changed again, to Washington and Lee. The next college president, aptly named for his maternal grandfather, was George Washington Custis Lee.

OVER HALF A CENTURY LATER, IN 1933, THE GARDEN CLUB OF VIRGINIA WAS asked to install the boxwood memorial garden, mentioned at the outset, adjacent to the Lee Chapel. According to Gillette's tactful description, "After study of the terrain it was realized that a boxwood walk or maze was not the solution, and a plan using other material was drawn for the chapel area."[8] The actual installation consisted of a wide concrete walkway in front of the chapel, with three narrower walks—leading from the campus, from the town, and from the parking lot at the bottom of the hill—converging on it.

Lee House

Having completed this phase, Gillette turned his attention to the entrance gates and parking lot below the chapel. This is the main entrance to the campus from Lexington's Jefferson Street. Gillette described it as having "very large gates leading to nothing but a parking space [with] no chance of ever carrying a roadway through these gates to the campus."[9] The "very large gates" to which Gillette referred are the War Memorial Gates, which were dedicated in 1920 as a memorial to alumni who had died in World War I. Today, plaques honor Washington and Lee alumni who died in World War II, Korea, Vietnam, and the Persian Gulf War as well. Gillette agreed that the area should be the place for some sort of memorial garden, and he suggested enclosing the parking lot with a hedge of tree box, paving it "properly" with cobblestone and brick, and fitting a statue of either Washington or Lee into the hillside opposite the entrance gates. This plan was considered too ambitious, but the Restoration Com-

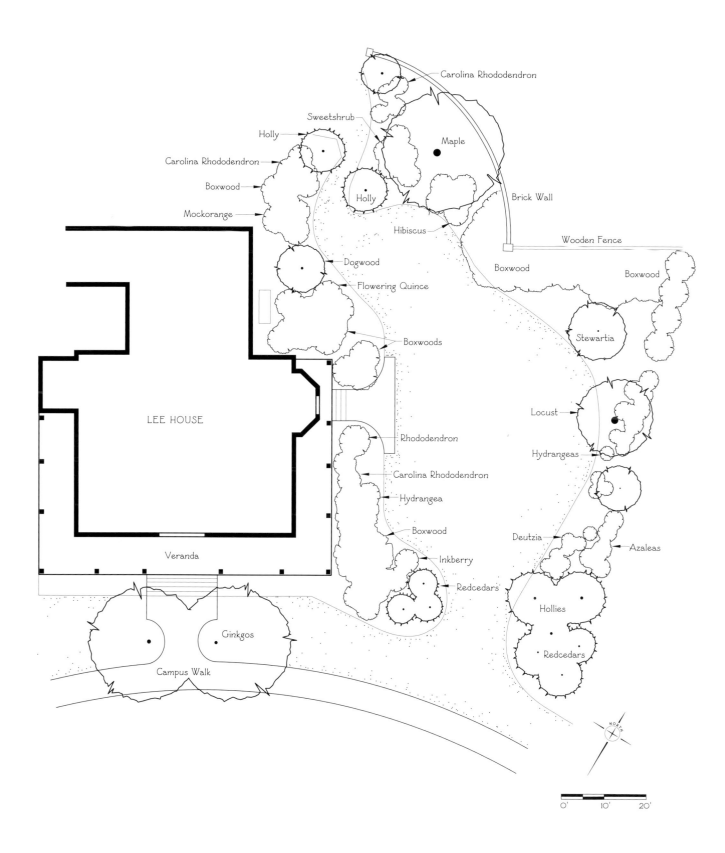

Carolina Rhododendron

Sweetshrub

Holly

Carolina Rhododendron

Boxwood

Mockorange

Maple

Holly

Hibiscus

Brick Wall

Wooden Fence

Boxwood

Boxwood

Dogwood

Flowering Quince

Stewartia

LEE HOUSE

Boxwoods

Rhododendron

Locust

Carolina Rhododendron

Hydrangeas

Hydrangea

Boxwood

Deutzia

Azaleas

Inkberry

Redcedars

Hollies

Veranda

Ginkgos

Redcedars

Campus Walk

NORTH

0'   10'   20'

WASHINGTON AND LEE UNIVERSITY

mittee agreed to a simplified version that kept the boxwood hedge, substituted a flag for the statue, left existing elms in place, and added shade and magnolia trees on the steep hillside leading to the chapel entrance.

Some forty-odd years later, in 1974, the Garden Club of Virginia received another request to underwrite improvements to the landscape around the chapel at Washington and Lee. The university had contracted with the firm of Griswold, Winters and Swain (later GWSM) to update the campus landscape. Ralph Griswold's hand is thus evident in the plan for the chapel entrance, the installation of which was supervised by the project architect, W. Thomas Borellis. Under the new plan, the old concrete walkway in front of the chapel was replaced by a semicircular brick platform. The terrain required that a retaining wall be cut into the hill to level the platform, but a more elegant solution was found by repeating the semicircle of broad brick steps connecting the chapel platform to the walk leading up to the colonnaded Washington Hall at the top of the hill.

The chapel doorway was flanked by rectangular planting beds set into the platform and outlined with brick coping; these were planted with yew and periwinkle. The simplicity of this unadorned green planting scheme balances that of the classical white colonnade of the academic buildings. It also reflects the dignity that was the

Shrub border defining garden

hallmark of General Lee and suits the simplicity of the Victorian chapel he helped to plan. The terrace and plantings were officially presented to Washington and Lee in September 1977.

In the 1990s, the campus was again renovated by the firm of GWSM. The renovations, designed by Thomas Borellis, included improvements to the parking lot. At that time, the brick wall that Gillette had suggested was built along Jefferson and Washington Streets and tied into the War Memorial Gates. As part of this renovation, the Garden Club of Virginia was asked to make a garden for entertaining next to the President's House. An old engraving shows this space bounded by a board fence, defining it as part of the lawn around the house. The restoration plan, drawn by Rudy J. Favretti in January 1998, separated the space on the east side of the house from the rest of the campus with a shrub border instead of a fence. The border, made up of spring-flowering shrubs, boxwood, hollies, cedars, and a small grove of stewartias, curves around to the northeast corner of the house, which is bolstered by an existing maple. The resulting lawn is an enclosed space suitable for private receptions, but one that can be open to the public when it is not being used for university entertainments. One can enter not only by the steps from the wide veranda of the house but also through an opening in the shrubbery from the front of the house and the driveway.

It is interesting to contemplate the changes in the role of a university and its president from one century to the next as reflected in the changes to its campus. The presidents of Washington and Lee have made these transitions carefully and gracefully. The university's greatly increased affluence and national reputation notwithstanding, Washington and Lee has remained faithful to the principles of the two remarkable Virginians whose names it bears.

Woodrow Wilson Presidential Library
at His Birthplace

An intricate landscape of terraces and parterre gardens

WOODROW WILSON WAS BORN IN THE PRESBYTERIAN MANSE IN STAUNTON, Virginia, in 1856.[1] His father, Dr. Joseph Ruggles Wilson, was pastor of Staunton's First Presbyterian Church from 1855 to 1857. The Manse, situated on top of the hill that rose above the church, had been built by the congregation in 1845. John Fifer, the contractor and builder, not only helped lay the bricks for the house, he also made them, in his yard on the turnpike just a mile from Staunton. Behind the new Manse, the land fell sharply away to the west. There was a path leading down the hill past the barn to the church, but there were no terraced gardens then for the Reverend Dr. Wilson to walk through.

Facing east on Coalter Street, a main artery of the town, the front of the plain Greek Revival dwelling has two stories. On the west side, the steep slope exposes an additional full lower story opening onto a flat terrace. Here, round pillars on pedestals extend the full height of the house, supporting porches for the two upper stories. The Manse is known in Staunton simply as "the Birthplace," no matter what more comprehensive title it may have. Having undergone significant renovations since 1979, it is now restored to its original appearance and provides a glimpse into life in the pre–Civil War Shenandoah Valley. Its surroundings and contents are plain but gracious, warm and dignified, a testament to the peaceful, harmonious, rich home life that cushioned the early years of our twenty-eighth president.

Inside the Manse are many Wilson family artifacts and period furnishings, authentic reproduction wallpaper, and mid-nineteenth-century Brussels and Scotch ingrain carpeting. The staid, unassuming dwelling brings President Wilson to life as an author, scholar, university president, governor, and statesman. The many personal possessions and memorabilia of his illustrious career provide an understanding of his family background and his life. His restored Pierce-Arrow limousine is now housed permanently in the museum garage beside the Manse.

The Manse from the garden at Woodrow Wilson Presidential Library

WOODROW WILSON PRESIDENTIAL LIBRARY

The Reverend Dr. Wilson's will, the family Bible in which he recorded the birth of his first son, at "12¾ o'clock at night," and the famous letter that Woodrow Wilson, then a young college professor, wrote to his father saying that he was the greatest influence in his life, are all back home in the Manse. In 1912, as a candidate for the presidency of the United States, Wilson made a great effort to emphasize his Staunton birth, a fact that did much to assuage the South's mistrust of his having served as governor of New Jersey, and which eventually won him the presidential election.

Reclaimed wrought-iron fence

The church sold the Manse to Mary Baldwin College in 1929, with the understanding that it could be conveyed at a later date to a "society for the perpetuation of the name and fame of Woodrow Wilson." Mary Baldwin held title to the Manse for the next ten years, during which time volunteers kept the house open to accommodate a growing number of visitors. Concurrently, a foundation to purchase the birthplace was organized, with contributions from Wilson's widow, the Virginia General Assembly, and other private donors.

IN 1932, THE GARDEN CLUB OF VIRGINIA RESPONDED TO REQUESTS TO HELP with the garden at the Manse. While there were no official records indicating what the gardens had looked like, the journal of the Manse's first resident, the Reverend Benjamin Mosby Smith, indicated the existence of a garden. Richmond landscape architect Charles Gillette, then retained by the Garden Club of Virginia, found in his own files a letter containing a plan for a garden at the Staunton Manse, drawn by the Reverend W. E. Baker sometime after the Wilsons' tenure there. Since he had no other guide, Gillette used the suggestions regarding plant material contained in this letter, incorporating them into his own design. Otherwise, the garden is pure Gillette, and there is no thought that it was a restoration or re-creation of an earlier garden. It is a 1930s Colonial Revival garden with Victorian accents.

The steep terrain begged for terraces, although there was no evidence to suggest that they had been there earlier. On the lowest of the terraces, Gillette designed Victorian bowknot flowerbeds outlined by low clipped boxwood, now overgrown. A flight of brick steps leads to the uppermost terrace, with a walk continuing directly to the Manse. A short allée of flowering trees shades the walk and provides spectacular clouds of white blooms in May. On either side of the central walk are two panels of lawn neatly edged with brick. At the far ends, Gillette suggested a Victorian sum-

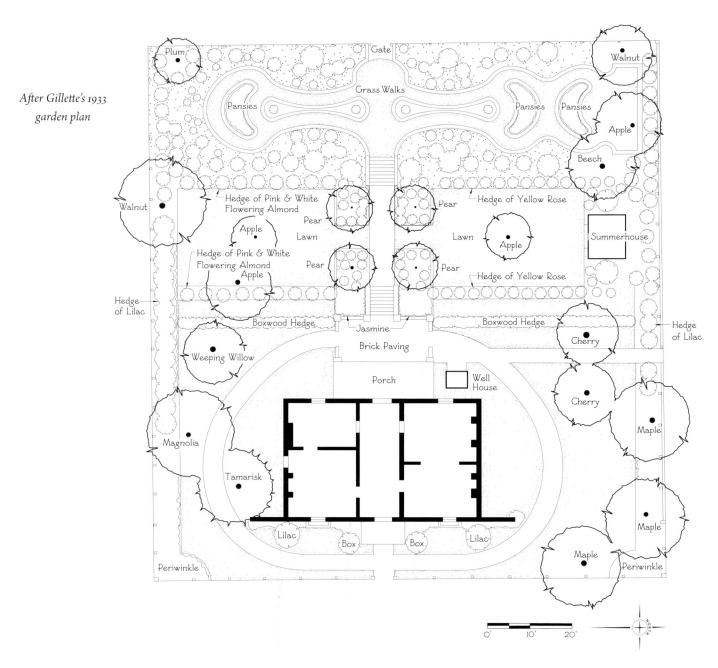

After Gillette's 1933 garden plan

merhouse, well house, and grape arbor, all brick-floored. Gillette's plan also called for replacing the existing concrete sidewalks near the house with brick, as concrete would not have been authentic to the period. After much debate, a brick wall was designed and built on the Frederick Street boundary; it replaced a wooden fence that required far too much maintenance. The rake of the brick wall followed the ground and was topped with a molded brick coping. Appropriate furniture was placed strategically to make the garden comfortably inviting.

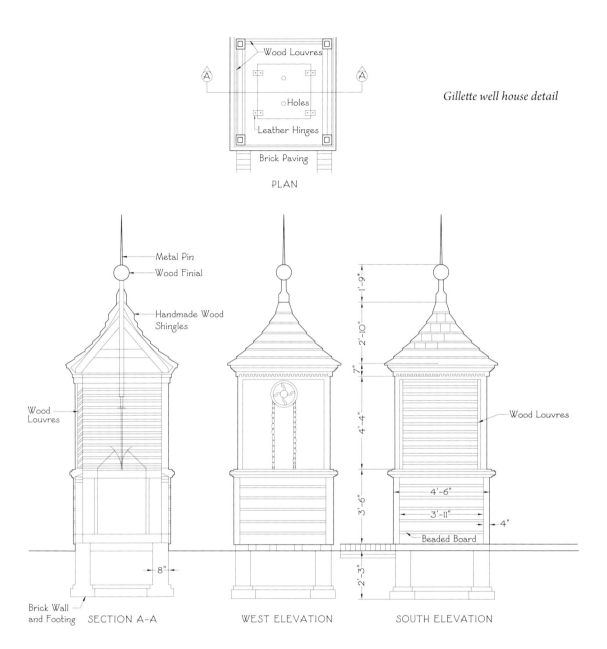

Gillette well house detail

PLAN

Wood Louvres

Holes

Leather Hinges

Brick Paving

Metal Pin

Wood Finial

Handmade Wood Shingles

Wood Louvres

Brick Wall and Footing

SECTION A-A

WEST ELEVATION

SOUTH ELEVATION

Wood Louvres

Beaded Board

1'-9"

2'-0"

7"

4'-4"

3'-6"

2'-3"

4'-6"

3'-11"

4"

8"

The 1933 garden restoration gift by the Garden Club of Virginia inspired other gifts greatly needed for renovating and furnishing the house itself. In 1940, a front porch was removed and replaced with one more appropriate to the period. The Garden Club of Virginia made further donations to help defray the cost of rebuilding the front wall on both sides of the new porch. GCV funds were also used to refine the planting of the Gillette plan of 1933. As visitation grew, the grass garden paths became difficult to maintain. In 1960, the Garden Club replaced many of them with brick. Old bricks were used, laid in sand and following Gillette's pattern of almost thirty years earlier. At the same time, Gillette refurbished the southwest end of the second terrace. He designed a simple white garden to set off the gift of a collection of pink tree peonies from a distinguished garden in Lexington that was being dismantled.

In 1967–68, the Garden Club of Virginia returned again to the Manse. This time, a lower terrace was added, connecting the garden with a newly constructed parking lot immediately below the Woodrow Wilson property. Ralph Griswold, the landscape architect engaged for this endeavor, managed successfully to blend the practical with the aesthetic; his transitional terrace preserved the Gillette garden while meeting the need for parking access.

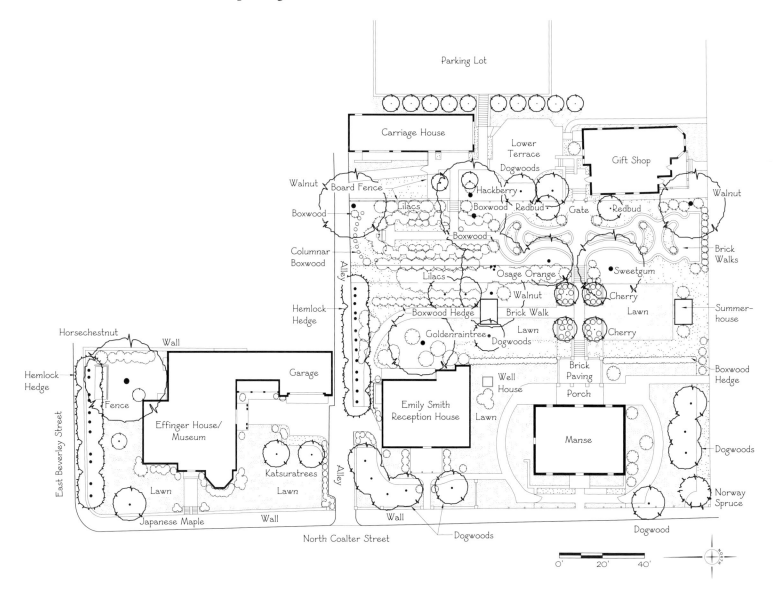

WOODROW WILSON PRESIDENTIAL LIBRARY

Gillette's bowknot
garden

In 1990, the Woodrow Wilson Museum opened in a handsome mansion in the same block. The museum contains exhibits of the life and times of the twenty-eighth president. The historic site complex actually consists of four separate sites brought together by a common landscape. The garden and the courtyard outside the museum are additional gifts of the Garden Club of Virginia, its third restoration project at the Manse. Designed in 1992 by Rudy J. Favretti, the new gardens replaced a parking lot and tied the museum building together with the older gardens behind the Manse and the Emily Smith Reception House. An iron and brass balustrade, originally a roof decoration, was reborn as a fence to frame a curved section of the paved museum forecourt; this space doubles as an area to accommodate the president's Pierce-Arrow and its maintenance. A lawn edged by a perennial garden was created between the forecourt and street. Two katsuratrees are planted within the garden.

In 2000, Will Rieley and Robert Self, the architectural conservator at Monticello, inspected the summerhouses. This inspection revealed that both structures, one a part of the original Gillette plan and the other a flanking one added by Ralph Griswold, were in a very bad state of disrepair. So too was the Colonial Revival well house

WOODROW WILSON PRESIDENTIAL LIBRARY

that Gillette had designed. As the buildings were carefully opened up and measured it became apparent that much of all three structures had to be replaced. Plans were drawn to reflect the exact configuration of each building; the rooflines of the two summerhouses were found to be slightly different, and this eccentricity was reproduced in the restoration. Complete Carpentry Services of Churchville rebuilt all three structures, retaining all of the original fabric that it was practical to keep. This renovation will extend the life of these charming and essential elements of the garden for generations to come.

In 2006, the foundation requested a rejuvenation of Gillette's white garden at the southwest end of the second terrace. Will Rieley's plan called for planting new white lilacs on the peripheries, trimming overgrown box, and restoring the white perennials under Mrs. Gilliam's tree peonies. The refurbished garden, implemented in 2007, was in full flower by the spring of 2008.

For some time now, the Woodrow Wilson Presidential Library has been bursting at the seams. After years of study, the foundation has purchased the house adjacent to the museum on Beverley Street. The rear of the newly purchased building, which will soon house the long-awaited expansion of the library, overlooks the refurbished white garden. The Garden Club of Virginia salutes the foundation for its commitment to the conservation of the fabric of historic Staunton and to the preservation of the restored garden, and it looks forward to working with the administration as the Woodrow Wilson Presidential Library expands into its new quarters.

The Manse from the garden gate

Looking into the garden
at Yeardley House

Yeardley House

*A commemorative garden on the site
of a 1920s rose garden*

ORDINARILY, THE DIRECTOR OR THE BOARD OF A HISTORIC PROPERTY COMES
to the Garden Club of Virginia with a request for help. But every now and then, just as
at the University of Virginia, a project comes up that is so important that the Garden
Club steps forward to help. Such was the case with the preparations for the 400th
anniversary celebrations at Jamestown Island. There were various ideas for possible
projects, and the Restoration Committee finally decided that the most useful and appropriate thing to do would be to create a garden at the Yeardley House. Built in 1907
for the 300th anniversary of the landing at Jamestown, the Yeardley House was originally designed as a caretaker's cottage, but it was named in honor of the governor who
established both the first representative body in America, which later became the Virginia House of Burgesses, and the individual ownership of land.

George Yeardley (1587–1627) served two terms as governor at Jamestown, from
1618 to 1621, and again from 1626 to 1627. He arrived in Virginia fresh from service in
the Lowlands as a young military officer, and his first trip to the American colony was
a decidedly roundabout one.[1] He was among a party of adventurers who left England in the spring of 1609 in a convoy of nine ships carrying a total of five hundred
passengers, all under the command of Sir George Somers. Yeardley, along with Sir
Thomas Dale and John Rolfe and his first wife (the widowed Rolfe would later marry
the princess Pocahontas), was on the *Sea Venture,* the admiral of the fleet, captained
by Christopher Newport. Another passenger was one William Strachey, whose 1610
letter "to a Noble Lady," describing the voyage, is thought to have been the inspira-
tion for Shakespeare's play *The Tempest.*[2] During the crossing, a hurricane scattered
the fleet, wrecking the *Sea Venture* on the island of Bermuda. Under Newport's command, the survivors managed to salvage timbers from the wreckage, and with the addition of Bermuda cedar taken from the island, they were able to build two small ships,
the *Deliverance* and the *Patience,* in which they continued their voyage, arriving at

Jamestown in 1610. When they got there, they found that four of the ships from the original fleet—the *Falcon*, the *Blessing*, the *Lion*, and the *Unity*—had arrived safely, more or less on schedule. The rest had been lost. One of the passengers on the *Falcon* was a thirteen-year-old girl named Temperance Flowerdew, who would return to England sometime before 1618, the year that she and George Yeardley were married there.

At the time of his arrival in Jamestown, Yeardley was only a young captain, but he was obviously a man of ability and courage. When, six years later, in 1616, Governor Sir Thomas Dale accompanied John Rolfe and his new bride, the Indian princess Pocahontas, on their trip to England, he put Yeardley in charge as acting governor of the colony until Dale's replacement should arrive.

George Yeardley also made the return trip to England, in 1617. The next year was a busy one for him: he was knighted, appointed governor of the Virginia colony, and married Temperance Flowerdew. The newlyweds then spent their honeymoon sailing back to Virginia.

In 1619, acting on instructions of the London Company, Governor Yeardley convened the first English colonial representative assembly in the New World. He also persuaded his superiors that individual land ownership would be a compelling incentive to bring more settlers to Virginia. Prior to that time, individual ownership of three acres per man had been reserved as a reward for hard work in the colony. Otherwise, all the land belonged to the Crown. The London Company paid quitrent to the crown, and reaped all the profits.[3]

Gateposts recycled from old Jamestown churchyard

YEARDLEY HOUSE

Yeardley was succeeded as governor in 1621 by Sir Francis Wyatt. By then, he had taken out his own patent on a large holding on the south side of the James, so he stayed on in Virginia to manage his plantation, Flowerdew Hundred, named for his bride. During the Massacre of 1622, Yeardley's plantation escaped major carnage and the Yeardleys were unharmed. When Wyatt went back to England in 1626, Sir George Yeardley returned to Jamestown to serve once again as governor, a post he held until his death in 1627.

Yeardley was a popular and successful governor. On his watch, new settlements were planted, new parishes were established, churches were built, courts met on a regular basis, and the balance of power in Virginia began to tilt away from the Crown in favor of the colonists.

Old sundial and new bower

IN 1907, IN FRONT OF THE HOUSE THAT HAD BEEN named in honor of George Yeardley, was a rose garden, with a rose for each state. The garden was bordered by a rectangle of boxwood and had a gate and a sundial. In 2005, the remains of that garden still had its boxwood edge, greatly overgrown, but grass panels had replaced the roses. The garden gate was gone, and two crossing paths bisected the rectangle. The sundial stood at the intersection of these two paths.

The new garden, designed and implemented by William D. Rieley, is not a restoration of the old one. There is no caretaker's wife to maintain it now, and a rose garden would not be useful, either as a ceremonial space or as a place for the other gatherings that take place in the garden today. The space is the same box-bordered rectangle; the remaining box bushes have been supplemented with new ones across the front. The paths divide now into an oval that defines a central space of grass with planting around the outside perimeter of the path. The sundial is still in the center, and arbors with benches are located at each end of the cross-path. They are patterned after architectural details on the Yeardley House and will eventually support roses, to recall the earlier garden. The posts of the new gate are the old gateposts from the yard of the seventeenth-century Jamestown church, a gift from the Association for the Preservation of Virginia Antiquities. Rieley was careful to leave open the wide view of the James River. The virgin forest is gone, but the James, though muddier, is still the

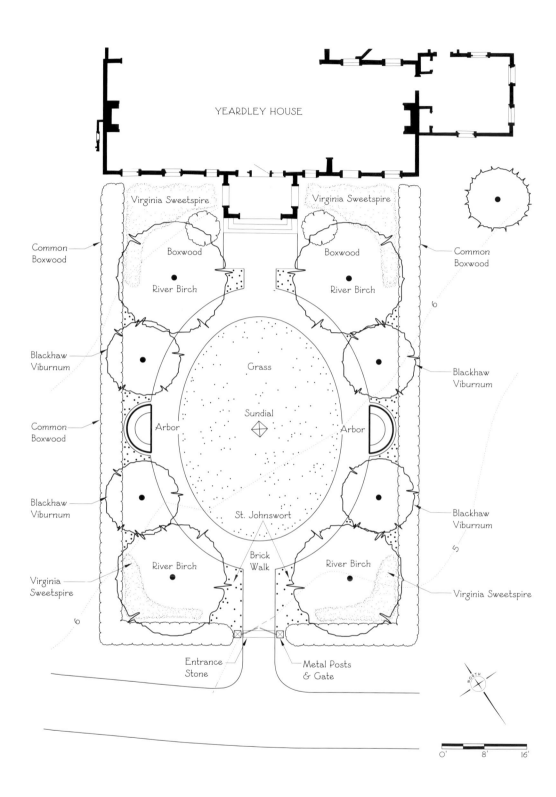

YEARDLEY HOUSE

Virginia Sweetspire

Virginia Sweetspire

Common Boxwood

Common Boxwood

Boxwood

Boxwood

River Birch

River Birch

Blackhaw Viburnum

Blackhaw Viburnum

Grass

Common Boxwood

Sundial

Arbor

Arbor

Blackhaw Viburnum

Blackhaw Viburnum

St. Johnswort

Blackhaw Viburnum

River Birch

Brick Walk

River Birch

Virginia Sweetspire

Virginia Sweetspire

Entrance Stone

Metal Posts & Gate

NORTH

0'   8'   16'

same river where the *Susan Constant,* the *Godspeed,* and the *Discovery* dropped sail and
anchor in 1607, putting their sea-weary passengers ashore to found a nation.

The archaeologists working at Jamestown under the direction of William Kelso
have made dramatic discoveries. They have verified the shape of the fort, uncovering
the "palisado" described by John Smith. They have discovered the foundations of a
government house that was grander and much more extensive than previously imag-
ined. Arthur Allen's brick house (see the essay on Bacon's Castle) is suddenly understood as part of a pattern, not the unique anomaly it was thought to be. In laying out
the Yeardley House garden, Rieley had to be constantly careful not to disturb the site
in any way that would destroy valuable archaeological evidence. When the garden was
put in, the archaeologists themselves dug the planting holes so they could be sure no
damage was done. This kind of meticulous attention is a far cry from the early days of
the preservation work of the Garden Club of Virginia.

At this writing, in the fall of 2007, the Yeardley House garden is very new. It is an
interesting time to visit it because the sophistication of the design is plain to see: the
repetitive arches of the gate and the two arbors mirror the arch of the porch leading to
the front door of the house, and this theme is emphasized by the curving sweep of the
brick walkway defining the central oval of grass. You can also see that the diamond pat-

terns on the bottom of the gate and the backs of the arbors echo the diamond panes of the windows of the house.

In a year or two, when the plants have filled in and festoons of roses have hidden the details of the arches, go back and stand on the steps of the house and look out toward the James River a few yards away. If the banks of the river had been cleared in 1610, George Yeardley's view would have been very much the same from that vantage point.

APPENDIX A

The Beginnings of Garden Week in Virginia

THE FIRST SO-CALLED "RESTORATION" OF THE GARDEN CLUB OF VIRGINIA was the Kenmore garden in Fredericksburg, which became the impetus for the beginning of Historic Garden Week in Virginia. The Kenmore garden is pure Colonial Revival. Few traces of an eighteenth-century garden could have survived the residential development that occurred on the Kenmore site, or its subsequent removal (see chapter 10). But as a Colonial Revival garden, its history includes most of the big names in the Colonial Revival period in Virginia: Arthur Shurcliff, James Greenleaf, Charles Gillette, Alden Hopkins, Ralph Griswold, and Rudy J. Favretti. Gillette, Hopkins, and Favretti produced three different master plans over a sixty-year span; Shurcliff and Greenleaf were early consultants; Griswold was asked by the GCV to address specific problems arising from a new building on the site.

The involvement of the Garden Club of Virginia in the Kenmore garden began on February 22, 1924, George Washington's birthday. He would have been 192 years old; the Garden Club of Virginia was four. Mrs. Thomas Wheelwright, then president of the GCV, visited Kenmore with her friend, Mrs. Frank Duke. According to Mrs. Wheelwright, Mrs. Duke "was interested in the re-furnishing of the house."

> I inadvertently remarked that the outside might be given a little attention with profit to the appearance of the place. Mrs. Smith,[1] now Field Secretary [of the DAR], was in the midst of a struggle to raise money for the purchase of the property. She is ever awake to the interest of Kenmore. It lies next to her heart, and my remark registered with her immediately. "Oh, Mrs. Wheelwright," she said, "you are the President of The Garden Club of Virginia, and if you ladies would undertake to improve the grounds, it would be a wonderful help and a splendid thing to do." I agreed with her. I wrote to Mr. Greenleaf, then President of the Landscape Architects of America to know if he would be interested enough to meet me at Kenmore with Mr. Gillette, and confer with us on a plan of planting and advise us how to proceed. I asked Mrs. Fairfax Harrison

and Mrs. Frank Duke to join us there. We had a very instructive and agreeable meeting at Kenmore, and a visit to Chatham, where the two gentlemen exchanged ideas and pointed out what was best to do. Mr. Greenleaf agreed to look over the completed plan and act as consultant with Mr. Gillette, who agreed to take over the work entirely as further visits to Kenmore and office work would be quite impossible for Mr. Greenleaf, he said.

At a subsequent meeting of the ladies at Kenmore, they suggested that we furnish them a good workable plan, acceptable to them and to the Garden Club of Virginia, which they could carry out from time to time as money was available. They would be deeply grateful for this help. You see how easy it is to start down the seemly [sic] short and open road, supposing you see the end, to find the horizon stretches ever farther along, with another hill ahead and another river to cross. Mr. Gillette agreed to make a survey and a planting plan; the office work cost, which he did not think would exceed $500.00, to be paid to him when the plan was accepted by Kenmore and the Garden Club of Virginia. Kenmore agreed to carry out the plan, as submitted, without changes except by consultation with him. The annual Meeting took place at Orange, Virginia the following May; the matter was laid before the members and was favorably voted upon. . . . Those present at the meeting in Orange were invited to participate in the celebration at Kenmore the next day when the last one thousand dollars of the purchase price was paid. Many Garden Club members accepted; enjoyed the luncheon and ceremonies, which were quite impressive; and looked forward with added interest to their part in making Betty Washington's home beautiful.

The $500.00 for the landscape plan was raised partly by a plant sale in Richmond the next autumn, and partly by a pro-rata contribution from each member club. During the following winter, the survey and landscape plan were made, approved and accepted with minor changes by both parties. It seemed our part was finished, but in the meantime, much was happening to the patriotic citizens of Fredericksburg, who had purchased Kenmore. Nation-wide interest had been aroused and advice and suggestions began to arrive from all quarters. A re-organization took place. The Kenmore Association was formed, with a Regent appointed in each State and the restoration of the outlying buildings was begun. Time went on and it seemed as though the Garden had to wait indefinitely. A second appeal was made to the Garden Club of Virginia to carry out the plan. An estimate was made by the Landscape Architect [Charles Gillette], who reported that it could be done for $5,000.00. This request of the Kenmore Association and the estimate of the cost was reported to the Garden Club of Virginia at their Annual Meeting in Charlottesville. Mrs. Massie, then

President, put the question to the members and it was voted that if the Kenmore Committee [of the GCV] could find a means of raising such a large sum of money, without taxing each club, they would be willing for the Committee to do so. That put it strongly up to the Committee, it seemed to me. I happened to be sitting next to Mrs. Andrew H. Christian at the luncheon at the Blue Ridge Club, following the meeting, talking over the ways and means of raising money—Lectures, plant sales and what not were suggested. She finally said that in one day at a pilgrimage to one of the James River places, a charitable organization had made over one thousand dollars. Here was an idea. Why not have historic places in all sections of Virginia open their homes to visitors simultaneously, then each Club could do its part without a great burden to any one. Mrs. Smith, the newly elected President of the Garden Club of Virginia, reappointed the same Committee and instructed us to go ahead. All you here present know where this road has led us. The first "Historic Garden Week" was the result . . .

It is scarcely necessary to go into the details of the organization and operation of this, our first Tour. Suffice it to say, we managed to exceed our goal of $5,000.00 by more than three-fold. The report was read at the next Annual Meeting at Winchester [in June 1929] amid great rejoicing. It happened that Mr. Arthur Shurtcliff [sic] of the Williamsburg Restoration, spoke at this meeting. He stressed the importance of exact reproduction in all restoration work on colonial places in Virginia. He made a great impression on all who heard him. There followed an informal meeting at Kenmore, and an unmistakable desire on the part of the Kenmore Association and the Garden Club of Virginia to restore the grounds as they were originally and not simply to embellish them, was apparent. The research and exploration work preliminary to such an undertaking seemed to me so long and so indefinite as to time and cost that I told the Kenmore Association that if they would do the necessary research, the Garden Club of Virginia would carry out the enlarged plan so far as the then available funds would permit. The result was a meeting at Kenmore with many experts in colonial restoration and landscaping present. . . . It was found that a true restoration of the grounds, as they probably existed in Col. Fielding Lewis's time, would be impossible, since the boundaries at present were so restricted, a modern town having sprung up on what were the original holdings of the Lewis estate. These gentlemen therefore suggested that we obtain from the court records a blue print of the original estate and from this make a plan which would eventually include the Mary Washington House; and that we would carry out the present plan on the property now owned by the Kenmore Association—that the present grounds be enclosed by a brick wall of appropriate colonial design. A letter was sent me by the President of the Kenmore Association requesting that we build the brick enclosure as soon as possible, and if there were not enough funds left to provide the necessary plant material, the enclosure would serve as the basis on which to build further and to embellish the grounds. They also requested, if possible, we complete the work by February 22, 1932, in time for the George Washington Bi-centennial celebration at Kenmore.

A search at once began for the best design for a brick wall of that period. The wall around Ware Church in Gloucester County was selected and approved. The plans were re-drawn, according to the suggestions of the Fine Arts Committee in Washington. These were shown at the annual meeting in Richmond, where Mrs. Leslie Gray was elected President. She decided "not to change horses in midstream," and the same Committee, already enlarged by those added for "Historic Garden Week" would continue to function, and in addition Mrs. Gari Melchers, Chairman of the Grounds Committee of the Kenmore Association.

The re-building of the old kitchen at Kenmore and all the disorder contingent to such work, caused another delay of one and a half years. The grounds were turned over to your committee in the spring of 1931. The wall was built, and during the late summer and autumn, the planting was done.

$19,104.15, the amount expended, includes all the money taken in at the gardens during the Tour, the sale of Guide Books, and the interest on the fund, which accrued during the years of waiting, the entire work having been paid for from this fund.

May I say right here that Mrs. Percy Falconer, who was the Treasurer . . . for the Kenmore Tour, has been of inestimable value. . . . Neither she nor I ever dreamed the office would cover a period of years or that the details would be so arduous. . . . I can only be deeply grateful [to all the many people involved who made it possible]. I am full of wonder that such a chain could be welded. It is strong because there is not a weak link in it; it is indestructible as it is more than material.

It serves to bind us irrevocably to Kenmore and we will always find there a center of interest and a feeling of satisfaction and pride. A letter was written by our President, Mrs. Gray, to Mrs. Fleming, President of the Kenmore Association, early in February telling her that the Garden was finished and *paid for*.

"The restoration of the grounds of Kenmore and the brick wall enclosing them is the gift of the Garden Club of Virginia. Begun February 22nd, 1924. Completed February 22nd, 1932."[2]

APPENDIX B

GCV's Two Fellowship Programs

IN THE MID-1990S IT BECAME APPARENT TO THE RESTORATION COMMITTEE OF the Garden Club of Virginia that, in addition to Virginia's wealth of public gardens in need of preservation, there are also a number of important gardens, either privately held or owned by private foundations, that also could benefit from historical documentation. Indeed, without documentation of these gardens, our gardening history would be incomplete. The result was the establishment of two separate fellowships, to be awarded to students enrolled in accredited academic programs of landscape architecture, landscape history, or horticulture. These are summer programs, during which the Fellows are given the opportunity to do measured drawings and perform historical research under the guidance of the landscape architect to the Garden Club of Virginia, currently, William D. Rieley.

The Rudy J. Favretti fellowship is named for the landscape architect who worked with the Garden Club of Virginia from 1978 until his retirement in 1998. Favretti Fellows document private gardens that are generally not open to the public. This fellowship was first awarded in 1996; since then, nine private gardens have been documented.

The Garden Club of Virginia Fellowship was created in 2004. It grew out of the work performed by Favretti Fellow Ginnifer McGill at Rosewell in the summer of 2003. McGill's work at Rosewell showed the Restoration Committee that there was a need to document valuable landscapes, not strictly in private hands, that might otherwise vanish or be lost to encroaching development.

Works of the Rudy J. Favretti Fellows

In 1996, Mario Herrada, of the University of California at Berkeley, drew measured drawings of the grand terraced garden overlooking the Rappahannock River at Sabine Hall, laid out by Landon Carter, in Richmond County; much of the original design of that garden remains.

In 1997, Darrin Alfred, of the University of Colorado at Denver, drew measured drawings of the large garden at Eyre Hall, established by Thomas Eyre on the Eastern

Crape myrtles (above) *in bloom at Eyre Hall* (right)

Bremo barn (above); *main house at Bremo* (right)

Shore, now beautifully restored by the current owner, a descendant of Thomas Eyre. It is open to the public.

No fellowship was awarded in 1998, but for the next three summers, Fellows worked to document the three gardens established by Jefferson's protégé, John Hartwell Cocke, at Bremo.

In 1999, Christopher Stevens, of the University of Virginia, documented the mid-nineteenth-century garden of Bremo Recess, the first Gothic Revival house in America.

In 2000, Brooke Whiting, of the University of Pennsylvania, through research with the Cocke Papers at the University of Virginia, documented the entire landscape of Bremo, John Hartwell Cocke's Palladian masterpiece.

In 2001, Adrian Fowler, of the University of Virginia, began the process of mapping the Bremo property, using Whiting's research; she discovered a drawing of the now vanished formal garden. Jocelyn Chorney, of the University of Manitoba, also a fellow in 2001, worked to document "Lucy's Garden" at Lower Bremo, the earliest house on the property.

In 2002, Sarah Trautvetter, of the University of Virginia, called her report on the mid-eighteenth-century grounds and house at Old Mansion, near Bowling Green in Caroline County, "A History of Change in the Virginia Landscape." It has been used by a recent buyer of the property to make plans for a refurbishing of the garden.

In 2003, Ginnifer McGill, of the University of Virginia, studied the landscape at Rosewell, concentrating on that area of the property held by the Rosewell Foundation. She was not able to uncover the vanished eighteenth-century garden itself, but her research is being used extensively by the archaeologists who work for the Foundation.

In 2004, Andrew Kohr, of Ball State College, documented the history of the landscape at Mirador, near Greenwood, west of Charlottesville. He described his work as "the documentation of the existing landscape, an examination of the landscape's evolution, and an exploration of its social and cultural context." The garden's heyday was during the period of Nancy Lancaster's ownership, in the years before the Second World War. Mrs. Lancaster, Lady Astor's niece, owned the London decorating firm Colefax and Fowler. Her gardens at Ditchley, Cliveden, and Haseley Court were as famous as the interior decoration of these three great houses, and of her remarkable apartment in London. Though

Rosewell ruins

APPENDIX B

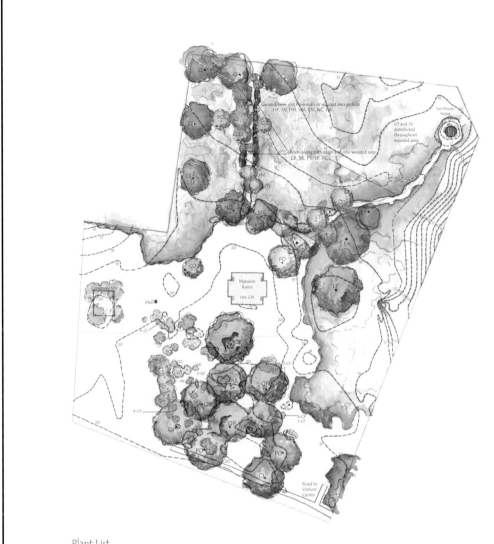

Plant List

Trees

AR	Acer rubrum	Red Maple
BS	Buxus sempervirens Aborescens	Tree Box
CF	Cornus florida	Flowering Dogwood
CI	Carya illinoinensis	Pecan
CO	Celtis occidentalis	Hackberry
FA	Fraxinus americana	White Ash
IO	Ilex opaca	American Holly
JN	Juglans nigra	Black Walnut
JV	Juniperus virginiana	Eastern Red Cedar
LT	Liriodendron tulipifera	Tulip Poplar
MA	Morus Alba	White Mulberry
MG	Magnolia grandiflora	Bullbay
PD	Populus deltoides	Eastern Cottonwood
PO	Platanus occidentalis	American Sycamore
PS	Prunus serotina	Wild Cherry
QP	Quercus phellos	Willow Oak
SV	Sassafras varifolium	Sassafras

Shrubs

BX	Buxus sempervirens	American Boxwood
FS	Forsythia sp.	Forsythia
LB	Lindera benzoin	Spicebush
PC	Philadelphus Coronarius	Mock Orange
SP	Spiraea sp.	Spirea
RB	Rubus sp.	Wild raspberry

Groundcover and Perennials

CM	Cymbalaria muralis	Kenilworth Ivy
FV	Fragaria virginiana	Wild Strawberry
HF	Hemerocallis fulva	Day Lily
HH	Hedera helix	English Ivy
NC	Narcissus sp.	Daffodil
PA	Polystichum acrostichoides	Christmas Fern
VM	Vinca major	Big-Leaf Periwinkle

Ginnifer L. McGill
Favretti Fellow
summer 2003

Rosewell
Gloucester, Virginia
The Garden Club of Virginia

Scale: 0'-1" = 40'-0"

she built her reputation as a decorator and gardener in England, Mrs. Lancaster always said that Virginia, and particularly Mirador, was its source.

In 2005, Jacqueline Luzar, of Ball State College, documented the impressive and virtually unknown terraced garden at Dan's Hill in Pittsylvania County, a part of Virginia well off the beaten tourist track.

In 2006, Joshua Meyer, of Temple University, digitized much of the copious documentation of Tuckahoe in Goochland County, where Thomas Jefferson spent much of his boyhood.

Sabine Hall, Eyre Hall, and the three houses at Bremo are all still owned and occupied by descendants of the original builders; the other places have changed hands.

Works of the Garden Club of Virginia Fellows

In 2005, two Garden Club of Virginia Fellows brought complementary qualifications to the documentation of the garden at Gay Mont, in Caroline County. Penelope Heavner, of George Washington University, had strong research experience, while Courtney Hinson, of North Carolina State University, was well qualified to do the measured drawings. This garden design was the result of a European grand tour by its young owner, John Bernard Hipkins, in 1825. The property is now held by APVA Preservation Virginia.

In 2006, Zachary Rutz, of the University of California at Berkeley, documented the much changed but still recognizable Ellen Biddle Shipman garden at Chatham, in Stafford County. Chatham is now the headquarters of Fredericksburg Battlefield National Park, and the emphasis is on interpretation of the Civil War years. Restoration of the garden is at present not in the Park Service's program, but should it ever be possible, Rutz's excellent work will be invaluable to augment a remarkable collection of Frances Benjamin Johnston photographs, taken of the garden at its height.

THE INSTRUCTIONS TO THE EARLIEST FAVRETTI FELLOWS DIRECTED THEM to provide detailed documentation of the gardens, not the houses or the builders. These early reports are nevertheless unique and valuable resources. In 1999, beginning with the research at Bremo Recess, the ground rules were changed. Since that time, the Fellows' reports have been more comprehensive. Along with the measured drawings of the gardens, they give, as far as possible, the complete and previously undocumented histories of the places.

All the reports, of both the Favretti Fellows and the Garden Club of Virginia Fellows, are deposited with the libraries of the Virginia Historical Society, the University of Virginia, and Colonial Williamsburg. It is the hope of the Garden Club of Virginia that these records will be a valuable resource for all future study of the history of landscape gardening in Virginia.

Fellows and Projects by Year

The Rudy J. Favretti Fellowship, Given to Execute Measured Drawings of Historic Gardens in Private Ownership

1996	Mario Herrada, University of California, Berkeley	*Sabine Hall, Warsaw*
1997	Darrin Alfred, University of Colorado, Denver	*Eyre Hall, Eastern Shore*
1999	Christopher Stevens, University of Virginia	*Bremo Recess*
2000	Brooke Whiting, University of Pennsylvania	*Bremo*
2001	Adriane Fowler, University of Virginia	*Bremo*
2001	Jocelyn Chorney, University of Manitoba	*Lower Bremo*
2002	Sarah Trautvetter, University of Virginia	*Old Mansion, Bowling Green*
2003	Ginnifer McGill, University of Virginia	*Rosewell, Gloucester County*
2004	Andrew Kohr, Ball State College	*Mirador, Greenwood*
2005	Jacqueline Luzar, Ball State College	*Dan's Hill, Danville*
2006	Joshua Meyer, Temple University	*Tuckahoe, Goochland County*
2007	Carrie Trebil, Clemson University	*Bloomsbury, Orange County*

The Garden Club of Virginia Fellowship, Given to Research Vulnerable Historic Gardens Not Held Privately

2005	Penelope Heavner, George Washington University	
	Courtney Hinson, North Carolina State University	*Gay Mont, Caroline County (APVA)*
2006	Zachary Rutz, University of California, Berkeley	*Ellen Biddle Shipman Garden at Chatham Manor, Fredericksburg (National Park Service)*

APPENDIX C

Alphabetical List of All GCV Restoration Projects,
1929–2007

ADAM THOROUGHGOOD HOUSE, PRINCESS ANNE COUNTY

1958–60   Garden—Alden S. Hopkins

2005   Because the City of Virginia Beach purchased the Adam Thoroughgood
         House from the City of Norfolk, with mutual agreement the Garden Club of
         Virginia has released the property while Virginia Beach considers its approach
         to interpreting and maintaining the garden.

BACON'S CASTLE, SURRY COUNTY

1984–89   Site archaeology, restored garden, and forcing wall—Rudy J. Favretti

THE BEALE GARDEN AT HOLLINS UNIVERSITY, ROANOKE

2006   Original design—Albert Farnham, given in memory of Lucy Preston Beale
         Restoration of garden—William D. Rieley

BELLE GROVE PLANTATION, MIDDLETOWN

1983–86   Landscape interpretation—Rudy J. Favretti

BELMONT, FREDERICKSBURG

1994   Restoration of Melchers-era formal grounds and gardens—Rudy J. Favretti

BLANDY EXPERIMENTAL FARM AND STATE ARBORETUM, BOYCE

2004   Rebuilding of stone wall along Dogwood Walk—William D. Rieley

BRUTON PARISH CHURCH, WILLIAMSBURG

1936   GCV worked directly with Bruton Parish Church to remove or prune existing
         trees and plant new ones in the churchyard

1939   Working with Colonial Williamsburg, landscape plan prepared—Arthur
         Shurcliff

1955   Expansion of terrace area and extensions of walls—Alden S. Hopkins

2003   Plan for brick terrace and memorial garden—William D. Rieley

BURWELL-MORGAN MILL, CLARKE COUNTY
1971–73   Landscape setting—Griswold, Winters and Swain

CENTRE HILL MANSION, PETERSBURG
1980–81   Immediate grounds and approach—Rudy J. Favretti

CHRIST CHURCH, MIDDLESEX COUNTY
1942   Brick walls along two sides of the churchyard—based on sketch by the Senior
           Warden

HISTORIC CHRIST CHURCH, LANCASTER COUNTY
1966–68   Landscape setting for the churchyard and surrounding area—Ralph E. Gris-
           wold

DANVILLE MUSEUM, SUTHERLIN MANSION, DANVILLE
2004   Restoration of nineteenth-century picket fence—William D. Rieley

EXECUTIVE MANSION, RICHMOND
1953   Garden design—Charles F. Gillette
2000   Restoration of garden design—William D. Rieley

FINCASTLE PRESBYTERIAN CHURCH, BOTETOURT COUNTY
1942   Restoration and repairs in the churchyard, built terrace and wall, plantings—
           no architect

GRACE ARENTS GARDEN, LEWIS GINTER BOTANICAL GARDEN, RICHMOND
1990   Restoration of formal garden with arbors, seated trellises, and garden
           house—Rudy J. Favretti

GUNSTON HALL, FAIRFAX COUNTY
1947–54   Gardens and grounds—Alden S. Hopkins

KENMORE, FREDERICKSBURG
1929   Gardens and grounds plan drawn—James Greenleaf and Charles F. Gillette
1930s &   Grounds, including Betty Washington Lewis's flower garden and enclosing
1940s   wall—Charles F. Gillette
1992–96   Renovation of Betty Washington Lewis's garden, herb demonstration garden,
           wilderness walk—Rudy J. Favretti

KENT-VALENTINE HOUSE, RICHMOND
1972–73   Grounds—Griswold, Winters and Swain
1996   Grounds—Rudy J. Favretti
2004   New planting design and rebuilding of brick wall—William D. Rieley

KER PLACE, ONANCOCK
1982   Grounds and garden—Rudy J. Favretti

LEE HALL, NEWPORT NEWS
2002–3   Trees and fencing—William D. Rieley

MARY WASHINGTON HOUSE, FREDERICKSBURG
1968–69   Garden—Ralph E. Griswold

MARY WASHINGTON MONUMENT, FREDERICKSBURG
1936   Landscape setting, including wall and planting—Alden Hopkins

MAYMONT, RICHMOND
1996–98   Mansion grounds, including trees, shrub labyrinth, and walks—Rudy J. Favretti
2006   Elm allée—William D. Rieley

MONTICELLO, CHARLOTTESVILLE
1936   West Lawn flower garden—Fiske Kimball, Architect; Garland A. Wood Jr.,
            planting plan
1991   Funding for analysis by Rieley & Associates of archival photographs relating
            to trees within the first roundabout

MONTPELIER, ORANGE
1992   Restoration of duPont-era terraced walled gardens and repointing of brick
            wall—Rudy J. Favretti

MOSES MYERS HOUSE, NORFOLK
2003   Federal period garden—William D. Rieley

MOUNT VERNON, MOUNT VERNON
2001   Restored perimeter plantings of George Washington's Bowling Green—Rudy
            J. Favretti

OATLANDS, LEESBURG
1991   Restoration of sixty-foot sections of early 1800s garden forcing wall—Rudy J.
            Favretti

PRESTWOULD PLANTATION, CLARKSVILLE
1980–81   Gardens delineated, grounds restored, and summerhouse furnished—Rudy J.
            Favretti
1989   Installation of water holding tank and irrigation system—Rudy J. Favretti
1991   Addition of reproduction eighteenth-century garden gates—Rudy J. Favretti
1998   Due to Prestwould's insufficient resources for maintenance of this garden, the
            Garden Club of Virginia released this property from its obligation.

POINT OF HONOR, LYNCHBURG

1978   Landscape restored—Meade Palmer

1996   Visitor Center reception terrace and plantings—Rudy J. Favretti

2006   New walk and planting—William D. Rieley

HISTORIC PORTSMOUTH COURTHOUSE, PORTSMOUTH

1979–82   Courthouse yard—J. P. C. Hanbury, in consultation with Rudy J. Favretti

ROLFE-WARREN HOUSE, SMITH'S FORT PLANTATION, SURRY COUNTY

1936   Seventeenth-century landscape setting for the house—Arthur Shurcliff

ST. JOHN'S MEWS, RICHMOND

1964–67   Cast-iron fencing and planting—Ralph E. Griswold

HISTORIC ST. LUKE'S CHURCH, ISLE OF WIGHT COUNTY

2006–7   Trees and shrubs for the churchyard, new entrance walk to the church, and
         improvements to the grounds of the Visitor Center—William D. Rieley

SCOTCHTOWN, HANOVER COUNTY

1968–69   Landscape setting of an eighteenth-century plantation—Griswold, Winters
          and Swain

SMITHFIELD PLANTATION, BLACKSBURG

1982–84   Fences, walks, colonial kitchen garden—Rudy J. Favretti

STRATFORD HALL, WESTMORELAND COUNTY

1930–32   Garden—Arthur Shurcliff and Morley Williams

1954–58   Renovation of garden—Alden Hopkins

2006   Restoration of garden gates and tree planting—William D. Rieley

SWEET BRIAR COLLEGE, AMHERST

2003   New entrance court at Sweet Briar House—William D. Rieley

UNIVERSITY OF VIRGINIA, CHARLOTTESVILLE

1947–53   West Lawn, five pavilion gardens—Alden Hopkins

1960–65   East Lawn, five pavilion gardens—Alden Hopkins and Donald Parker, with
          Ralph E. Griswold, consultant

1977   East Lawn and the north forecourt of the Rotunda—J. Patrick Graham IV,
        Nancy Takahashi, and the University Planning Office

2002   Pavilion III, refurbishment of garden—William D. Rieley

2006   Pavilion VI, refurbishment of garden—William D. Rieley

Washington and Lee University, Lexington

1933   Lee Chapel planting—Charles F. Gillette

1977   Half-circle brick wall, steps, and terrace—Griswold, Winter and Swain

1994   Lee House, nineteenth-century gardens and grounds—Rudy J. Favretti

Wilton, Richmond

1936   Grounds—Arthur Shurcliff

1959   Additional planting—Alden Hopkins

1960   Pair of iron gates—Alden Hopkins

Woodlawn Plantation, Fairfax County

1953–60   Garden and grounds—Alden Hopkins

1967   Implementation, orchard paths—Alden Hopkins's design

1974   Implementation, kitchen garden—Alden Hopkins's design

1977   Visitor reception area—Meade Palmer

2005   Replacement of fences and gates—William D. Rieley

Woodrow Wilson Birthplace/Presidential Library, Staunton

1932–34   Garden—Charles F. Gillette

1960   Brick paths—Charles F. Gillette

1968   Terraces—Ralph E. Griswold

1991   Museum forecourt and walk—Rudy J. Favretti

1999   Reconstruction of summerhouses—William D. Rieley

2006   Refurbishing of south end of second terrace—William D. Rieley

Yeardley House, Jamestown Island

2006   Garden setting for 1907 house and offices—William D. Rieley

APPENDIX D

*Chronological List of All GCV Special Gifts
and Contributions, 1940–2007*

1940   Hammond-Harwood House, Annapolis, Maryland

1941   British Mobile Kitchen

1941   English war rehabilitation, specifically, Plymouth, England

1947   Planting of trees and shrubs at the Barter Theater, Abingdon, Virginia

1950   St. John's Church churchyard tree planting, Richmond, paid through Massie-Christian Fund

1974   Publication of *Historic Virginia Gardens,* by Dorothy Hunt Williams, in collaboration with Ralph E. Griswold

1989   Donation made to fund established for the replacement of trees in Charleston, South Carolina, following Hurricane Hugo

1989/   Tree planting, Virginia Union University, Richmond—Rudy J. Favretti
1991

1991   Front landscape plantings, signs, and indoor interpretive exhibit, Carlyle House, Alexandria—Rudy J. Favretti

1993   Publication of *Gardens and Landscapes of Virginia,* photography by Richard Cheek, text by Rudy J. Favretti

1994   Publication of illustrated brochures on twenty of the restored gardens, to be distributed at the gardens

1996   Small demonstration garden and arbor at the Ball-Sellers House, Arlington

1996   Original plans of restoration projects placed in archives at the Virginia Historical Society

2002   Paid for the services of William D. Rieley to prepare a master plan and documents for work funded by the TEA-21 program, for Dodona Manor, Leesburg

2002   Donation toward landscape plan for Capitol Square, Richmond

2004   Digitizing of archived drawings at the Virginia Historical Society to make them accessible via the Web

2006   Donation made to the New Orleans Botanical Garden Foundation for replacement greenhouses at City Park, following the devastation from Hurricane Katrina

APPENDIX E

Plants Used in 1975–2007 GCV Preservation Work

Trees Native to Virginia or Introduced in the 1600s

Acer negundo	Boxelder	*Melia azedarach*	Chinaberry
Acer rubrum	Red maple	*Morus* sp.	Mulberry
Aesculus octandra	Yellow buckeye	*Pinus* sp.	Pine
Cedrus libani	Cedar of Lebanon	*Platanus × acerifolia*	London planetree
Celtis occidentalis	Hackberry	*Platanus occidentalis*	Sycamore
Cercis canadensis	Redbud	*Prunus armeniaca*	Apricot
Cornus florida	Dogwood	*Prunus cerasus*	Cherry
Cornus mas	Corneliancherry dogwood	*Prunus domestica*	Plum
Fagus sylvatica	Copper beech	*Prunus persica*	Peach
'Atropurpureum'		*Prunus serotina*	Black cherry
Juglans nigra	Black walnut	*Pyrus communis*	Pear
Juniperus virginiana	Eastern redcedar	*Quercus alba*	White oak
Laburnum anagyroides	Common laburnum	*Robinia pseudoacacia*	Black locust
Larix decidua	Common larch	*Sassafras albidum*	Sassafras
Liquidambar styraciflua	Sweetgum	*Thuja occidentalis*	Arborvitae
Liriodendron tulipifera	Tuliptree, Tulip poplar	*Tilia* sp.	Linden
Magnolia virginiana	Sweetbay magnolia	*Tsuga canadensis*	Canadian hemlock
Malus pumila	Apple		

Shrubs Native to Virginia or Introduced in the 1600s

Berberis vulgaris	Barberry	*Hypericum* sp.	St. Johnswort
Buxus sempervirens	Common box	*Ilex glabra*	Inkberry
Euonymus americanus	Strawberrybush	*Ilex verticillata*	Winterberry
Ficus carica	Fig	*Lindera benzoin*	Spicebush
Hamamelis virginiana	Witchhazel	*Myrica cerifera*	Southern waxmyrtle
Hibiscus syriacus	Althea, Rose-of-Sharon	*Philadelphus coronarius*	Mockorange

Prunus laurocerasus	Cherrylaurel	*Rosa eglanteria*	Eglantine
Punica granatum	Pomegranate	*Rubus idaeus*	Raspberry
Pyracantha coccinea	Scarlet firethorn	*Sambucus canadensis*	American elderberry
Pyracantha fortuneana 'Graberi'	Firethorn	*Syringa vulgaris*	Lilac
		Viburnum opulus var. *roseum*	Guelder-rose viburnum
Ribes sativum	Currant		
Ribes uva-crispa	Gooseberry	*Vitex negundo*	Chastetree
Rosa damascena	Damask rose	*Yucca* sp.	Yucca

Vines Native to Virginia or Introduced in the 1600s

Campsis radicans	Trumpet vine	*Lonicera sempervirens*	Honeysuckle
Gelsemium sempervirens	Carolina yellow jessamine	*Parthenocissus quinquefolia*	Virginia creeper
Lonicera periclymenum	Woodbine	*Vitis vinifera*	Grape

Herbaceous Plants Native to Virginia or Introduced in the 1600s

Alcea rosea	Hollyhock	*Hyacinthus orientalis*	Hyacinth
Amaranthus caudatus	Love-lies-bleeding	*Lavandula angustifolia*	Lavender
Asparagus officinalis	Asparagus	*Matthiola incana*	Gillyflower
Aster sp.	Aster	*Mimosa pudica*	Sensitive plant
Campanula persicifolia	Peachleaf bellflower	*Mirabilis jalapa*	Four-o-clock
Colchicum autumnale	Crocus	*Narcissus jonquilla*	Narcissus
Cucumis sativus	Cucumber	*Narcissus* sp.	Daffodil
Cucurbita sp.	Squash	*Pisum sativum*	Pea
Dianthus barbatus	Sweet William	*Polemonium caeruleum*	Jacob's-ladder
Dianthus sp.	Clove	*Primula auricula*	Primrose
Fragaria virginiana	Strawberry	*Tagetes* sp.	Marigold
Gladiolus communis	Sword lily	*Teucrium chamaedrys*	Germander
Hemerocallis fulva	Tawny daylily	*Tulipa* sp.	Tulip
Hibiscus moscheutos	Rose mallow		

Trees Introduced in the 1700s

Acer platanoides	Norway maple	*Amelanchier canadensis*	Shadblow
Acer saccharinum	Silver maple	*Betula nigra*	River birch
Acer saccharum	Sugar maple	*Carpinus caroliniana*	American hornbeam
Aesculus hippocastanum	Horsechestnut	*Carya illinoinensis*	Pecan
Aesculus pavia	Red buckeye	*Catalpa bignonioides*	Southern catalpa
Albizia julibrissin	Mimosa	*Catalpa speciosa*	Hardy catalpa
Amelanchier arborea	Downy serviceberry	*Chionanthus virginicus*	Fringetree

Cladrastis kentukea	Yellowwood	*Pinus echinata*	Shortleaf pine
Cornus alba	Tatarian dogwood	*Pinus taeda*	Loblolly pine
Cornus florida var. *rubra*	Pink flowering dogwood	*Pinus virginiana*	Virginia scrub pine
Crataegus phaenopyrum	Washington hawthorn	*Prunus padus*	Birdcherry
Crataegus viridis	Green hawthorn	*Prunus virginiana*	Chokecherry
Fagus grandifolia	American beech	*Quercus falcata*	Southern red oak
Franklinia alatamaha	Franklinia	*Quercus nigra*	Water oak
Fraxinus americana	White ash	*Quercus palustris*	Pin oak
Gymnocladus dioicus	Kentucky coffeetree	*Quercus phellos*	Willow oak
Halesia tetraptera	Carolina silverbell	*Quercus rubra*	Red oak
Ilex aquifolium	English holly	*Quercus virginiana*	Live oak
Ilex decidua	Possumhaw	*Salix babylonica* 'Pendula'	Weeping willow
Ilex opaca	American holly	*Salix caprea*	Goat willow
Ilex vomitoria	Yaupon	*Sophora japonica*	Pagodatree
Lagerstroemia indica	Crape myrtle	*Stewartia malacodendron*	Silky stewartia
Magnolia grandiflora	Southern magnolia	*Stewartia ovata*	Mountain stewartia
Malus coronaria	Sweet crabapple	*Styrax americanus*	American snowbell
Nyssa sylvatica	Black tupelo	*Taxodium distichum*	Baldcypress
Ostrya virginiana	Hophornbeam	*Ulmus americana*	American elm
Oxydendrum arboreum	Sourwood	*Ulmus parvifolia*	Chinese elm, Lacebark elm

Shrubs Introduced in the 1700s

Aesculus parviflora	Bottlebrush buckeye	*Daphne cneorum*	Rose daphne
Aronia arbutifolia	Red chokeberry	*Dirca palustris*	Leatherwood
Buxus sempervirens 'Suffruticosa'	Dwarf box	*Euonymus atropurpureus*	Eastern wahoo
Callicarpa americana	American beautyberry	*Fothergilla gardenii*	Dwarf fothergilla
Calycanthus floridus	Sweetshrub	*Hydrangea arborescens*	Smooth hydrangea
Camellia japonica	Japanese camellia	*Hypericum calycinum*	Aaronsbeard St. Johnswort
Camellia sinensis	Tea	*Hypericum prolificum*	Shrubby St. Johnswort
Caragana arborescens	Siberian peashrub	*Itea virginica*	Virginia sweetspire
Castanea pumila	Chinquapin	*Jasminum fruticans*	Common yellow jasmine
Cephalanthus occidentalis	Buttonbush	*Jasminum officinale*	White jasmine
Chaenomeles speciosa	Flowering quince	*Kalmia latifolia*	Mountain laurel
Chimonanthus praecox	Wintersweet	*Leucothoe axillaris*	Dog-hobble
Clethra alnifolia	Clethra, Summersweet	*Leucothoe fontanesiana*	Fetterbush
Cytisus scoparius	Scotch broom	*Lonicera tatarica*	Tatarian honeysuckle
Danae racemosa	Alexandrian-laurel	*Myrica pensylvanica*	Northern bayberry
		Physocarpus opulifolius	Ninebark

Prunus maritima	Beach plum	*Rosa spinosissima*	Scotch rose
Rhododendron calendulaceum	Flame azalea	*Rosa virginiana*	Virginia rose
		Rubus odoratus	Flowering raspberry
Rhododendron canescens	Sweet Piedmont azalea	*Sorbus aucuparia*	European mountain ash, Rowan
Rhododendron catawbiense	Catawba rhododendron		
Rhododendron indicum	Indica azalea, Indian azalea	*Symphoricarpos orbiculatus*	Indiancurrant, Coralberry
Rhododendron maximum	Rosebay rhododendron		
Rhododendron minus	Piedmont rhododendron	*Syringa × persica*	Lilac
Rhododendron periclymenoides	Pinxterbloom azalea	*Taxus baccata*	English yew
		Vaccinium stamineum	Deerberry
Rhododendron viscosum	Swamp white azalea	*Viburnum acerifolium*	Mapleleaf viburnum
Rhus aromatic	Fragrant sumac	*Viburnum alnifolium*	American Wayfaringtree
Rhus glabra	Smooth sumac	*Viburnum cassinoides*	Witherod
Ribes hirtellum	Currant	*Viburnum dentatum*	Arrowwood
Robinia hispida	Bristly locust	*Viburnum prunifolium*	Blackhaw viburnum
Rosa laevigata	Cherokee rose	*Vitex agnus-castus*	Chastetree

Vines Introduced in the 1700s

Celastrus sp.	Bittersweet	*Hedera helix*	English ivy
Clematis virginiana	Virginsbower	*Vinca minor*	Periwinkle
Clematis vitalba	Traveler's joy	*Vitis labrusca*	Fox grape

Herbaceous Plants Introduced in the 1700s

Amaranthus tricolor	Amaranth	*Mertensia virginica*	Virginia Bluebells
Aruncus dioicus	Goatsbeard	*Narcissus pseudonarcissus*	Jonquil
Dianthus chinensis	China pink	*Polemonium reptans*	Greek valerian
Dianthus plumarius	Grass pink	*Polygonatum* sp.	Solomon's seal
Dianthus superbus	Double pink	*Polygonum orientale*	Prince's-feathers
Dicentra cucullaria	Dutchman's breeches	*Reseda odorata*	Mignonette
Galanthus nivalis	Snowdrop	*Saponaria officinalis*	Bouncing bet, Soapwort
Gaultheria procumbens	Wintergreen	*Scilla bifolia*	Two-leaved squill
Gentiana sp.	Gentian	*Scorzonera hispanica*	Spanish salsify
Iberis sempervirens	Candytuft	*Sternbergia lutea*	Fall daffodil
Iris cristata	Crested Iris	*Tiarella cordifolia*	Foamflower
Jeffersonia diphylla	Twinleaf	*Vicia faba*	Broad bean
Leucojum aestivum	Summer snowdrop	*Viola canadensis*	Violet
Lilium speciosa	Lily	*Viola tricolor*	Pansy

Trees Introduced in the 1800s

Alnus glutinosa	Common alder	*Paulownia tomentosa*	Empress tree
Amelanchier laevis	Allegheny serviceberry	*Phellodendron amurense*	Amur corktree
Castanea dentata	American chestnut	*Picea abies*	Norway spruce
Cedrus deodara	Deodar cedar	*Picea pungens*	Colorado spruce
Celtis laevigata	Sugar hackberry	*Populus tremuloides*	Quaking aspen
Cercidiphyllum japonicum	Katsuratree	*Prunus avium*	Mazzard cherry
Chamaecyparis sp.	Falsecypress	*Prunus subhirtella*	Weeping Higan cherry
Cornus kousa	Kousa dogwood	'Pendula'	
Cryptomeria japonica	Japanese cryptomeria	*Pseudolarix amabilis*	Golden-larch
Koelreuteria bipinnata	Bougainvillea goldenraintree	*Stewartia pseudocamellia*	Japanese stewartia
Parrotia persica	Persian parrotia	*Toona sinensis*	Chinese cedrela

Shrubs Introduced in the 1800s

Buxus microphylla	Littleleaf box	*Poncirus trifoliata*	Hardy-orange
Cotoneaster microphyllus	Littleleaf cotoneaster	*Rhododendron carolinianum*	Carolina rhododendron
Deutzia gracilis	Slender deutzia		
Enkianthus perulatus	White enkianthus	*Rhododendron mucronulatum*	Korean rhododendron
Fothergilla major	Large fothergilla		
Hydrangea quercifolia	Oakleaf hydrangea	*Rhododendron prinophyllum*	Roseshell azalea
Jasminum nudiflorum	Winter jasmine		
Ligustrum japonicum	Japanese privet	*Rhododendron vaseyi*	Pinkshell azalea
Nandina domestica	Nandina, Heavenly bamboo	*Sarcococca hookeriana*	Sweetbox
Osmanthus × fortunei	Fortune's osmanthus	*Tamarix ramosissima*	Tamarisk
Philadelphus coronarius 'Aureus'	Sweet mockorange	*Taxus cuspidata*	Japanese yew
		Viburnum dilatatum	Linden viburnum
Photinia villosa	Oriental photinia	*Viburnum opulus*	European cranberrybush
Pieris floribunda	Mountain pieris		

Vines Introduced in the 1800s

Campsis grandiflora	Chinese trumpetcreeper	*Lonicera periclymenum* var. *Belgica*	Dutch woodbine
Hydrangea anomala var. *petiolaris*	Climbing hydrangea		

Herbaceous Plants Introduced in the 1800s

Allium unifolium	Oriental onion	*Liriope muscari*	Lilyturf
Anemone blanda	Windflower	*Trillium grandiflorum*	Giant trillium

Trees and Shrubs Introduced in the 1900s

Buxus sempervirens 'Jensen'	Jensen boxwood	*Prunus laurocerasus 'Otto Luyken'*	Otto Luyken laurel
Clethra alnifolia 'Rosea'	Pink summersweet	*Rhododendron atlanticum*	Coast azalea
Heptacodium miconioides	Seven-son flower	*Rhododendron bakeri*	Cumberland azalea
Ilex × attenuata 'Fosteri'	Foster's holly	*Styrax americanus*	American snowbell
Ilex crenata 'Rotundifolia'	Round-leaf Japanese holly	*Symphoricarpos microphyllus*	Pink coralberry
Ilex crenata 'Soft Touch'	Soft Touch Japanese holly		
Ilex × 'Nellie Stevens'	Nellie Stevens Holly	*Ulmus americana 'Valley Forge'*	Valley Forge American elm
Kolkwitzia amabilis	Beautybush		
Magnolia × 'Butterflies'	Butterflies magnolia		
Photinia glabra	Japanese photinia		

NOTES

Bacon's Castle

1. The quotation is taken from the subtitle of Leighton's book, *Early American Gardens: For Meate or Medicine* (1970).

2. See Luccketti, "Archaeological Excavations at Bacon's Castle," 35.

3. *Virginia Landmarks Register,* 516.

4. 1843 Morrison survey, in Garden Club of Virginia, Restoration Committee, Papers, 1924–97, Section 2, Bacon's Castle folder, Virginia Historical Society, Richmond.

5. The term "regular" was used to describe a garden laid out in a symmetrical and geometrical pattern. It was synonymous with "formal," and such gardens were the antithesis of the irregular, naturalistic gardens that became fashionable in eighteenth-century England (see Reynolds, *The Treatment of Nature in English Poetry Between Pope and Wordsworth*).

6. See Kevin P. Kelly, "The Allens of Bacon's Castle: A Report for the APVA," April 1, 1974, in Garden Club of Virginia, Restoration Committee, Papers, 1924–97, Section 2, Bacon's Castle folder, Virginia Historical Society, Richmond [hereafter cited as Kelly Report].

7. All the archaeological data presented here is taken from Luccketti, "Archaeological Excavations at Bacon's Castle, Surry County, Virginia."

8. Kelly Report, 30–38.

9. Unknown person to Nicholson, 20 February 1704/5, MS43.04: Francis Nicholson Papers, Institute of Early American History and Culture, Williamsburg, Va., http://research.history.org/CWDLArchive/Manuscripts/Html/M4304303.htm.

10. Ibid.; see also s.v. "Arthur Allen," *Encyclopedia of American History.*

11. Kelly Report, 5.

12. Ibid.

13. *Richmond Times Dispatch,* July 15, 1995.

14. Unknown person to Nicholson, 20 February 1704/5, MS43.04: Francis Nicholson Papers, Institute of Early American History and Culture, Williamsburg, Va., http://research.history.org/CWDLArchive/Manuscripts/Html/M4304303.htm.

15. Kelly Report, 10–20.

16. Ibid.

17. See Kinnexions.com, http://kinnexions.com/smlsource/evelyn.htm; information about the Evelyn family on this Web site is taken from *My Southern Families,* by Hiram Kennedy Douglass (1967: World Nobility and Peerage, The Blackmore Press, Gillingham, Dorset).

18. Author's conversation with Nicholas Luccketti, the archaeologist who led the team working at Bacon's Castle, summer 2005.

19. Rudy J. Favretti, in an e-mail dated June 19, 2007, says, "This is what we assumed was a forcing wall, but there is not proof that it was. We made this assumption because of its position at the north end of the garden. I tried in designing the wall to make it simple, not over-stated. . . . I researched my slide collection of forcing walls

and used as the prototype the simple forcing wall in the kitchen garden at Blicking Hall, Norfolk, England."

20. Luccketti, "Archaeological Excavations at Bacon's Castle," 32.

21. Ibid.; author's conversations with Nicholas Luccketti and Rudy J. Favretti.

22. William L. Kelso, quoted in *Garden History*, 34.

23. See Boggs, *Prints and Plants of Old Gardens*, 35–54.

24. The linear land measurement unit most common in seventeenth-century Virginia was the pole of 16.5 feet (less commonly, the chain of 33 feet, and, later, of 66 feet). The north-south dimension of the garden, as shown on the archaeologist's measured drawing of the site, is 20 poles, or 330 feet long. The measurement from the northern edge of the southernmost path to the northern edge of the next path to the north is 6 poles, or 99 feet. Similarly, the same measurement, taken in the east-west direction, is 5 poles, or 82.5 feet. The east-west dimension of each planting bed is very nearly 70 feet. This dimension, taken with the 99-foot north-south dimension, yields a proportion of 1:1.4142857..., or 1 to the square root of 2, a proportion known and used from antiquity. The angles of the garden are 90 degrees, and the garden is orthogonal with the house. So this garden was laid out in a very intentional, regular, and formal way.

Belle Grove

1. The following historical narrative is taken from conversations and e-mail correspondence with Elizabeth McClung, director of Belle Grove; the HABS building survey report, in Garden Club of Virginia, Restoration Committee, Papers, 1924–97, Section 2, Belle Grove folder, Virginia Historical Society, Richmond; and from "Jost Hite—Shenandoah Pioneer," at Suite101.com, www.suite101.com/article.cfm/colonial-america-retired/48664.

2. E-mail to author from Rudy J. Favretti, June 19, 2007.

Belmont

1. The historical narrative is taken from conversations with Joanna Catron, Belmont's curator, and Beate Jensen, Belmont's director of grounds, who provided references from and access to the unpublished letters and diaries of Corinne Melchers; as well as from e-mail correspondence with Rudy J. Favretti, and conversations with William D. Rieley.

2. Frances Benjamin Johnston's original black-and-white photographs of Belmont are part of the Historic American Buildings collection at the Library of Congress.

3. E-mail to author from Beate Jensen, July 2006.

4. From Corrinne Melchers's unpublished diaries, housed at Belmont. All subsequent diary quotations are taken from this source.

5. In an e-mail of June 19, 2007, Rudy J. Favretti wrote, "It is important to mention that I wanted to use all Liberty Elms, to reproduce what had been there, but the staff/management was reluctant to do so, fearing that the Elms would not survive."

Blandy

1. Historical information in this chapter is from Nancy St. Clair Talley, a very knowledgeable historian from Millwood, Virginia.

2. Margaret T. Peters, "Blandy Experimental Farm" (National Register of Historic Places Nomination Form), Virginia Department of Historic Resources, Richmond, 1992.

Bruton Parish Churchyard

1. The historical narrative for this essay was gleaned from the Garden Club of Virginia, Restoration Committee, Papers, 1924–97, Section 2, Bruton Parish Churchyard folder, Virginia Historical Society, Richmond; from vestry reports; and from conversations with William D. Rieley and members of the Bruton Parish Vestry.

2. "Act of Assembly," 1633, in Virginia, *The Statutes at Large*, 1:208–9.

3. Report of Rudy J. Favretti, Landscape Architect, August 11, 1997, in Garden Club of Virginia, Restoration Committee, Papers, 1924–97, Section 2, Bruton Parish Churchyard folder, Virginia Historical Society, Richmond.

4. *Bruton Parish Church Bulletin,* 2000.

5. William D. Rieley's notes, in author's possession.

Centre Hill

1. The historical information for this essay was taken from Garden Club of Virginia, Restoration Committee, Papers, 1924–97, section 2, Centre Hill folder, Virginia Historical Society, Richmond; and from Edward A. Wyatt's *Petersburg, A History.*

2. Robert Buckner Bolling to Petersburg, Va., Common Council, 1858, Bolling Family Papers, 1785–1875, Section 2, Centre Hill folder, Virginia Historical Society, Richmond.

3. *Virginia Landmarks Register,* 376.

4. Rudy J. Favretti to Angela Barksdale, president of the Petersburg Garden Club, July 19, 1994, Garden Club of Virginia, Restoration Committee, Papers, 1924–97, Section 2, Centre Hill folder, Virginia Historical Society, Richmond.

5. William J. Martin to Constance Ingles, January 5, 1993, Garden Club of Virginia, Restoration Committee, Papers, 1924–97, Section 2, Centre Hill folder, Virginia Historical Society, Richmond.

The Executive Mansion

1. Except as otherwise noted, the information in this chapter was largely gleaned from conversations with previous governors and first ladies, and from e-mail correspondence with landscape architect William D. Rieley and architect John Paul C. Hanbury.

2. Seale, *Virginia's Executive Mansion,* 12.

3. This brief biography of Alexander Parris is synthesized from information on the website of the Alexander Parris Digital Project (see www.parrisproject.org/About.htm).

Grace Arents Garden

1. The historical information for this essay was gleaned from Lewis Ginter Botanical Garden literature; and from e-mail correspondence with landscape architect Rudy J. Favretti and Frank Robinson, director of the Lewis Ginter Botanical Garden.

2. E-mail to author from Rudy J. Favretti, June 19, 2007.

3. E-mail to author from Frank Robinson, director of Lewis Ginter Botanical Garden, November 2007.

4. Ibid.

Hollins University

1. The historical narrative for this essay was gleaned from Hollins University literature and from conversations with members of the administration. Much of the literature can be found online, including photographs of the newly restored Beale Garden (see www.hollins.edu).

2. Lucy Preston Beale was the great-granddaughter of William Preston, the builder of "Smithfield" (see the "Smithfield" essay in this volume), where her grandfather, James Patton Preston, was born. Her father, William Ballard Preston, was a member of the U.S. Congress (elected in 1846), secretary of the navy (1849–50) under Zachary Taylor, and, finally, a senator in the Confederate congress (see Biographical Directory of the U.S. Congress, s.v. "Preston, William Ballard," http://bioguide.congress.gov/scripts/biodisplay.pl?index=P000518).

Kenmore

1. The historical information for this essay was taken from Garden Club of Virginia, Restoration Committee, Papers, 1924–97, Section 2, Kenmore folder, Virginia Historical Society, Richmond; Felder, *Fielding Lewis and the Washington Family;* Felder, *Forgotten Companions;* and conversations with Paula Felder and with the administration at Kenmore. See also the Kenmore website, http://www.kenmore.org/kenmore/history.html; and the Charles F.

Gillette Papers at the Library of Virginia, Richmond.

2. In 1671, Thomas Royston and John Buckner, both from Essex County, patented a large swath of land from the Rappahannock River westward to what is now Winchester Street. The then Governor Spotswood, to protect his own waterfront, engineered the taking by eminent domain of the Buckner-Royston waterfront in the 1720s. This became the original town of Fredericksburg. John Lewis's 1742 purchase from James Thornton wrapped around the Royston land and shared over a mile of common boundary with the Buckner-Royston patent (Felder, *Forgotten Companions,* 133).

3. "Four Unpublished Letters from Washington's Family Correspondence," *Magazine of American History,* vol. 2, 1884.

4. George Washington Diary, January 1–May 16, 1785, image 110, part of the George Washington Papers at the Library of Congress, 1741–99: Series 1b, http://memory.loc.gov/cgi-bin/ampage.

5. The events related here leading up to the first renovation of the Kenmore landscape have been gleaned from the report of Mrs. Thomas Wheelwright to the annual meeting of the Garden Club of Virginia in 1932. The report was written several years after some of the facts, and it telescopes those facts in the most tactful way (see Final Report of Mrs. Thomas S. Wheelwright [to the Annual Meeting of the Garden Club of Virginia], May 18, 1932, Garden Club of Virginia, Restoration Committee, Papers, 1924–97, Section 2, Kenmore folder, Virginia Historical Society, Richmond).

6. Charles Moore, U.S. Commissioner of Fine Arts, to Mrs. R. K. Smith, Secretary, The Kenmore Association, August 7, 1927, box 39, folder 9, Charles F. Gillette Papers, 1918–69, Library of Virginia, Richmond.

7. Emily W. Fleming [then president of the Kenmore Association] to Charles Gillette, September 28, 1927, box 39, folder 9, Charles F. Gillette Papers, 1918–69, Library of Virginia, Richmond.

8. Letter, Mrs. Francis B. Crowninshield, Chairman, [Kenmore] Board of Regents, to Mrs. H. O. Swanson, Rappahannock Valley Garden Club, April 12, 1937, Garden Club of Virginia, Restoration Committee, Papers, 1924–97, Section 2, Kenmore folder, Virginia Historical Society, Richmond.

9. According to Dorothy Hunt Williams, Gillette had seen a letter mentioning "two bowers." As a model, he copied the summerhouse at Federal Hill, outside of Fredericksburg, but the eighteenth-century existence of bowers at Kenmore could not be proven, so they were later removed (*Historic Virginia Gardens,* 8).

10. "Notes on the Joint Meeting of the Kenmore Association and the Restoration Committee of the GCV," May 27, 1964, Garden Club of Virginia, Restoration Committee, Papers, 1924–97, Section 2, Kenmore folder, Virginia Historical Society, Richmond.

Kent-Valentine House

1. The historical narrative for this essay is taken from Green, Loth, and Rasmussen, *Lost Virginia;* the *Virginia Landmarks Register;* and from conversations with Calder Loth, senior architectural historian of the Virginia Department of Historical Resources. See also Garden Club of Virginia, Restoration Committee, Papers, 1924–97, Section 2, Kent-Valentine House folder, Virginia Historical Society, Richmond.

2. In 1840 Rogers designed the Greek Revival Exchange Hotel at Fourteenth and Franklin Streets (visited in 1842 by Charles Dickens, and later Thackeray, Jenny Lind, and the Prince of Wales, who became King Edward VII). The Exchange Hotel was demolished in 1901, put out of business by the new Jefferson Hotel (Green, Loth, and Rasmussen, *Lost Virginia,* 175).

3. *Virginia Landmarks Register,* 431.

Ker Place

1. Historical information for this essay is taken from the literature of the Eastern Shore Historical Society; conversations with the Ker Place administration; and from the *Virginia Landmarks Register.*
2. E-mail to author from Rudy J. Favretti, July 2007.
3. Ibid.

Lee Hall Mansion

1. Genealogy for the Lee family is from Cary Young Adams, "Genealogical notes on the Lee family of York and Warwick counties, Va.," Manuscript collection no. Mss6:1 L5167:8, Virginia Historical Society, Richmond. For Richard Lee's life and times, see Goldberger and Moore, "From Antebellum Farm to Twenty-first Century Museum." Additional information about the mansion and its restoration is available at the Mansion's website, www.leehall.org.
2. There are counties, cities, and streets across America named either "Decatur" or "Decauter," most of them dating from the early nineteenth century, the period of Stephen Decatur's much-heralded heroics. In works about U.S. Naval history, the name is generally spelled "Decatur," but one of the early commands of another naval hero, Admiral Chester W. Nimitz (whose son and namesake followed in his father's footsteps during World War II), was the "USS Decauter." In 1908, the *Decauter,* a "mothballed destroyer in the Philippines," was recalled into action in response to a war threat from Japan (see *Army and Navy Club Bulletin,* April 2005, 9).
3. In April 1862 Lee's Mill was the scene of a brief engagement "which prompted Major General George B. McClellan to besiege Magruder's Warwick River–Yorktown Line" (see "The 1862 Peninsula Campaign: Campaign Sites," www.peninsulacampaign.org/sites.shtml).
4. E-mail to author from Sarah Goldberger, September 19, 2006

Mary Washington House

1. The historical narrative for this essay was developed from numerous sources, including conversations with Gail Braxton, president of the Fredericksburg chapter of APVA Preservation Virginia, with Fredericksburg historian Paula Felder, and with landscape architect William D. Rieley, as well as e-mail correspondence from landscape architect Rudy J. Favretti. See also Garden Club of Virginia, Restoration Committee, Papers, 1924–97, Section 2, Mary Washington House folder, Virginia Historical Society, Richmond. And on the development of Fredericksburg and Fielding Lewis's involvement, see Felder, *Fielding Lewis and the Washington Family.*
2. See Williams, *Historic Virginia Gardens,* 235.
3. Ibid., 237.
4. Ralph Griswold to the Garden Club of Virginia, May 28, 1969, in Garden Club of Virginia, Restoration Committee, Papers, 1924–97, Section 2, Mary Washington House folder, Virginia Historical Society, Richmond.
5. Williams, *Historic Virginia Gardens,* 237.
6. Report of W. Thomas Borellis from Ralph Griswold's office, Garden Club of Virginia, Restoration Committee, Papers, 1924–97, Section 2, Mary Washington House folder, Virginia Historical Society, Richmond.
7. E-mail to author from Rudy J. Favretti, July 2007.

Maymont

1. Historical information in this essay was gleaned from conversations with historian Mary Lynn Bayliss, who is James Henry Dooley's biographer; with the director of Maymont, Dale Cyrus Wheary; and with the museum's director of grounds and horticulture, Peggy Singlemann. See also Garden Club of Virginia, Restoration Committee, Papers, 1924–97, Section 2, Maymont folder, Virginia Historical Society, Richmond; and Otis, *Grounds for Pleasure.*
2. Testimony of J. H. Dooley in the annexation

case "City of Richmond vs. S. M. Dooley and Others," Henrico County, Virginia, Circuit Court, January 19–February 17, 1906, pp. 1812–38, Henrico County Court Records, Library of Virginia.

3. Otis, *Grounds for Pleasure,* 39–40.

4. Author's conversation with Dale Wheary, June 2007.

5. E-mail to author from Rudy J. Favretti, July 2007.

6. Ibid.

Monticello

1. The following historical and horticultural narrative is adapted from *Thomas Jefferson's Garden Book,* annotated by Edwin Morris Betts (1944); and Hatch, *The Gardens of Thomas Jefferson's Monticello.*

2. Garrett, Preface to *Thomas Jefferson's Monticello,* xviii.

3. *Thomas Jefferson's Garden Book,* 461.

4. Ibid., 1.

5. Ibid., 6.

6. Ibid., 33.

7. Jefferson to M. de Marbois, reproduced in *Thomas Jefferson's Garden Book,* 644.

8. "A Tour to Some of the Gardens in England" (Jefferson Memorandum), reproduced in *Thomas Jefferson's Garden Book,* 111.

9. *Thomas Jefferson's Garden Book,* 111.

10. Lucia C. Stanton, "A Botanical Anniversary," *Twinleaf Journal,* 1992, online at http://www.twinleaf.org/articles/jeffersonia.html.

11. Hatch, *The Gardens of Thomas Jefferson's Monticello,* 9.

12. Helferich, *Humboldt's Cosmos,* 298.

13. Typescript (1969) by Mrs. James Bland Martin, from penciled, handwritten, 1939 desk book of Mrs. W. Allan Perkins, in collection of Peter J. Hatch, current director of gardens and grounds at Monticello.

14. Thomas Jefferson to Anne Cary Randolph, June 7, 1807, in the collection of the Massachusetts Historical Society.

15. Typescript (1969) by Mrs. James Bland Martin, from penciled, handwritten, 1939 desk book of Mrs. W. Allan Perkins, in collection of Peter J. Hatch, current director of gardens and grounds at Monticello. This entry seems to be of March 9 (the typescript was bent and the month obscured), but subsequent entries are dated in March of 1939.

16. Wood's undergraduate degree was from VPI. He had also obtained a master's degree in city planning from MIT in 1947, and he subsequently served as head of the city of Richmond's planning commission, from 1947 to 1956.

17. *Bulletin of the Virginia Outdoors Foundation* 8, no. 1 (Fall/Winter 2005): 4.

18. The entry in *Jefferson's Garden Book* for November 12, 1772 reads: "In making the Round-about walk, 3 hands would make 80. yds in a day in the old feild but in the woods where they had stumps to clear, not more than 40. & sometimes 20.yds." Edwin Morris Betts's annotation to the entry notes, "This is the first mention of Roundabouts." Thirty-four years later, Jefferson would write to William Hamilton from the White House: "The grounds which I destine to improve in the style of the English gardens are in a form very difficult to be managed. They compose the northern quadrant of a mountain for about 2/3 of its height & then spread for the upper third over its whole crown. They contain about three hundred acres, washed at the foot for about a mile, by a river of the size of the Schuylkill. The hill is generally too steep for direct ascent, but we make level walks successively along it's side, which in it's upper part encircle the hill & intersect these again by others of easy ascent in various parts. They are chiefly still in their native woods, which are majestic, and very generally a close undergrowth, which I have not suffered to be touched, knowing how much easier it is to cut away than to fill up" (Thomas Jefferson to William Hamilton, July 1806, in Jefferson's *Letters,* 1167).

Montpelier

1. The historical narrative of Madison and his life at Montpelier is taken from conversations with Ann Miller at Montpelier; from *The Selected Letters of Dolley Payne Madison*, ed. David B. Mattern and Holly C. Shulman; and from *The Dolley Madison Digital Edition*, ed. Holly C. Shulman.

2. The entrepreneurial Spotswood had himself patented a huge swath of land looping around Fredericksburg to the west and north. It included the site of Fort Germanna, a Lutheran community that had been set up for German miners around 1714. Though the miners were not technically imported by Spotswood, he had certainly arranged for them to come, through an intermediary, and he had shepherded their settlement through the Council of Virginia. Germanna was also the name of Spotswood's elaborate Georgian house and terraced gardens. The house was built sometime during the 1720s and burned in the 1740s, soon after Spotswood's death (see Green, Loth, and Rasmussin, *Lost Virginia*, 12).

3. Dolley Payne Todd Madison to Anna Maria Brodeau Thornton, 18 May [1808], in *Dolley Madison Digital Edition*, http://rotunda.upress.virginia.edu/dmde/DPM0168.

4. Anna Maria Brodeau Thornton to Dolley Payne Todd Madison, 21 August 1809, in ibid., http://rotunda.upress.virginia.edu/dmde/DPM0218.

5. Dolley Payne Todd Madison to Anna Payne Cutts, [ca. 1] August [1811], in ibid, http://rotunda.upress.virginia.edu/dmde/DPM0290.

6. Thomas Jefferson to James Madison, April 19, 1809, Series 1: General Correspondence, microfilm reel 11, James Madison Papers, Library of Congress, Manuscript Division, Washington, D.C.

7. Memoir of Mary Estelle Elizabeth Cutts, Cutts Family Collection of Papers of James and Dolley Madison, 1794–1845 [microfilm], Library of Congress Manuscript Division Washington, D.C.

8. William Maury to James Madison, September 17, 1831, Series 1: General Correspondence, microfilm reel 23, James Madison Papers, Library of Congress, Manuscript Division, Washington, D.C. Brackets within quoted material indicate gaps in the text.

9. Miller, "The Weather Log of James Madison."

10. According to Margaret Bayard Smith, "One wing of the house, during her lifetime, was exclusively appropriated to the venerable and venerated mother of Mr. Madison, to which was attached offices and gardens, forming a separate establishment, where the aged matron preserved the habits and the hours of her early life, attended by old family slaves and surrounded by her children and grandchildren" (Smith, "Mrs. Madison," 9).

11. Bagby, "The Home of Madison in 1877," 473. According to Ann Miller at Montpelier, the person being quoted was probably Colonel John Willis, Madison's great nephew, whom Bagby referred to as "a gentleman living in the neighborhood." Historian and Madison family biographer Ralph Ketchum accepted this theory about the origins of the garden's design, but landscape historians today do not.

12. Anne Hyde de Neuville, the artist who painted the watercolor, was the wife of the Minister of France; she and her husband had visited Montpelier in 1818.

13. Memoir of Mary Estelle Elizabeth Cutts, Cutts Family Collection of Papers of James and Dolley Madison, 1794–1845 [microfilm], Library of Congress Manuscript Division Washington, D.C.

14. Mrs. duPont is quoted by Rudy J. Favretti in his e-mail to the author, July 2007. Favretti gave no further information about the original source of the duPont quote.

15. Memo from Frank Sanchis to Christopher Scott, February 14, 1989, Garden Club of Virginia, Restoration Committee, Papers, 1924–97, Section 2, Montpelier folder, Virginia Historical Society, Richmond.

16. Mrs. Robert Hopkins to Mrs. Wyatt Williams,

January 9, 1990; and Lawrence Goldschmidt to Mrs. Robert Hopkins, January 12, 1990, Garden Club of Virginia, Restoration Committee, Papers, 1924–97, Section 2, Montpelier folder, Virginia Historical Society, Richmond.

17. Favretti to Mrs. Robert Hopkins, chairman of the Restoration Committee, October 24, 1989, Garden Club of Virginia, Restoration Committee, Papers, 1924–97, Section 2, Montpelier folder, Virginia Historical Society, Richmond.

18. Notes e-mailed to the author by Rudy J. Favretti, July 2007.

19. Rudy J. Favretti to Mrs. Robert Hopkins, October 24, 1989, Garden Club of Virginia, Restoration Committee, Papers, 1924–97, Section 2, Montpelier folder, Virginia Historical Society, Richmond.

Moses Myers House

1. The historical narrative for this essay is taken from the website of the Chrysler Museum of Art, which administers the Moses Myers House (http://www.chrysler.org/myers_house.asp); as well as from conversations with Jeanne M. Bollendorf, Myers House curator, and with Calder Loth, senior architectural historian of the Virginia Department of Historical Resources; as well as interviews with collateral descendants of Moses Myers.

Mount Vernon

1. Griswold, *Washington's Gardens at Mount Vernon* (quotation, 11).

2. *George Washington's Mount Vernon,* (quotations, 120 and 114).

3. E-mail to author from Rudy J. Favretti, July 2007.

4. Ibid.

5. Ibid.

6. Charles Sprague Sargent was a professor of botany at Harvard University and the first director of the Arnold Arboretum. His report, "The Trees at Mount Vernon," was published in the Mount Vernon Ladies' Association Annual Report of 1926.

7. The historical and horticultural narrative presented here is taken from conversations with Dean Norton, director of grounds and horticulture at Mount Vernon; as well as from e-mail correspondence with landscape architect Rudy J. Favretti. See also James River Garden Club, Richmond, *Historic Gardens of Virginia.* On Washington's purchase and use of gardening, agricultural, and animal husbandry books from England, see Fusonie and Fusonie, "George Washington: Pioneer Farmer."

8. See James River Garden Club, Richmond, *Historic Gardens of Virginia,* 191.

9. George Washington to Lund Washington, December 25, 1782, in *The Writings of George Washington from the Original Manuscript Sources,* vol. 25, http://etext.virginia.edu/washington/fitzpatrick/.

10. Ibid.

11. *The Diaries of George Washington,* 4:75, 78, 79, 86, 88, 96, respectively. Available online at the American Memory Web site of the Library of Congress, http://memory.loc.gov/ammem/gwhtml/gwseries1.html.

12. Ibid., 4:121.

13. Griswold, *Washington's Gardens at Mount Vernon,* 53.

14. Thomas Jefferson to George Washington, April 16, 1784, online at The Avalon Law Project at Yale Law School, The Letters of Thomas Jefferson, www.yale.edu/lawweb/avalon/jefflett/let24.htm.

15. George Washington to Catherine Macaulay Graham, January 9, 1790, in vol. 25 of *The Writings of George Washington from the Original Manuscript Sources,* http://etext.virginia.edu/washington/fitzpatrick/.

Oatlands

1. Information for the historical narrative in this essay comes from James River Garden Club, Richmond, *Historic Gardens of Virginia;* and from conversations with the Oatlands staff.

2. *Virginia Landmarks Register,* 274.

3. James River Garden Club, Richmond, *Historic Gardens of Virginia,* 248–49.

4. The story of how the Garden Club of Virginia came to participate in the repair of the north wall is in Garden Club of Virginia, Restoration Committee, Papers, 1924–97, Section 2, Oatlands folder, Virginia Historical Society, Richmond.

5. E-mail to author from Rudy J. Favretti, July 2007.

Old Portsmouth Courthouse

1. Peters and Peters, *Virginia's Historic Courthouses*, 116.

2. Ibid., 118.

3. Mr. Hanbury was elected a Fellow of the American Institute of Architects for his "dedication and activism to save historic architecture in Portsmouth and the Commonwealth."

4. Author interview with John Paul C. Hanbury, August 2007.

Point of Honor

1. The information for this essay comes from the Cabell Family Papers at the Albert and Shirley Small Special Collections Library at the University of Virginia, available online at www.lib.virginia.edu/small/collections/cabell; and from the Garden Club of Virginia, Restoration Committee, Papers, 1924–97, Section 2, Point of Honor folder, Virginia Historical Society, Richmond.

Smithfield

1. The following historical narrative was gleaned from the exhibits at Historic Smithfield Plantation, and from an interview with the museum's garden coordinator, Lori Tolliver-Jones, which took place on April 24, 2006. In 2007, Ms. Tolliver-Jones became the administrative director at Historic Smithfield Plantation; the new garden coordinator is Don Bixby.

St. Luke's Churchyard

1. *Virginia Landmarks Register,* 237. The following historical narrative has been gleaned from the literature of Historic St. Luke's, and from con-versations with Calder Loth, senior architectural historian of the Virginia Department of Historical Resources, and with Carl Lounsbury, of Colonial Williamsburg. Concerning the creation of Newport Parish, see Cocke, *Parish Lines, Diocese of Southern Virginia.*

2. Virginia Council, *Minutes of the Council and General Court of Colonial Virginia,* 200.

3. See Virginia, *Statutes at Large,* vol. 1, no. 122: Act I; vol. 1, no. 168: Act XXXIII.

4. Upton, *Holy Things and Profane,* 38–39, 60–61; for Wilson's opinion, see *Buildings of Virginia,* 471; Lounsbury and Loth both expressed their opinions in personal conversations with the author.

5. Conversation with author. Loth bases his date on the use of Flemish bond, which was not used in England before the 1630s, and "was very rare until the end of the century."

6. The deed can be found in the Isle of Wight County courthouse.

7. Robert Fulghum, St. Luke's Church 50th Annual Pilgrimage Address, given May 20, 2007.

8. For those unfamiliar with the full verse of this bit of doggerel, it goes like this: "Be civil to all your relations / Be kind to all parish priests / You never can tell when you'll need them / For weddings or funerals or feasts."

9. From William D. Rieley's notes for St. Luke's, in possession of author.

Sutherlin House

1. The following historical narrative was gleaned from the exhibits at the Danville Museum of Fine Arts and History, and from an interview with the museum's director, Lynne Bjarnesen, which took place on April 12, 2006.

Sweet Briar College

1. The historical narrative for this chapter is taken from the literature of Sweet Briar College and conversations with its administrative staff.

2. Mrs. Robert Carter to Elisabeth Muhlenfeld, January 23, 2003, Garden Club of Virginia, Restoration Committee files.

3. Remarks of Mrs. Robert Wood at the formal presentation of the Sweet Briar restoration, April 28, 2005, Garden Club of Virginia, Restoration Committee files.

University of Virginia Pavilions III and VI

1. Thomas Jefferson to Destutt Tracy, 1820, no. 8731 in *The Jefferson Cyclopedia*, http://etext.virginia.edu/jefferson/quotations/foley/.
2. Much of the historical narrative for the creation of "Mr. Jefferson's University" is taken from the Thomas Jefferson Digital Archive of the University of Virginia Library, http://etext.virginia.edu/jefferson; and from Grizzard, "Documentary History of the Construction of the Buildings at the University of Virginia," especially chapter 1: "Genesis of the Academical Village, 1814–17." The "dry communcation" quote is from Thomas Jefferson to Hugh White, 1810, Thomas Jefferson Digital Archive of the University of Virginia Library, http://etext.virginia.edu/jefferson/. The original sources for information about the restoration of the gardens can be found in Garden Club of Virginia, Restoration Committee, Papers, 1924–1997, Section 2, University of Virginia folder, Virginia Historical Society, Richmond. Information about the latest round of restorations, the gardens of Pavilions III and VI, came from personal observation and conversations with landscape architects Mary Hughes and William D. Rieley.
3. For the correspondence between Jefferson and Thornton and Latrobe, see the notes to chapter 1 of Grizzard, "Documentary History"; available online at http://etext.lib.virginia.edu/jefferson/grizzard/cho1note.html#N_40_.
4. Ibid.
5. Ibid.
6. The tulip poplar characterization is from a letter Jefferson wrote to Mme La Comtesse Tessé, October 27, 1805 (see *Thomas Jefferson's Garden Book*, 306).
7. The UNESCO citation reads, in part: "Thomas Jefferson (1743–1826), author of the American Declaration of Independence and third president of the United States, was also a talented architect of neoclassical buildings" (see http://whc.unesco.org/en/list/442).

Washington and Lee University

1. See Garden Club of Virginia, Restoration Committee, Papers, 1924–1997, Section 2, Washington and Lee University folder, Virginia Historical Society, Richmond.
2. The plans and the detailed drawing of the brick wall separating the parking lot from Lexington's Main Street are now part of the Charles Freeman Gillette, Papers, ca. 1880–1985 (bulk 1918–1969), Series III: Drawings, 1902–1968, accession no. 34472, at the Library of Virginia; see "Wall Detail, Washington & Lee, Lexington, Virginia" (pencil and red pencil on tracing paper), October 9, 1933, control no. 867, Gillette drawing no. 460-3; "A Study for the Arrangement of Grounds about the Lee Chapel at Washington & Lee made for the Garden Club of Virginia" (pencil and colored pencils on tracing paper), October 9, 1933, control no. 867, Gillette drawing no. 460-2; "Proposed Memorial Box Garden, Robert E. Lee's Tomb, Washington & Lee University, Lexington, Virginia . . ." (Diazo print), n.d., control no. 867, Gillette drawing no. 460-1; and "A Sketch suggesting an Arrangement and Planting of Parking Areas for Washington & Lee University, made for the Garden Club of Virginia" (blueprint), October 9, 1934, control no. 867, Gillette drawing no. 460-5.
3. The historical information presented here is taken from Washington and Lee's literature and from its website (http://www.wlu.edu/x22.xml); as well as from conversations with and e-mails from the university's grounds staff, and from correspondence with landscape architect Rudy J. Favretti. See also Freeman, *Robert E. Lee, A Biography*.
4. Freeman, *R. E. Lee, A Biography*, 4:215.
5. Ibid., 4:218.
6. Ibid., 4:226.

7. Ibid., 4:266.

8. Williams, *Historic Virginia Gardens,* 39.

9. Ibid., 40.

Woodrow Wilson Presidential Library at His Birthplace

1. The following narrative is taken from interviews with staff at the Woodrow Wilson Presidential Library, and from conversations with landscape architects Rudy J. Favretti and William D. Rieley.

Yeardley House

1. The story of Yeardley's voyage to America is taken from Vaughan, "Shakespeare Discovers America, America Discovers Shakespeare." For Yeardley's time as governor of Virginia, see Keith, *The History of the British Plantations in America,* 134.

2. See Vaughan, "Shakespeare Discovers America, America Discovers Shakespeare," 2.

3. The system of land ownership in the colony was a complicated, hierarchical one. Until 1781, ownership was not in fee simple; lands were "owned" under long-term leasehold with quitrent paid in the beginning to the London Company, a stock company chartered by the Crown in 1606 to settle the Americas. The company received a second charter in 1609, but it was finally disbanded in 1624, when Virginia became a Crown colony. In 1619, the "individual ownership" proposed by Yeardley was still a leasehold that required quitrent to the London Company, but the owner could keep at least some of the benefits of his labors for himself (see Yonge, "The Site of Old James Towne," chapter 10, available online at www.jamestown.us/Yonge-TheSiteofOldJamesTown/10-The%20New%20Towne.htm).

Appendix A.

The Beginnings of Garden Week

1. Mrs. H. H. Smith, member of the DAR, who with her mother, Mrs. Fleming, was one of the determined ladies who saved Kenmore from the developers' wrecking ball in 1922. It had been sold in 1860 as Block 38 of the subdivision of Kenmore Farm, so the town had been growing around it for years by that time. Kenmore served as a hospital during the civil war, then as a boys' school. After that it had a succession of private owners including the Howard family of Maryland (1884 to 1914) until 1922 when it was threatened with destruction and saved by the remarkable ladies of the Fredericksburg chapter of the DAR, which they had formed for that purpose.

2. Final Report of Mrs. Thomas S. Wheelwright [to the Annual Meeting of the Garden Club of Virginia] May 18, 1932, Garden Club of Virginia, Restoration Committee, Papers, 1924–1997, Section 2, Virginia Historical Society, Richmond.

BIBLIOGRAPHY

Adams, Denise W. *Restoring American Gardens: An Encyclopedia of Heirloom Ornamental Plants, 1640–1940.* Portland, OR: Timber Press, 2004.

The Avalon Project at the Yale Law School: Documents in law, history and diplomacy. An electronic publication of the Avalon Project; William C. Fray and Lisa A. Spar, Co-Directors. New Haven, CT: Avalon Project, 1996–.

Bagby, George W. "The Home of Madison." *Lippincott's Magazine,* April 1872.

Bemiss, Samuel M. *Ancient Adventurers.* Richmond, VA: Garrett and Massie, 1959.

Birnbaum, Charles A., and Robin Karson, eds. *Pioneers of American Landscape Design.* A project of the National Park Service Historic Landscape Initiative, Library of American Landscape History, Catalog of Landscape Records in the United States at Wave Hill. New York: McGraw Hill, 2000.

Boggs, Kate Doggett. *Prints and Plants of Old Gardens.* Richmond, VA: Garrett and Massie, 1932.

British and American Gardens in the Eighteenth Century: Eighteen Illustrated Essays on Garden History. Edited by Robert P. Maccubbin and Peter Martin. Williamsburg, VA: Colonial Williamsburg Foundation, 1984.

Buildings of Virginia: Tidewater and Piedmont. Edited by Richard Guy Wilson; with contributions by Sara A. Butler et al. New York: Oxford University Press, 2002.

Cocke, Charles Francis. *Parish Lines, Diocese of Southern Virginia.* Richmond: Virginia State Library, 1964.

Cooper, Nicholas. *Houses of the Gentry, 1480–1680.* New Haven, CT: Published for the Paul Mellon Centre for Studies in British Art in association with English Heritage by Yale University Press, 1999.

Cothran, James R. *Gardens and Historic Plants of the Antebellum South.* Columbia: University of South Carolina Press, 2003.

Dirr, Michael. *Manual of Woody Landscape Plants: Their Identification, Ornamental Characteristics, Culture, Propagation, and Uses.* Champaign, IL: Stipes Publishing Co., 1983.

Encyclopedia of American History. Edited by Richard B. Morris. New York: Harper, 1953.

Felder, Paula S. *Fielding Lewis and the Washington Family: A Chronicle of Eighteenth-Century Fredericksburg.* Fredericksburg, VA: American History Co., 1998.

———. *Forgotten Companions: The First Settlers of Spotsylvania County and Fredericksburg Town (with Notes on Early Land Use).* Fredericksburg, VA: American History Co., 1982.

Fithian, Philip Vickers. *Philip Vickers Fithian, Journal and Letters, 1767–1774, Student at Princeton College, 1770–72, Tutor at Nomini Hall in Virginia, 1773–74.* Vol. 1. Edited for the Princeton Historical Association by John Rogers Williams. Princeton, NJ: The University Library, 1900.

Freeman, Douglas Southall. *R. E. Lee, A Biography.* 4 vols. New York: C. Scribner's Sons, 1934–35.
———. *George Washington.* 7 vols. New York: C. Scribner's Sons, 1948–54.
Fusonie, Alan, and Donna Jean Fusonie. "George Washington: Pioneer Farmer" [pamphlet]. Mount Vernon, VA: Mount Vernon Ladies Association, 1998.
Garden History: Issues, Approaches, Methods. Dumbarton Oaks Colloquium on the History of Landscape Architecture (13th: 1989), edited by John Dixon Hunt. Washington, DC: Dumbarton Oaks Research Library and Collection, 1992.
Garrett, Wendell. Preface to *Thomas Jefferson's Monticello.* Charlottesville, Va.: Thomas Jefferson Foundation, 2002.
George Washington's Mount Vernon. Edited by Wendell Garrett; photography by Robert C. Lautman; collection photography by Edward Owen; essays by Susan Gray Detweiler et al. New York: Monacelli Press, 1998.
Goldberger, Sarah M., and J. Michael Moore. "From Antebellum Farm to Twenty-First Century Museum: Lee Hall Mansion, Newport News." *Virginia Cavalcade Magazine,* Spring 2002, 84–95.
Green, Bryan Clark, Calder Loth, and William M. S. Rasmussen. *Lost Virginia: Vanished Architecture of the Old Dominion.* Charlottesville, VA: Howell Press, 2001.
Griswold, Mac K. *Washington's Gardens at Mount Vernon: Landscape of the Inner Man.* Boston: Houghton Mifflin, 1999.
Grizzard, Frank Edgar, Jr. "Documentary History of the Construction of the Buildings at the University of Virginia, 1817–1828." Ph.D. diss., University of Virginia, 1996. Available online at http://etext.lib.virginia.edu/jefferson/grizzard/.
Hatch, Peter J. *The Gardens of Thomas Jefferson's Monticello.* Charlottesville, VA: Thomas Jefferson Foundation, 1992.
Helferich, Gerard. *Humboldt's Cosmos: Alexander von Humboldt and the Latin American Journey that Changed the Way We See the World.* New York: Gotham Books, 2004.
Henderson, Paula. *The Tudor House and Garden: Architecture and Landscape in the Sixteenth and Early Seventeenth Centuries.* New Haven: Published for the Paul Mellon Centre for Studies in British Art by Yale University Press, 2005.
Hobhouse, Penelope. *Gardening Through the Ages: An Illustrated History of Plants and Their Influence on Garden Styles—from Ancient Egypt to the Present Day.* New York: Simon and Schuster. 1992.
James River Garden Club, Richmond, comp. *Historic Gardens of Virginia.* Edited by Edith Tunis Sale. Richmond: William Byrd Press, 1923.
Jefferson, Thomas. *The Jeffersonian Cyclopedia: A Comprehensive Collection of the Views of Thomas Jefferson Classified and Arranged in Alphabetical Order under Nine Thousand Titles Relating to Government, Politics, Law, Education, Political Economy, Finance, Science, Art, Literature, Religious Freedom, Morals, etc.* Edited by John P. Foley. New York: Funk & Wagnalls, 1900. Online at http://etext.lib.virginia.edu/jefferson/quotations/foley/.
———. *Thomas Jefferson's Garden Book, 1766–1824, with Relevant Extracts from His Other Writings.* Annotated by Edwin Morris Betts. Philadelphia: American Philosophical Society, 1944.
———. *Letters.* Edited by Merrill D. Peterson. Library of America, no. 17. New York: Literary Classics of the U.S., distributed to the trade in the U.S. and Canada by the Viking Press, 1984.
John Evelyn's "Elysium Britannicum" and European Gardening. Edited by Therese O'Malley and Joachim Wolschke-Bulhmahn. Washington, DC: Dumbarton Oaks Research Library and Collection, 1998.
Keith, William, Sir. *The History of the British Plantations in America: With a Chronological Account of the most remarkable Things, which happen'd to the first Adventurers in their several Discoveries of that New*

World, part I, *Containing the History of Virginia, with Remarks on the Trade and Commerce of that Colony.* London: Printed at the Expence of the Society for the Encouragement of Learning, by S. Richardson; and sold by A. Millar, J. Nourse, and J. Gray, 1738.

Lawson, William. *A new Orchard and Garden* with *The Country Housewifes Garden* (1618) England. Prospect Books, 2003.

Leighton, Ann, *Early American Gardens: For Meate or Medicine.* Amherst: University of Massachusetts Press, 1970.

———. *American Gardens in the Eighteenth Century: "For Use or for Delight".* 1976; reprint, Amherst: University of Massachusetts Press, 1988.

———. *American Gardens of the Nineteenth Century: "For Comfort and Affluence."* Amherst: University of Massachusetts Press, 1987.

Leiner, Frederick C., *The End of Barbary Terror, America's 1815 War against the Pirates of North Africa.* New York: OxfordUniversity Press, 2006.

Luccketti, Nicholas. "Archaeological Excavations at Bacon's Castle, Surry County, Virginia." In *Earth Patterns: Essays in Landscape Archaeology.* Charlottesville: University Press of Virginia, 1990.

Madison, Dolley. *The Dolley Madison Digital Edition.* Edited by Holly C. Shulman. Charlottesville: University of Virginia Press, 2004, 2007. http://rotunda.upress.virginia.edu:8080/dmde/default.xqy.

———. *The Selected Letters of Dolley Payne Madison.* Edited by David B. Mattern and Holly C. Shulman. Charlottesville: University of Virginia Press, 2003.

Maymont Notes, Fall 2001.

Meade, William, D.D. [Bishop Meade]. *Old Churches, Ministers, and Families of Virginia.* 2 vols. Philadelphia: J. B. Lippincott, 1857.

Miller, William B. "The Weather Log of James Madison." *Journal of Presbyterian History* 40 (December 1962): 209–12.

Nichols, Frederick Doveton, and Ralph E. Griswold. *Thomas Jefferson, Landscape Architect.* Charlottesville: University Press of Virginia, 1978.

Otis, Denise. *Grounds for Pleasure: Four Centuries of the American Garden.* New York: Harry N. Abrams, 2002.

Pierson, William H., Jr. *American Buildings and Their Architects,* vol. 1, *The Colonial and Neoclassical Styles.* Garden City, NY: Doubleday, 1970.

Peters, John O., and Margaret T. Peters. *Virginia's Historic Courthouses.* Charlottesville: University Press of Virginia, 1995.

Reynolds, Myra. *The Treatment of Nature in English Poetry Between Pope and Wordsworth.* 1909; reprinted, New York: Gordian Press, 1966.

Sarudy, Barbara Wells. *Gardens and Gardening in the Chesapeake, 1700–1805.* Baltimore: Johns Hopkins University Press, 1998.

Seale, William. *Virginia's Executive Mansion: A History of the Governor's House.* Richmond: Published for the Citizens Advisory Council for Interpreting and Furnishing the Executive Mansion by the Virginia State Library and Archives, 1988.

Smith, Margaret Bayard Smith. "Mrs. Madison." In vol. 3 of *The National Portrait Gallery of Distinguished Americans,* conducted by James B. Longacre and James Herring; under the superintendence of the American Academy of the Fine Arts. Philadelphia: H. Perkins; New York: M. Bancroft; London: O. Rich, 1837.

Upton, Dell. *Holy Things and Profane: Anglican Parish Churches in Colonial Virginia.* 1986; reprint, New Haven, Conn.: Yale University Press, 1997.

Vaughan, Alden T. "Shakespeare Discovers America, America Discovers Shakespeare." In *Shakespeare in American Life* (exhibition catalog). Washington, D.C.: Folger Shakespeare Library, 2007. Available online at http://www.shakespeareinamericanlife.org/identity/shipwreck/seaventure.cfm.

Virginia. *The Statutes at Large; being a collection of all the laws of Virginia, from the first session of the Legislature in the year 1619.* By William Waller Hening. New York, Printed for the editor, 1819–23. 13 vols. Charlottesville: Published for the Jamestown Foundation of the Commonwealth of Virginia by the University Press of Virginia, 1969.

Virginia. Council. *Minutes of the Council and General Court of Colonial Virginia 1622–1632, 1670–1676: With notes and excerpts from original Council and General Court records, into 1683, now lost.* Edited by H. R. McIlwaine. Richmond: [The Colonial Press, Everett Waddey Co.], 1924.

Virginia Landmarks Register. Edited by Calder Loth. 4th ed. Charlottesville: Published for the Virginia Department of Historic Resources by the University Press of Virginia, 1999.

Washington, George. *The Diaries of George Washington.* Edited by Donald Jackson and Dorothy Twohig. 6 vols. Charlottesville: University Press of Virginia, 1976–79.

———. *The Writings of George Washington from the Original Manuscript Sources, 1745–1799.* Edited by John C. Fitzpatrick. Prepared under the direction of the United States George Washington Bicentennial Commission and published by authority of Congress; reprint of the 1931–44 edition. 39 vols. Westport, CT: Greenwood Press, 1970. Available online at the Electronic Text Center, University of Virginia Library, http://etext.virginia.edu/washington/fitzpatrick/.

Weishan, Michael. *The New Traditional Garden: A Practical Guide to Creating and Restoring Authentic American Gardens for Homes of All Ages.* New York: Ballantine Publishing Group, 1999.

Williams, Dorothy Hunt. *Historic Virginia Gardens: Preservations by The Garden Club of Virginia.* Charlottesville: Published for the Garden Club of Virginia by the University Press of Virginia, 1975.

Wyatt, Edward A., and James G. Scott. *Petersburg's Story: A History.* Petersburg: Titmus Optical Co., Petersburg, Publisher, 1960.

Young, Samuel H. "The Site of Old James Towne—1607–1698." 1907. Available online at http://www.jamestown.us/Yonge-TheSiteofOldJamesTown/TitlePage-The_Site_of_Old_James_Towne.htm.

INDEX

Page numbers in italics refer to illustrations.

Warsaw, Va.
 Sabine Hall, 233, 237
Washington, Betty. *See* Lewis, Betty Washington
Washington, George, 71–74, 97–99, 143–45, 147–51, 206
Washington, Lawrence, 147
Washington, Lund, 149
Washington, Martha Dandridge Custis, 147
Washington, Mary Ball, 97–100, 147, 241
Washington, Samuel, 72–73
Washington and Lee University (Lexington, Va.), *204*, 205–12, *207–11*, 243
Westmoreland County, Va.
 Stratford Hall, 242
Wheary, Dale, 108, 111
Wheelwright, Mrs. Thomas, 77, 121, 229
White, Edwin, 5
Whiting, Brooke, 234–35
Whitney, Gertrude Vanderbilt, 56
Wickham, John, 53
Williams, Daisy, 189, 191
Williams, Dorothy Hunt, xi, xiii, 75–76, 97, 99
Williams, Indiana Fletcher, 189, 191

Williams, Morley, 124, 242
Williamsburg, Va., 6
 Bruton Parish Church, *36*, 37–44, *39–41, 43*, 177, 239
Williamsburg Garden Club, 40
Wilson, John Ruggles, 213
Wilson, Orme, Jr., 34
Wilson, Richard Guy, 177
Wilson, Woodrow, 213
Wilton (Richmond, Va.), 243
Winchester-Clarke Garden Club, 35
Wood, Garland A., Jr., 124–25, 241
Wood, Mrs. Robert C., III, 192
Woodlawn Plantation (Fairfax County), 243
Woodrow Wilson Museum (Staunton, Va.), 219
Woodrow Wilson Presidential Library/Birthplace (Staunton, Va.), 213–21, *214–21*, 243

Yeardley, George, 223–25
Yeardley House (Jamestown Island), *222*, 223–27, *224–27*, 243
Yost, Pearl, 93
Young, George, 27

Designed by Martha Farlow and typeset by Chris Harrison in Arno Pro
with Artcraft display. Typeface used for plans designed by William D. Rieley.
Printed on 150 gsm Lumi Silk by Everbest Printing Company Ltd.